COLLECTIVE BARGAINING IN EDUCATION

COLLECTIVE BARGAINING IN EDUCATION

Win/Win, Win/Lose, Lose/Lose

Jerry J. Herman, Ph.D.

Area Head, Administration and Educational Leadership
The University of Alabama

Gene E. Megiveron, Ed.D.

Superintendent, Vermilion Parish School Ditrict
Abbeville, Louisiana

TECHNOMIC
PUBLISHING CO., INC.

LANCASTER · BASEL

Collective Bargaining in Education

a **TECHNOMIC**® publication

Published in the Western Hemisphere by
Technomic Publishing Company, Inc.
851 New Holland Avenue
Box 3535
Lancaster, Pennsylvania 17604 U.S.A.

Distributed in the Rest of the World by
Technomic Publishing AG

Printed in the United States of America
10 9 8 7 6 5 4 3 2 1

Main entry under title:
    Collective Bargaining in Education: Win/Win, Win/Lose, and Lose/Lose

A Technomic Publishing Company book
Bibliography: p. 263
Includes index p. 269

Library of Congress Card No. 92-61292
ISBN No. 0-87762-964-1

WE wish to acknowledge the contributions that Dr. Janice L. Herman has made to this effort. She proofread each chapter and made helpful suggestions, she assisted in the collection of pertinent reference materials, and she provided encouragement throughout the entire project. Janice, we sincerely thank you.

WHAT THIS BOOK IS ABOUT

COLLECTIVE bargaining is a dynamic, important, and very serious process. Preparing for it, doing it, and living with its results will determine to a large degree the organizational structure that will exist in a school district and the day-to-day procedures that will be followed. Because of the impact on structure and procedures, collective bargaining will have a significant effect on the climate and culture of the school district. In addition, the way it is conducted by union and management and the results achieved can strongly influence the attitudes of the students, parents, and taxpayers of the school district. It is extremely important, and it must be handled carefully by all parties involved.

School-based or site-based management promotes the direct involvement of employees and citizens in management decisions related to the individual school buildings. With the advent of these reforms, both union and management representatives who are responsible for collective bargaining must be even more mature and sophisticated in their contract negotiations and contract management responsibilities. If the school district allows school-based management teams to have authority over the selection of employees, the structure of the school day, and some budgetary areas, then the union and management representatives who are responsible for negotiating and managing the master school district contract must take these matters seriously when managing or renegotiating a master contract. Business-as-usual approaches will not suffice, because it is not a business-as-usual environment in which collective bargaining is taking place.

This book is a how-to-do-it road map, which presents practical details on all the important aspects of collective bargaining at the local school district level. It sets the stage by discussing how administrators and employees live and work together in the school district environment. It then quickly details all of the strategies, tasks, events, and influences that bear on the collective bargaining process from the initial certification election of a union through the preparation for, negotiation of, and administration of a union/management collective bargaining agreement.

This book is about administrators, teachers, and nonteaching employees, and it is about union and management groups who participate in a dynamic, emotional, and intellectually stimulating and draining process called collective bargaining. It is also about win/win, win/lose, and lose/lose situations which affect the individuals and groups who work within the school district and which affect those who are served by the employees of the school district. That is, it is about successes, losses, hurts, and happinesses felt by the individuals and groups who comprise the union's and management's bargaining teams, and it is about the individuals and groups who profit from the successful results of the process or who lose from the failures of the collective bargaining process.

FOR WHOM IS THIS BOOK WRITTEN?

This book is written for three purposes. First, it is written as a self-contained, easily read comprehensive manual for those administrators and board members who are inexperienced in general labor/management relations and in the specifics of collective bargaining. Second, it is written as a university textbook for graduate education courses in collective bargaining. Third, it is written for use as a reference book by anyone who is responsible for or who has an interest in any phase of the collective bargaining process as it relates to the local school district level.

BY WHOM IS THIS BOOK WRITTEN?

The authors each have in excess of thirty years of experience in education, and each has over twenty-five years in educational administration. They each have been teachers, principals, central office administrators, superintendents of schools, and university graduate professors in the field of educational administration.

Both began their experience with collective bargaining in 1965 in the State of Michigan, and they have been involved with trade unions, municipal unions, teachers' unions, classified employees' unions, and administrators' unions in the states of Michigan, New York, and Louisiana. They have experienced numerous contract negotiations as spokespersons, as negotiating team members, and as CEOs. They also have experienced mediations, arbitrations, fact-findings, and strikes.

They share their wealth of on-the-line, practical experiences in a comprehensive, yet easily understood manner. They write about collective bargaining through the eyes of the local school district's collective bargainer. They explain terms, strategies, and tactics for win/win, win/lose, and lose/lose situations, and they do this with real-life examples and with exercises to be utilized by the reader.

LIVING AND WORKING WITH INDIVIDUALS AND GROUPS

Section One consists of three chapters. Chapter 1, *Working Together with People and Groups*, presents information about the beliefs one holds about individuals and groups, and discusses the needs of individuals and groups. It also discusses intergroup relations, communication among and between individuals and groups, and the development of groups into winning teams.

Chapter 2, *Living Together Every Day in the Workplace*, covers the topics of employee empowerment, employee recognition structures, methods of involving union/management teams, and a variety of group structures. It ends by presenting a list of ways to create and maintain a productive and satisfying work environment.

Chapter 3, *Considering the Students, the School District, and the Community*, answers the following questions. Who are the stakeholders? What are the clients' needs? What is the responsibility of the district's management and the employees' union to the school district's clients? How is client input obtained? How do you communicate with the school district's clients?

Working Together with People and Groups

CHAPTER 1 develops a philosophical and pragmatic base about people and groups, and the development of an environment within which collective bargaining will take place and within which the educational and personal lives of students, employees, and management representatives will be affected. Chapter 1 discusses: (1) beliefs about people, (2) needs of people, (3) beliefs about groups, (4) growth patterns of groups, (5) development of groups into winning teams, and (6) intergroup formal and informal communications. The chapter also includes a summary, exercises, and selected references.

BELIEFS ABOUT PEOPLE

How one acts as a member of a union's or board of education's (management's) collective bargaining team, and how one administers or lives with the negotiated master contractual agreement, depends to a large degree on what one believes about people—about employees or board members and administrators, about members of the union or of management, about those persons who serve on the other party's collective bargaining team, and those persons who do not serve on either party's collective bargaining teams but who are seriously affected by the results of collective bargaining and by the way in which the negotiated master contractual agreement is administered. Therefore, it is very important to discern the beliefs, either by conversation or by analysis of actions, of all members of the collective bargaining teams of both the union and the management who serve within an individual school district.

If the board of education members, the superintendent of schools, and the board of education's collective bargaining team's members have the following beliefs about people and employees, they will exhibit positive collaborative behaviors during negotiations and during the administration of the master contractual agreement between negotiation periods.

- People are basically good, honest, and hardworking.

3

- Employees wish to perform well, serve students in a quality manner, and assist the school district to achieve its performance goals.
- Union representatives want to be fair to their membership, fair to the students, fair to the community, fair to taxpayers, and fair to management.
- Union representatives prefer to approach negotiations of a master contractual agreement and day-to-day union business with management's representatives in a win/win, collaborative manner [1,2].

On the other hand, if the members of the union's collective bargaining team, or more importantly, the employees of the school district, feel that the board of education's members or the school district's administrators or the members of the management's collective bargaining team, harbor negative beliefs about people, employees, and the union, then collective bargaining will almost always be doomed to a hard-line, win/lose relationship between labor and management. In this case, the threat of a lose/lose strike situation looms large as the collective bargaining relationship runs its course under the adversarial interpersonal and intergroup relationships created by these negative beliefs. If management harbors the following negative beliefs or if the members of the union's collective bargaining team feel that management harbors the following negative beliefs, labor and management are almost always doomed to a difficult adversarial relationship.

- People are lazy, selfish, and have no concern for the quality of their work.
- Employees feel no loyalty to the school district's organization, nor to the students, nor to the community in which they work.
- Union representatives are not concerned about the quality of the students' environment nor about the degree of achievement attained by the school district's students.
- Union representatives are only concerned about enhancing their power and about getting more money and more of everything they can conjure up, regardless of the effect on students' programs or the community's, administration's, or board of education's attitudes towards the union [3].

Not only will the beliefs of the board of education's members, the superintendent of schools, the administration, or the members of the board of education's collective bargaining team have a profound effect on the climate within which contract negotiations take place and within which the day-to-day union/management relationships function, but the union's beliefs about people, management, board of education members, and the members of the board of education's collective bargaining team will also dramatically affect what takes place during the negotiations of a collective bargaining master contract and the day-to-day relations between union and management once the master contract is negotiated. If the union's representatives and the employees hold the following beliefs, the labor/management environment during and after negotiations of a master contractual agreement will, in all likelihood, be a positive one [4].

- Members of the boards of education appreciate the employees and trust them; realize that employee unions represent an important and necessary countervailing force; and want to be fair to employees and provide them with good salaries, fringe benefits, and working conditions.
- Superintendents of schools believe employees are hardworking; wish to achieve; want to assist the students; want to assist in improving all aspects of the school district; and want to be fair to students, to management, and to the community.
- Managers see themselves in the role of helpers of employees and students, and they perceive that they act within a consulting and helping framework.
- Members of the board of education's collective bargaining team desire to work in a collaborative, win/win environment that assists the members of the union's bargaining team in solving problems and in achieving reasonable union and employee collective bargaining goals [5].

On the other hand, if employees and union representatives hold the following negative beliefs toward board of education members, administrators, and the members of the board of education's collective bargaining team, the environment within which contractual negotiations take place and within which the day-to-day union/management relations will function, will probably be an adversarial, win/lose one. In all likelihood the threat of a lose/lose strike situation will also loom large on the horizon [6].

- Boards of education will adamantly refuse to share any power, and they will attempt to provide the lowest salaries and fringe benefit costs possible.

- Superintendents of schools and the board of education's chief negotiator will attempt to maintain control for the boards and they will attempt to keep new money expenditures to a minimum, whether the financial condition of the school district is average or exceptionally good.
- Administrators play the roles of autocratic managers, not of educational leaders, and they manage by "snoopervision" and intimidation.
- Board members, superintendents, administrators, and members of the board of education's collective bargaining team believe that employees are lazy, selfish, not concerned about the students, not concerned about the school district, and not concerned about the community at large. They are only concerned about their selfish interests and how much of everything their union representative can take from the board of education, management, and the taxpayers.

Not only will the belief that one holds about people influence the collective bargaining process and labor relations in general, but the knowledge of and the consideration given to the needs of people will also influence the collective bargaining and labor relations within school districts. Let's now examine some of the most crucial people needs that must be addressed if one is to perform well within a collective bargaining environment.

NEEDS OF PEOPLE

All persons have needs for security, for social acceptance, and for self-esteem. In addition, employees have needs for: (1) adequate salary and fringe benefits, (2) job security, (3) interesting work, (4) opportunities for input into matters that affect them, (5) recognition by peers and management personnel, (6) opportunities for growth, and (7) self-satisfaction and self-actualization [7].

Whether one is dealing with a union's negotiation team or with employees on a day-to-day basis, these people needs are important variables that must be kept in mind. Of course, the union's negotiation team and the employees have to realize that many of the management personnel with whom they deal have identical or similar needs.

The way that individuals are treated depends on the beliefs one has about individuals, but, in addition, one must recognize the beliefs one holds about groups and about the needs of groups [8].

BELIEFS ABOUT GROUPS

If boards of education, superintendents of schools, and school administrators hold the following beliefs about groups, they will act in a mature, collaborative, win/win manner during the negotiations of a master contractual agreement and during the day-to-day relations with employees and union leadership.

- The union's collective bargaining team serves the legitimate purpose of representing all of its employees' interests.
- The union's leadership groups are mature, logical, and fair.
- The union's leadership groups will consider the financial ability of the district and the community; the legitimate leadership and management requirements of the board of education and the district's administrators; and, most importantly, the needs of the students, who are the sole reason for the existence of the school districts [9].

On the other hand, if the boards of education, superintendents of schools, and school administrators hold the following beliefs about the union's negotiation teams and about the union's leadership groups, they will act in an adversarial, win/lose mode that may eventually lead to strikes by the school districts' employees.

- The union's collective bargaining teams are only concerned about getting more of everything regardless of any negative effect those moves may have on students, taxpayers, community relations, or on labor/management long-term relations [10].
- The union's leadership groups are self-serving, power-hungry groups whose only purpose is to increase their power and increase their own benefits. If the union's membership receives gains through the collective bargaining process, those gains are incidental to the main goals of increasing leadership power, control, and benefits [11].

Union leaders and employees, in general, react to the management's negotiation team and to the board of education and the school district administration in a positive or negative manner based upon their beliefs about boards and administrators [12].

The following positive beliefs about boards, the management's collective bargaining teams, and administrators, by union leaders and employees, will lead to a collaborative win/win approach to collective bargaining and to positive day-to-day labor/management relationships [13].

- School board members, administrators, and members of the management's collective bargaining team believe that the union has a legitimate right to request those working conditions that promote a positive, happy, and productive work environment for the employees it represents.
- They realize that it is necessary to provide good salaries, good fringe benefits, and a positive labor/management image in order to attract and retain excellent employees.
- They realize that a collaborative, positive, win/win approach in conjunction with union leaders is the best way to realize the goals of the school district and to enhance the probability of achieving the quality of education desired for all the district's students.
- School board members, administrators, and members of the management's collective bargaining team must represent the interests of students, taxpayers, and the community; but they will not do this by undermining or neglecting the legitimate interests of employees or the employees' union.

On the other hand, if the union leadership and the school district's employees harbor the following negative beliefs about boards of education, administrators, and members of the management's collective bargaining team, the result will be protracted and adversarial negotiations that may very well end in a lose/lose, strike situation. In addition, these negative beliefs will probably lead to a day-to-day win/lose relationship between union leaders and employees, and administrators and board of education members [14].

- Board of education members are only concerned about keeping taxes low and pacifying community power figures in order to promote their own future political aspirations.
- Administrators view employees as lower level workers who must be closely monitored, given orders, and snoopervised.
- Management's negotiation team members will lie, use dirty tricks,

attempt to discredit union leaders, and do whatever they deem necessary to get a win for management and a loss for the union.

Not only are one's beliefs about individuals and groups predictors of one's probable future behavior, and not only is the knowledge of the needs possessed by individuals and groups a predictor of one's potential future behavior, but, also, one's understanding of the growth patterns of groups will probably determine the strategies and tactics one utilizes in dealing with labor/management situations.

GROWTH PATTERNS OF GROUPS

As individuals grow from birth through adolescence, through adulthood, and through old age, so do groups move through stages. Groups move through the stages of infancy, adolescence, and maturity. It is crucial that those dealing with collective bargaining of a master contract agreement or with day-to-day labor/management relations, whether from the union's or the management's viewpoint, carefully analyze the growth stage of the group with which they are dealing. Some of the major characteristics of the three stages in the growth pattern of groups are:

- During the *infancy stage* of group growth a careful observer will see that: (1) the group is not clear about the role of the individuals who comprise the group, (2) the group has no clear goals or objectives, (3) leadership within the group is undetermined, (4) strategies and tactics are not discernible, (5) communications are amoeba-like and clarity of communications is left to chance, and (6) problem-solving methodologies are nonexistent. Certainly during its infancy stage, the group (whether it be a labor or a management group) is ill-prepared to handle intergroup relations.
- During the *adolescent stage* of group growth a careful observer will recognize that the group: (1) realizes the necessity of leadership, but the leadership role changes from time to time and from person to person, (2) goals are determined, but they are changed or modified frequently, (3) members' knowledge of one another is improving, and communications are beginning to be stabilized, (4) strategies and tactics are developed, but they are moving targets, (5) problem solving is only of the short-term variety, and (6) roles of the various members who comprise the group are beginning to evolve.
- During the *maturity stage* of group growth even a casual observer

will realize that: (1) roles of the various group members are clarified and stabilized, and they form the basis for the smooth operation of the group, (2) strategies and tactics are developed for both the short term and long term, (3) problem-solving techniques are highly sophisticated, and they successfully lead to the attainment of the desired results, (4) each person understands well the other members of the group, and each person understands the personalities, strengths, and weaknesses of all the other members of the group, (5) communications are clear and they are those of an open system, (6) leadership of the group is clearly identified, and the leadership is supported by all members of the group, (7) input is requested from all members and the members' input is accepted as valuable by all members of the group and (8) the group works as a cohesive unit which is well prepared to deal with intergroup relations in a professional and productive manner [15].

Once both the union's and management's groups are in the maturity stage of growth, they can combine to create a mature win/win, collaborative relationship. This relationship will serve both groups well as they collectively bargain a master contractual agreement, and this relationship will serve both groups well in their day-to-day labor/management relations. Contrary to the potential success of win/win by mature groups, the probability of successful win/win relations with adolescent groups is limited, and the potential for successful win/win, collaborative labor/management relations with immature groups is almost nonexistent [16].

When both union and management groups reach the maturity stage, they are prepared, for all practical purposes, to become a single win/win, collaborative working group. Let's now briefly turn to the differences among a group, a team, and a "winning" team.

DEVELOPMENT OF GROUPS INTO WINNING TEAMS

A *group* is a collection of two or more people who are placed in a single environment for a period of time [17]. A group may be together for a short time period, and the group may not possess any goals. An example is a group of people at a shopping mall.

A *team* is a collection of two or more individuals who share a common purpose. An example is a sports team. The members of a team may have a common purpose and they may have agreed-upon goals, but the team may not achieve its goals and there might be dissention among the team members [18].

A *winning team* is a collection of two or more individuals who share a common purpose, have a set of agreed-upon goals and objectives, have a shared vision and mission, and work together in a collaborative and positive manner. This team achieves its vision, mission, goals, and objectives at a satisfactory level. The individuals who comprise the team feel a sense of accomplishment and they also feel a sense of caring and respect from the other team members [19].

We have established the definition of a winning team and have stressed that once the union's team and the management's team reach the maturity stage of growth, they can combine into a single problem-solving and program-development winning team. Let's explore the descriptors that define the intergroup relations, and the intergroup formal and informal communications patterns that identify an environment where union and management function as a winning team.

INTERGROUP FORMAL AND INFORMAL COMMUNICATIONS, AND INTERGROUP RELATIONS

Intergroup relations within a win/win, collaborative union/management environment can best be described as consisting of mutual goal-setting, mutual problem-solving actions, and a high level of achievement related to the goals that have been mutually established. In addition to this general picture of factors that discriminate between a win/win, collaborative team and a lose/lose, adversarial team, a listing of those descriptors that identify, in detail, a winning team comprised of both union and management members will further describe this positive union/management operation [20].

Formal and informal communications are open, honest, and frequent. Trust and understanding is fostered, and the success of both the union's and management's members is enhanced.

SUMMARY

In order to be effective players within the environment of collective bargaining, it is crucial that management's representatives work within their beliefs about people, about groups, about unions, about members of the union's negotiation team, about union leadership, and about employees. It is just as crucial that employees and union leaders, if they wish to be effective within the environment of collective bargaining, work within their beliefs about boards of education, board of education members, superintendents of schools, school district administrators and members of the management's negotiation team. In addition, it is important that both parties in collective bargaining clearly understand the needs of individuals and of groups.

The stages of group growth are: (1) infancy, (2) adolescence, and (3) maturity. Stress was placed on the fact that the mature union and management groups can combine into a single win/win, collaborative problem-solving and program-developing group. However, the probability of a win/win, collaborative union/management environment existing is greatly diminished when the union and management groups are in the adolescent stage of growth, and a win/win union/management process is next to impossible when either the union or management groups are in the infancy stage of growth.

A winning team is one that possesses: (1) an agreed-upon vision, mission, goals, and objectives, (2) an open and clear system of communications, (3) strategic and tactical plans, (4) excellent problem-solving methodologies, and (5) a high level of achievement related to its vision, mission, goals, and objectives. The members of a winning team feel a sense of accomplishment, are individually productive, and feel a sense of caring, respect, and recognition from all other members of the team.

When a winning team comprised of both management members and union members exists, informal and formal communications are positive, clear, and occur at a high level, and intergroup relations are those of respect, common concern, and caring. In addition, winning teams and winning team members:

- are comfortable in sharing leadership functions, and make decisions within a collaborative atmosphere
- feel that a strong sense of interdependence is necessary if the vision, mission, goals, and objectives are to be achieved at a high level
- solicit the best input from all members of the team
- participate consistently and comprehensively in communications on matters related to issues, goals, and problems
- are dedicated to creating a collaborative, win/win, rather than an adversarial, win/lose environment
- join forces to solve critical operating and long-term problems

relating to the welfare of the district's students, the union's membership, and the district's management
- use informal as well as formal continuous communication channels and use ad hoc problem solving and program development subgroups comprised of membership from both union and management
- look at the level of positive functioning of the team, and each individual looks at her/his role and performance within the team as a means of assessing her/his level of performance as a team member
- feel a unity of purpose, a sense of ownership, and a requirement to be the best they can be as a unit and as members within the team

EXERCISES

1. Describe methods you can use to assist a group of individuals who are in the infancy stage of group development to quickly develop into a productive group.
2. Describe the methods you can use to assist a group of individuals who are in the adolescent stage of group development to quickly develop into a mature and successful group.
3. What techniques can you utilize to assess the level of achievement of a mature group and of the contribution(s) of each member of this mature group?
4. Define the differences among a group, a team, and a winning team.
5. Describe the indicators of a winning team.
6. List your beliefs about people, unions, employees, boards of education, board of education members, superintendents of schools, administrators, members of a union's collective bargaining team, and members of a management's collective bargaining team.
7. What do you know about the needs of individuals and of groups?
8. What type of informal and formal communications techniques would you use when dealing with union/management relations?
9. List some primary descriptors that will characterize the infancy, adolescent, and maturity stage of groups.

REFERENCES

1. McGregor, D. M. 1960. *The Human Side of Enterprise.* New York, NY: McGraw-Hill Book Co., pp. 33–34.

2. Herman, J. J. and J. L. Herman. 1991. *The Positive Development of Human Resources and School District Organizations*. Lancaster, PA: Technomic Publishing Co., Inc., pp. 183 – 184.

3. Herman, J. J. and J. L. Herman, pp. 168 – 169.

4. Kearney, R. C. 1984. *Labor Relations in the Public Sector*. New York, NY: Marcel Dekker, Inc., p. 237.

5. Helsby, R. D., J. Tener and J. Lefkowitz, eds. 1985. *The Evolving Process — Collective Negotiations in Public Employment*. Fort Washington, PA: Labor Relations Press, p. 442.

6. Eberts, R. W. and J. A. Stone. 1984. *Unions and Public Schools*. Lexington, MA: D. C. Heath and Company, pp. 30 – 31.

7. Herman, J. J. and J. L. Herman, pp. 138 – 139.

8. Barrett, J. T. 1985. *Labor-Management Cooperation in the Public Service: An Idea Whose Time Has Come*. Washington, DC: International Personnel Management Association, p. 30.

9. Helsby, R. D., J. Tener and J. Lefkowitz, eds., p. 442.

10. Webster, W. G., Sr. 1985. *Effective Collective Bargaining in Public Education*. Ames, IA: Iowa State University Press, pp. 82 – 83.

11. Webster, W. G., Sr., pp. 10 – 13.

12. Webster, W. G., Sr., pp. 44 – 47.

13. Eberts, R. W. and J. A. Stone, pp. 30 – 31.

14. Coleman, C. J. 1990. *Managing Labor Relations in the Public Sector*. San Francisco, CA: Jossey-Bass Publishers, pp. 284 – 285.

15. Herman, J. J. and J. L. Herman, pp. 42 – 43.

16. Bacharach, S. B., J. B. Shedd and S. C. Conley. 1989. "School Management and Teacher Unions: The Capacity for Cooperation in an Age of Reform," *Teachers College Record*, 91(1):97 – 105.

17. Johnson, D. W. and F. P. Johnson. 1982. *Joining Together — Group Therapy and Group Skills, Second Edition*. Englewood Cliffs, NJ: Prentice-Hall, Inc., p. 4.

18. Bucholz, S. and T. Roth. 1987. *Creating the High Performance Team*. New York, NY: John Wiley & Sons, Inc., pp. 30 – 31.

19. Bucholz, S. and T. Roth, pp. 30 – 31.

20. Herman, J. J. and J. L. Herman, pp. 182 – 183.

Living Together Every Day in the Workplace

CHAPTER 2 discusses empowerment methodologies, and a variety of group and team configurations that can be used to implement a philosophy of empowerment for employees. It also presents information related to employee recognition structures and methods of involving union/management teams in day-to-day problem solving and decision making, and it discusses ways of creating and maintaining a productive and satisfying work environment. It ends with a discussion of methods involving union/management teams in day-to-day problem solving and decision making.

EMPLOYEE EMPOWERMENT

The late 1980s ushered in a change-oriented movement in schools which was given the popular name of *restructuring*. Restructuring was the name given to any idea that dramatically changed the structure of school districts or that changed the manner in which they operated [1].

In the 1990s, some legislatures, such as those of the states of Kentucky and Texas, mandated that school districts implement a restructuring plan entitled School-Based or Site-Based Management [2]. This movement is picking up steam as individual school boards mandate SBM, or individual school districts or individual schools voluntarily implement SBM. The theory that underlies SBM is that those closest to the action are those who are best able to make wise decisions related to the education of the children in the individual school building. Obviously, the SBM restructures a traditional school district by allowing bottom-up rather than top-down decision making. Many of the decisions that were previously made at the central level regarding personnel, budget, policy, and instruction are now delegated to the individual school building's SBM committee [3].

Although some SBM models include parents and community members, all SBM models give a great deal of decision-making power to teachers. Teacher empowerment and employee empowerment is clearly a trend of the 1990s [4], but this trend has some precedential configurations, and all of these shall be discussed next. The first of these precedential configurations is that of vertical work teams.

Vertical Work Teams

Historically, in school districts, vertical teams have been organized for relatively short time periods to accomplish a specific task. Traditionally, vertical teams of teachers, building administrators, and central office curriculum supervisors have been organized to develop a local school district's curriculum guides. Also, various categories of site level employees, site level administrators, and central level administrators have been, voluntarily or forcibly, formed into vertical teams for the purpose of training or staff development [5].

Not only have vertical teams been historically utilized to involve employees, but focus groups have also been created as a means of involving employees.

Focus Groups

Focus groups comprised of employees and management are usually assembled to deal with a problem that is facing the school district. Focus groups usually meet for very short periods of time, and the task of a focus group is usually one of isolating a problem, analyzing the variables that impact the problem, and brainstorming possible solutions. This input is then utilized by management in arriving at an action plan to resolve the problem that has been discussed [6].

Another historical method of involving employees is by assembling project groups.

Project Groups

Project groups are comprised of a variety of employees who are relieved of their basic duties, part time or full time, for the length of time necessary to complete the project. In school districts, project groups or task forces can be comprised of teachers, classified employees, administrators, or a combination of any of the three categories. Also in school districts, project groups many times meet after normal student school hours, or the members are employed during the summer months to work on the project [7].

This traditional form of employee empowerment utilizes the knowledge and skills of selected employees to develop a program modification, to solve a problem, or to create an innovative school building level or school district level service. Some examples of projects are: (1) to initiate a business/school partnership, (2) to solve the problem of lowering the adult/pupil ratio by modification of the volunteer program to recruit a large number of retired community members, and (3) to modify the existing school district's public relations program by creating a new marketing advisory committee comprised of representatives of each category of employee. This project group is charged with the responsibility of developing, implementing, and evaluating the success of the marketing efforts of each school building and of the school district as a whole [8].

Another vehicle for empowering employees that was initiated by some large American industries during the 1970s and 1980s is entitled QWL (Quality of Work Life). QWL has a subcategory called Quality Circles. Some school leadership districts in the 1970s and 1980s also developed QWL programs, and they found this structure and process, which was originally influenced by the success of Japanese industry, to be a very successful way of empowering employees [9].

Quality of Work Life

Quality of Work Life can be defined (1) as a *philosophy* that states that employees are capable and desirous of improving their work environment and level of production, (2) as a *goal* that attempts to make the work environment for employees the best possible work environment, and (3) as a *structure and process* that involves employees in continuously improving the quality of their work life. *Quality circles,* generally, are groups of six to eight employees who identify problems within their workplace; develop potential solutions to each problem; present their proposed solution to management and if management approves, the circle implements its solution [10].

Before discussing the details of QWL and quality circles, it is important to emphasize that this process is a voluntary one on the part of employee unions or employee groups and management. QWL central groups and their subset quality circles are also comprised of individual employees who volunteer their time to serve within this process. Let's now explore some of the classical details of this structure and process.

Characteristics of Quality of Work Life include the following.

- It is voluntary.
- It is a long-term continuous process, *not a quick fix.*
- Union and nonunion employees, as well as management, must voluntarily work to evolve the specific form and substance to implement QWL within their own school district.
- Decisions are made by consensus and all participants have equal status.
- Activities of QWL groups should never infringe on any right established by collective bargaining agreements.
- Members should participate in ongoing leadership skills development and in training for interpersonal communications and problem-solving methodologies.
- The QWL groups should be provided with the necessary budgetary, temporal, and other resources that are required for them to be successful.
- A trained central liaison should be available to assist the elected leadership, to help with training needs, and to coordinate the building level quality circles [11].

Some of the detailed housekeeping needs, which will enhance the probability of a successful implementation and maintenance of a QWL program, include the following.

(1) Start with a high-level activity to provide knowledge of and to enhance interest in the possibility of creating a QWL program for the school district.

(2) Get concurrent prior approval of the board of education, employee union leaders, and administrators to go ahead with the program.

(3) Establish budget accounts, naming the persons who are authorized to draw upon the budget, and determining the categories of activities for which expenditures can be made.

(4) Hire substitute employees when QWL or quality circle meetings are held on school district time.

(5) Hire consultants, especially during the initiation year, if the internal school district liaison or other school district employees are unable to provide members with the training required or desired.

(6) Have the QWL central committee develop and adopt bylaws before starting the entire QWL program. These initial bylaws may need to be modified later, but they will provide clear-cut guidelines for the conduct of QWL business.
(7) Conduct a needs assessment to determine the types of training required and desired by employees and management [12].

Given that QWL and quality circles provide a structure and process for empowering employees, let's turn to some of the major advantages of QWL. The most important advantage of a QWL approach to employee involvement is that it improves employee/management relations by utilizing the full intelligence of every employee who volunteers to participate in improving the school district's work climate, which, in turn, improves the school climate for students and lets every employee know that she/he is valued, cared for, and respected.

A QWL process opens the communications system among employees and between employees and administration. It eliminates much of the top-down communication, and it allows problems to be solved at the level at which the work is performed. It creates a team approach to planning, training, innovation, communication, problem solving, productivity, and quality control.

- It creates a collaborative approach between employee unions and the school district's management, rather than wallowing in an adversarial labor/management relationship. It also allows both labor leaders and administrators to bask in the sunshine of success, realizing that they assisted employees in improving their work environment.
- It creates an employee empowerment structure and process that allows for innovative programming, training, and problem solving, which result in productive short-term operational and long-term strategic collaborative planning.
- It allows for both district-wide and work site (quality circle) components, and it is geared to improving the work climate at the individual employee, subgroup, and district levels.
- It is people-oriented, process-saturated, and success-reinforced, and it stresses the worth and dignity of the human element, while the organization's health will improve as a welcomed bonus [13].

However, the most current popular program of employee involvement is called school-based or site-based management. Let's now turn to a detailed discussion of this very popular restructuring procedure, which emphasizes the wise and productive use of all employees.

SCHOOL-BASED MANAGEMENT

Although QWL diminished, to some degree, the power of union leaders and school district administrators in school districts that have officially recognized unions who are empowered to collectively bargain with management, one of the bylaws that controls QWL structures and processes always states that QWL activities cannot conflict with or replace any activities that are reserved to the union under a collective bargaining master contractual agreement [14]. On the other hand, school-based management structures and processes, especially if they involve parents, taxpayers, and some of the community's power people, have the potential to seriously impact the environment within which collective bargaining takes place. This potential, if activated, may cause conflict within the school district, lessen the power of union leaders and school district administrators, and may impact both board of education policies and collective bargaining master contractual agreements. These master contracts may be affected during the process of negotiations, and they may be affected during the operation of a previously negotiated master contract [15].

To realize the potential impact on collective bargaining and union/management relations, one only has to review the current state of affairs related to SBM legislation. After defining school-based management, we shall next turn to an overview of legislative action in the arena of restructuring, specifically related to the structure and process of school-based management.

School-based management is a structure and a process that delegates greater decision-making power regarding any or all of the areas of instruction, budget, policy, personnel, and all matters related to governance at the local school building level, and it is a process that involves a variety of stakeholders, including employees, in the decisions that relate to the local individual school building's programs and operations [16].

The legislatures of Kentucky and Texas have mandated school-based management as a portion of dramatic educational restructuring legislation. Also, many school boards and administrative leaders are mandating school-based management within their school districts, and many teachers, teacher unions, principals, and superintendents are voluntarily entering the process and structure of school-based management [17]. Many of these districts are involving parents and community members, as well as teachers and other employees, in the composition of their school-based management teams, but all SBM structures empower teachers in the process.

The most dramatic and far-reaching mandate is that passed by the Kentucky Legislature and entitled the Kentucky Education Reform Act of 1990. Although the act made many other dramatic changes, such as transitioning from an elected state superintendent of public instruction to an appointed commissioner of education, and abolishing the existing state department of education structure, an elaboration of the provisions of the act related to school-based management will demonstrate Kentucky's commitment to using the SBM structure and process as a means of restructuring schools for the purpose of improving the education of children [18].

The basic provisions of the Kentucky Education Reform Act of 1990 are numerous. Those that impact a local Kentucky school district through mandating a form and structure Kentucky has termed School-Based Decision Making (SBDM) are included in Appendix G at the end of the book.

In consideration of the dramatic changes required by the implementation of school-based management, let's discuss the questions that anyone considering SBM should ask before entering into an SBM structure and process.

The September, 1990 issue of the National Association of Secondary School Principals' *Bulletin* includes an article entitled "School-Based Management: A Checklist of Things to Consider," and this checklist is repeated below as an aid for any school district's or school building's decision makers who are investigating the possibility of entering into an SBM structure and process. Answer "yes" or "no" to each question.

(1) Do you really believe in shared decision making?
(2) Are you willing to take full responsibility (accountability) for your decisions?
(3) Have you decided which stakeholders should be given the power to make final decisions?
(4) Have you decided which stakeholders will be given a role in the decision-making process?

(5) Have the central decision makers reached agreement with the building decision makers on the policies, procedures, and methodologies to implement the process of school-based management?

(6) Have the local decision makers been given maximum decision-making power and flexibility related to staffing, instruction and operation budget decisions?

(7) Have you allowed sufficient time to reflect on all important decision areas before establishing a date to implement?

(8) Do you realize that this may cause an additional workload to be placed on the principal and the school building's employees?

(9) Have the local decision makers clearly defined, in operational terms, what they mean by school-based management; have they developed the bylaws and policies that are necessary for implementation?

(10) Have you determined the outcome measures that will be assessed to decide whether or not your locally designed program of school-based management is working well, or whether or not it requires modification?

(11) Are the roles of the central personnel and the building personnel crystal clear in each area of decision making?

(12) Is it clear, on the continuum of decision-making possibilities, which decisions are totally school-based, which are totally district-based, and which are shared?

(13) Have you budgeted time and money to conduct training or staff development programs for those persons who are to become involved with school-based management for the first time?

(14) Have you decided upon methods to perform formative and summative evaluations?

(15) Will each school be able to develop its own school-based management procedures, or will there be a district structure applied to all school buildings within the school district?

(16) Do you have realistic expectations of what school-based management can do, and do you realize that it is not a ''cure-all'' for everything that is happening in the schools?

(17) Do you realize that this is not a ''quick fix,'' and that it will take considerable time and effort to implement and improve the process that you initially use?

(18) Do you realize that over a long time period, not only will the decision-making process change, but there will be a dramatic

(hopefully, positive) change in the entire culture of the organization?

(19) Are you prepared to collect "hard" and "soft" data to make a yearly report of the degree of success of the school-based decision process in your school building?

(20) Do you really believe that the process of school-based management will improve the effectiveness and efficiency of your school and your school district, or are you involved simply because it is the thing to do?

(21) Do you believe that school-based management will improve communication, trust, and collaboration between the school building and the school district levels?

(22) Do you believe that school-based management will create a greater feeling of ownership and greater support from the employees and the community at large?

(23) Do you really like and respect people, and are you willing to depend on them to help you make important decisions?

(24) Do your employee union leaders and your board of education members buy into school-based management?

(25) Do you believe that dispersed leadership is the best type of leadership, and do you believe that school-based management nurtures and stimulates new leadership at all levels of the organization?

(26) Do you realize that school buildings and school districts are open systems, and that school-based management is a process that improves the schools' ability to become more open?

(27) Do you believe in "loosely coupled" organizations?

(28) Do you believe that school-based management can promote continuous school renewal?

(29) Do you believe in promoting entrepreneurial efforts?

(30) Again, do you really believe and trust people, and are you willing to share your decision-making power?

(31) What types of training are you going to provide the school-based management team? Are they related to:
(a) Communication skills?
(b) Planning skills?
(c) Decision-making skills?
(d) Problem-solving skills?
(e) Other skill areas?

(32) What specific procedures will you put in place to arrive at decisions related to:
   (a) Staffing?
   (b) Budget?
   (c) Instruction?
   (d) Building level governance?
   (e) Other? [19]

An important factor in any work environment is recognizing the positive contributions of individual employees and groups of employees, including union groups. We shall now discuss ideas related to employee recognition and the creation and maintenance of this type of a work environment.

EMPLOYEE RECOGNITION AND THE CREATION AND MAINTENANCE OF A PRODUCTIVE AND SATISFYING WORK ENVIRONMENT

A work environment, to be both productive and satisfying, has to maintain a positive balance between the *positive feeling tone* among employees and a *positive level of quality output and outcomes*. An environment with a positive feeling tone but with a low level of outputs and outcomes, is one that eventually will lead employees to a feeling of defeat, and it will also lead to a reduction in morale regarding their own contributions and about the quality of the school district in which they work. On the other hand, an environment that produces acceptable outputs and outcomes but which leaves employees with an attitude that no one recognizes their contributions or is concerned about their well-being, will eventually become an organization with low morale and with low productivity [20].

To create and maintain a positive work environment, employees must feel that they:

- are trusted by their peers and by the administration
- have interesting work to do
- are wanted, cared for, and respected
- have an opportunity for self-growth
- have security in their positions
- are provided the opportunity to give input into matters concerning them and into matters of importance to their school and school district
- are challenged and are making an important contribution

- are crucial elements in a high-quality school district that produces high-achieving students, very productive employees, and a community that supports and respects the educational efforts of the school district [21]

Finally, it is important for management to plan celebrations for employees' successes and to recognize good contributions by individual employees, groups of employees, and the employees' unions [22]. Although the administrators and boards of education of school districts can develop recognition programs, such as employee of the week or month, designation as a master employee, or merit or performance pay for highly productive individuals, more significant and accepted forms of employee recognition are those wherein the administration creates programs for students, parents, business and industry groups, and professional groups to find specific ways to recognize employees. The most important source of employee recognition is one in which management creates a program for employees to select and publicize individual employees and groups of employees who perform in an extraordinary manner, by the visible evidence of the quality of their work [23].

Now that we have discussed ways of empowering employees, let's end by discussing a formal means of empowering members of the employees' unions and managements' representatives to avoid potential union/management problems or to solve existing problems within the school districts where they work.

METHODS OF INVOLVING UNION/MANAGEMENT TEAMS

Union/management teams are variously sized groups that are comprised of official representatives of the employees' union and the official administrative representatives of the school district. The union/management teams meet for a variety of time periods, depending on the issue upon which the team is focusing. This approach allows for continuous and formal communications between union and management, and it promotes trust and respect between the union's and management's official representatives as they work collaboratively, rather than in an adversarial manner, to improve conditions for employees and to improve the operations of the local school district [24].

Some of the major tasks that can be undertaken by union/management teams are:

- to solve employee grievances without getting into adversarial positions or going to grievance arbitration

- to discuss items that might well be problem areas in upcoming contract negotiations, in a manner that informs each party of the needs of the other so that both parties may work towards eliminating impasse possibilities prior to formally sitting across the table from one another during collective bargaining sessions
- to discuss and resolve union/management problems that currently exist in the school district
- to plan specific approaches to improving the school district
- to jointly collect accurate information related to specific grievance situations, upcoming potential collective bargaining issues, and to collect comparative information from comparable school districts about salary, fringe benefits, and other matters related to teachers and classified employees

Through a myriad of cooperative endeavors, the union's and management's officials will avoid negative feelings towards one another, will provide a model of conduct for the total group of employees and administrators within the district to emulate, and will display a mature, professional approach to union/management operations that will be recognized and appreciated by the school district's patrons [25].

SUMMARY

The chapter discussed a variety of means of empowering employees. Specifically, brief discussions about vertical teams, focus groups, and project groups were presented. More lengthy discussions were provided related to the very popular 1970s and 1980s innovation called QWL (Quality of Work Life) and its subset technique entitled quality circles, and an extensive presentation was provided on the current important and popular restructuring program entitled school-based or site-based management. The highlights of the mandates related to SBM included in the Kentucky Reform Act of 1990 were related, as well as a series of questions to be reviewed by local school district decision makers, prior to entering into an SBM structure and process.

The importance of recognizing the contributions of employees was emphasized, and the factors that are important in creating a productive and satisfying employee work environment were presented. Although management's involvement in employee recognition programs was mentioned, stress was placed upon the belief that the strongest role of management is one in which management assists other groups, especially employees themselves, in developing programs that recognize the positive contributions of individual employees and groups of employees.

The chapter ends by stressing the advantages of creating union/management teams that collaboratively explore problem solutions and program improvements. The resultant improvement in day-to-day union/management relations when union/management teams are operative was emphasized.

EXERCISES

1. What forms of employee empowerment exist in your organization, and what forms do you feel can be added to improve the employees' work environment?

2. What detailed steps would you place in your plan if you wished to install a QWL (Quality of Work Life) and quality circles operation in your school district?

3. What categories of stakeholders would you involve in an SBM (school-based management) team in your school district, and why would you include each category?

4. How would you go about initiating an SBM program in your school district?

5. What scales could you use to measure the impact of a QWL or SBM program in your school district?

6. What are the advantages of creating union/management teams in your school district?

REFERENCES

1. Lewis, A. 1989. *Restructuring America's Schools.* Arlington, VA: American Association of School Administrators, pp. 3−4.
2. Herman, J. J. 1991. "School-Based Management: a Primer," *NASSP Bulletin.*
3. Herman, J. J. and J. L. Herman. (In press.) "The School Business Official's Roles, Opportunities, and Challenges Related to School-Based Management," *School Business Official.*
4. Herman, J. J. and J. L. Herman. 1991. *The Positive Development of Human Resources and School District Organizations.* Lancaster, PA: Technomic Publishing Co., Inc., p. 232.
5. Metz, E. J. 1981. "The Verteam Circle," *Training and Development Journal,* 35(12):79−85.
6. Herman, J. J. and J. L. Herman. 1991, pp. 30, 33.
7. Herman, J. J. and J. L. Herman. 1991, pp. 149, 160−162, 220.

8. Pace, R. W., P. C. Smith and G. E. Mills. 1991. *Human Resource Development — The Field.* Englewood Cliffs, NJ: Prentice-Hall, Inc., p. 46.

9. Herman, J. J. and J. L. Herman, 1991, p. 109.

10. Herman, J. J. and J. L. Herman, 1991, p. 153–162.

11. Herman, J. J. 1982. "Improving Employee Relations with QWL," *Michigan School Board Journal,* 29(7):10–13.

12. Herman, J. J. 1984. "The Quality of Work Life: Has it Come of Age?" *Journal of the New York State School Boards Association* (August):19–21.

13. Beer, M. et al. 1985. *Human Resource Management.* New York, NY: Macmillan, pp. 581–582.

14. Kaufman, R. and J. Herman. 1991. *Strategic Planning in Education.* Lancaster, PA: Technomic Publishing Co., Inc., pp. 109, 163, 167.

15. Herman, J. J. and J. L. Herman. (In press.) "What's New in Educational Administration, Part Two — School-Based Management," *The Clearing House.*

16. Herman, J. J. 1990. "School-Based Management," *Instructional Leader,* Texas Elementary Principals and Supervisors Association, 3(4):1–5.

17. Lewis, A. 1989, pp. 173–175.

18. Van Meter, E. J. 1991. "Kentucky Mandate: School-Based Decision Making," *NASSP Bulletin,* 75(527):52–62.

19. Herman, J. J. 1990. "School-Based Management: A Checklist of Things to Consider," *NASSP Bulletin,* 74(527):67–71.

20. Herman, J. J. and J. L. Herman, 1991, p. 188.

21. Herman, J. J. and J. L. Herman, 1991, p. 188.

22. Guthrie, J. W. and R. J. Reed. 1986. *Educational Administration and Policy — Effective Leadership for American Education, Second Edition.* Boston, MA: Allyn and Bacon, p. 348.

23. Herman, J. J. and J. L. Herman, 1991, pp. 219–220.

24. Venter, B. M. and J. Ramsey. 1990. "Improving Relations: Labor Management Committees in School Districts," *School Business Affairs,* 56(12):20–23.

25. Herman, J. J. and J. L. Herman, 1991, pp. 183–184.

26. Miller, M. H., K. Noland and J. Schaaf. 1990. *A Guide to the Kentucky Education Reform Act.* Frankfort, KY: Legislative Research Commission.

Considering the Students, the School District, and the Community

CHAPTER 3 addresses the following questions. (1) Who are the stakeholders? (2) What is the responsibility of the district's management and of the employees' union to the school district's clients? (3) How is community input obtained? (4) How do you communicate with the school district's clients during normal day-to-day school district operations and during times of negotiations for a master contractual agreement?

To provide a brief historical note, the loss of confidence in management, in administration, in leadership, and in supervision of personnel in American education came about soon after the loss of confidence in big business management and the management of the labor unions during the early 1960s. Costs began to spiral, and legislatures began to feel the pinch of finances and could no longer fund the schools in the manner required. Higher salary demands to meet the marketplace expenses and basic survival needs became reasoned and reasonable expectations. The need for effective management became a reasonable expectation. Management in education (superintendent and central cadre) tied to the public coffers of property, income, and sales taxes had little recourse but to expect the state to better fund the educational process.

With the increasing costs in goods and materials needed to operate the very broad education spectrum (food service, office materials, books, transportation, insurance, construction, and renovation of facilities, and oftentimes having the largest payroll in town), there was not enough money left for salaries. State efforts had to be increased, but it was not enough. Therefore, the states passed legislation to permit public sector employees to reap the same benefits as those employed in industry. Conditions of work and salary could then be bargained. The results were varied, and all degrees of success and failure were realized.

Once a state legislature approves a collective bargaining law for public school employees [1], the result of each local contract negotiation can vary in accordance with the skill, attitude, and ability of both the union's

29

and the board of education's players in the serious game of negotiations. What are the possible results of each contract negotiation in terms of the stakeholders? Who loses and who wins when bargaining ends in a win/lose arrangement? Who loses when the bargaining ends in a lose/lose arrangement? Let's explore three scenarios and the impact of each on the district's stakeholders.

- *Win/win* is the result when there is a collaborative approach to problem solving by both the union and management representatives. The outcome results in students winning a better school environment, the employees having a better work environment, and the community attitude remaining at the status quo stage or improving in support of the school district [2].
- *Win/lose* is the result of an adversarial approach to contract negotiations, wherein each party to the negotiations, union and management, wins some and loses some. In this case, the outcome effect usually results in students losing some opportunities because of ever-tightening contractual mandates, employees losing some control over their individual day-to-day professional destinies, administrators and the board of education losing some control over the operation of the district for which they hold ultimate responsibility, and the community, perhaps, developing a decreasing attitude of support when strategies and tactics used during the negotiation process imply that either the union's or the board of education's representatives are not honest, are greedy, don't care about students, or any other negative strategic or tactical publicity that is released to the general public [3].
- *Lose/lose* usually results when an adversarial approach to negotiations by the union's and the board of education's representatives has gotten out of control. The negotiations have entered a serious impasse that may even end in a strike. In this case, the effect on all stakeholders is a serious negative one, and the negativism may carry over for years in the future. Students lose a great deal, as employees (teachers and others who are members of a union) may refuse to perform those duties that are normally expected. In addition, the environment in which students are to learn, assuming that the impasse has not yet led to a strike, is one that is extremely negative. Employees exist in a very negative work environment, and their focus will be on union tactics and their own job security. The board of education and its administrative staff will

be under great stress as employees work-to-rule, picket meetings, or utilize other similar strategies. Finally, the community, especially parents who have children attending the district's schools, will become upset with employees and the board of education for not achieving a reasonable contractual settlement. The effects on attitudes due to this serious impasse condition can well hinder progress of the school district's programs and negatively affect human relationships of the various stakeholders for years to come [4].

Now that we have explored the potential results of win/win, win/lose, and lose/lose collective bargaining on various stakeholders, let's discuss in more detail who these stakeholders are and what their interests are in the school district. Stakeholders, by the way, may consist of individuals and of groups.

WHO ARE THE STAKEHOLDERS?

The community residents are stakeholders but in a larger sense the entire country's residents are important stakeholders. Often during national and state level political races those running for office talk about the importance of education and the requirement that we improve our current system of education. Indeed, some presidential candidates and gubernatorial candidates sell themselves as the education candidate. This is also true of many candidates for seats in the national and state senate and house of representatives.

Obviously, community residents and civic, business, industrial, and other community organizations are immediate stakeholders because they produce the students and they pay the taxes to support schools. The parents and nonparents who reside in the local school district may be satisfied with the quality of their schools, or they may become upset with the way the district is operating and with the skills and knowledge that the district's students possess upon graduation. If supported, they may vote additional taxes to enrich an already good educational system, or they may withdraw financial support if they do not feel they are getting their money's worth. Businesses, industrial, civic, and other organizations are stakeholders because they have to have excellent schools in order to attract the quality of employees they desire, and, to a large extent, the quality of their employees will determine the quality and profitability level of their products [5].

Students, of course, are the most important of all stakeholder groups. Students, without a doubt, are the primary reason for school districts being in existence. They are the future; when they are amassed across the entire United States, they truly become our "nation in waiting." They will provide energy and the knowledge to propel the nation into a preeminent position in the world, and they will be the determining factor in our maintaining that leadership for succeeding generations. At the local community level, they will assume leadership, and, in large measure, they will determine the quality of life that will exist in the communities in which they choose to reside [6].

Teachers, classified employees, and administrators, when grouped together, are another important stakeholder group. The conditions under which they work are crucial to their meeting basic economic, social, and professional needs. If the negotiated contract improves upon these needs, the employees can spend more time and energy on improving the educational delivery systems for students. If the negotiated contract negatively affects these needs, the employees will have to spend more time and energy on satisfying these needs. Also, if the newly negotiated contract is perceived as a negative one, morale, efficiency, and effectiveness will suffer [7].

The final group of important stakeholders consists of the board of education and the individual members who comprise it. If contractual negotiations are conducted in an atmosphere of trust and cooperation and if a fair contractual settlement is reached as the end product, the board of education and its members will retain and perhaps improve the respect they have in the eyes of the general public and in the eyes of their employees. If, however, the contractual negotiations become adversarial and bitter and the negotiated contract is either unfair to the employees or the community, the board and its members will be the recipients of complaints, distrust, and disrespect. The conditions could deteriorate to the point that board members would resign or a totally new board of education would be elected as soon as board elections are held [8].

Looking at the best result, we find that the contract negotiated is a fair one to all parties and it is designed to assist students and to satisfy both employee and community needs. Finally, let's assume that the contract was negotiated through the collaborative efforts of the union's and the board of education's representatives. If this is true, what then are some elements of a positive scenario that would immediately result from this contractual settlement? From our wide-angle lens view of the school district, we can observe the following.

- The school year starts on time.
- Teachers and other employees are anxious to help students to learn.
- New students are anxious, and returning students are renewing old friendships and are eager to begin their classes and participate in their co-curricular activities.
- Nursery school and kindergarten students are dressed in their finest and are wondering what this new adventure is all about.
- Parents are anxious for their children to once again begin their formal learning, and those parents who are working outside of the home are relieved to be free of child care costs and the concern about where their children are and what the children are doing.
- The community at large begins a more normal pattern that will last approximately nine months of the year.
- Parents and nonparents begin to support the school district's students by becoming volunteers or members of booster groups for various types of student activities.
- Businesses, industrial firms, civic groups, and nonprofit groups assist the school district by offering student visits, by offering lecturers to classes, by participating in ''adopt-a-school'' programs or by involvement in a wide variety of other supportive activities [9].

Now let's turn to elements in a negative scenario, when the parties to negotiation are in a serious impasse situation, and when the negotiation has been adversarial and negative in tone. From our wide-angle lens view we can perceive the following elements.

- Teachers refuse to sponsor sport teams and other co-curricular activities because the union has decided this is a tactic that can be utilized to apply pressure on the board of education.
- School sites are picketed before and after normal school hours, and all meetings of the board of education are picketed.
- Both the board of education and the union slant communications and media releases to paint the other party as the villain.
- Employees ''work-to-rule.'' That is, they do such things as refuse to give homework, refuse to attend meetings called by the administration, or eliminate any voluntary activity. They only do what is absolutely legally required.
- Students are upset because employees have poor morale, refuse to give students extra help when it is requested, and spend a lot of time and energy on nonstudent-related matters.

- Parents and nonparents are disgusted with the situation, and they are complaining about the leadership of the district.
- Civic, business and industrial, and other community groups are concerned that their community will acquire a tarnished reputation that will have a negative effect into the future.
- Media sources have a field day.

If the negative scenario exists, all parties must pull together after a master contractual agreement is finally signed in order to get the district back on a positive note. Although all parties have a stake in recreating a positive environment, the two individuals who will have the most direct impact on the actions taken to improve the situation are those who work directly in each individual school building. These two important players are the union steward for the building and the school principal. Working together they can improve the morale of the staff as well as the school building's climate for students and employees. The principal's actions will also, to a large degree, determine whether or not the parents and residents of that school attendance area will again buy into a supportive stance.

Now that we have elaborated upon the stakeholders' identities, let's turn more directly to the clients' needs. Clients are the customers or recipients of what the schools within the district deliver.

WHAT ARE THE CLIENTS' NEEDS AND WHAT ARE THE RESPONSIBILITIES OF THE DISTRICT'S MANAGEMENT AND EMPLOYEES' UNIONS TO THESE CLIENTS?

At the local school district level, the clients are the students and the taxpaying residents of the local school district. The needs or rights of the clients should be well met by the providers, who consist of the employees of the school district and the board of education. For example, the students need to be ensured that the school to which they are assigned is ready for their occupancy. The school must be guaranteed to be neat, clean, well-repaired, bright, and cheerful. They ought to fulfill the need (or right) to be educated by the best staff using the latest and best equipment and supplies. They need to have a nonconfrontational setting or environment in which to learn and recreate. They need to have the resources spent in the best manner they can in order to derive the most from them. They need to have the proper time (both clock and calendar) allotted for the educative process. Diagnostic, instructional, assessment, or evaluative tools need to be at their disposal to assure that each is obtaining the highest level of assistance from the education. In short, students need and should be provided a minimum of:

- a safe and healthy environment in which to learn
- teachers and other school employees who care about them and respect them
- teachers and other school employees who have high aspirations for each student's academic achievement and social behavior, and who demand the best efforts from each student
- teachers and other school employees who possess a high degree of skill and knowledge related to subject areas taught and also related to the psychological, physiological, and social growth patterns of children and youth
- an expectation that when they graduate from high school, they will be able to obtain a good job and perform that job well, or that they will be well-prepared to enter and succeed at an institute of higher education

If these items represent the needs of student clients, what, then, are the needs of the clients of the district—the residents of the community? These clients need to be considered by both the union leadership and the administrative staff of the district, as it is usually the management group that bargains for the board of education, and thus represents the community and students by the virtue of management's position during the year and throughout bargaining. The clients, from both sides of the table, present a responsibility to both sides to be considerate of clock and calendar, curriculum and course, time and teachers, finances and fair play for the employees, and, certainly, a contract done on time. The responsibility of management is an onerous one to carry to the table.

The needs of the school district's clients include the following.

- The requirement to receive a product equal to or in excess of their investment. In other words, the community should expect that those responsible for the education of the community's students should turn out productive citizens who contribute in a positive manner to the community. They are academically well educated, economically productive, and conscious of their societal responsibilities.
- The expectation that the employees of the school district and the

members of the board of education see the school district as an integral and important part of the larger community, and that they cooperate with other elements in the community.

- The financial and other resources provided the school district by the residents of the community are spent wisely, efficiently, and productively [10].

Both the students' needs and the needs of the community's residents are responsibilities of the union members and of the district's management team. The two parties must work together and must reach a contractual master agreement that allows the needs of these clients to be met to the highest degree reasonable. To do otherwise is to neglect collective responsibility and to fail in an important professional obligation.

Now that we have identified stakeholders and discussed the needs of our two basic local client groups, we will turn our attention to means of obtaining client input.

HOW DO YOU OBTAIN CLIENT INPUT?

Prior to sitting down at the table to negotiate a master contractual agreement between the board of education and the union, it is wise to determine the expectations that the clients have for the school district. In this context, the clients of the union leadership are the members of their union. For the board of education, the clients are the community residents and the description of the quality of school district they desire and the components that they expect to be delivered by their school district [11]. Although many times forgotten in the heat of negotiations, the most important clients are the students of the school district, and both union and management share the responsibility of assuring that the student clients' needs are adequately represented during the negotiations dialogue.

Although obtaining reliable and useful input is a difficult task for both the union's negotiation team and management's negotiation team, it appears to be an even more difficult task for management than it does for the union. Time and information are the two elements of negotiating power, and both of these elements generally favor the union. Use of these power factors is made difficult for management. The time factor is taken from management in education because of the historical calendar and because the corresponding funds are not an issue, since the law dictates the number of days of attendance in most, it not all, of the states. Information is hard to protect due to the public nature of the operation of the district. The district's open budget and enrollment and programmatic data are examples of this. There is little the management team brings to the table beyond the undisclosed outer concession limits that the board has set. There is very little, on the other hand, that the union brings to the table that is known in advance to management; the surprise element can only be essentially on one side.

Once adequate input information is gathered, both the union and management should establish specific objectives to be achieved during the upcoming negotiations. Once the objectives are clearly in mind, both the union and management should go about the task of developing tactics and support materials designed to achieve those objectives.

The union negotiators usually have three sources of information related to the planning of their goals and objectives for upcoming contract negotiations. Through a national network, the union negotiators can obtain information on national trends, comparative national data, and any priorities that the national union wishes their local affiliates to address. Through the union's state organization, the negotiators can also obtain information on state level contract trends, suggested language for proposals, comparative state contractual data, and any priorities that the state's union leadership wishes the local units to address. Indeed, in many local school districts, a state representative (uniserve director) is an integral part of the local negotiation team's membership. Finally, the local union leadership usually conducts a needs assessment by polling or discussing priorities with all its local members. Traditionally, this is achieved by a questionnaire or by a series of meetings with focus groups. Following the needs assessment, the leadership decides on the priorities, goals, and objectives for the upcoming negotiations. The local union negotiators will also collect comparative information from other districts in their geographical region.

The board of education's negotiating team receives its direction only from the board of education. However, the negotiating team can collect data on the history of negotiations in the district, an analysis of grievances filed during the current and previous master contractual agreements, and comparative information from other local school districts in their geographical area or in their state.

The board of education and its administrative staff may also wish to collect broader-based information from the public at large [12]. Some of the possibilities for this broader-based input are as follows.

(1) The board of education may distribute questionnaires wherein some items can be ranked or prioritized by its clients – students and community residents. However, the board must be careful to protect the usefulness of the results in order that they can be placed in somewhat of a prioritized listing; otherwise the negotiation team will not be clear on the direction to take at the bargaining table.

(2) Another technique sometimes used by boards of education involves placing questions in newspapers. The board asks citizens to mail responses back to the school district's administrative offices. A caution has to be stressed at this point: children should not be used to deliver negotiation-related materials home, or to courier information back to the administration or board members.

(3) Another means of obtaining input is to survey the business and civic clubs by attending their meetings and asking to be placed on their agenda to obtain suggestions and feedback related to the school district and the upcoming contract negotiations [13].

Once the board of education has collected information from the various sources available, it must establish its goals, objectives, and priorities for the upcoming contract negotiations. Once this is done, the board provides this information to its negotiating team, and the negotiating team develops language proposals, strategies, and tactics to achieve the goals and objectives outlined by the board of education.

Once it has received input from its clients, the board must develop a plan to communicate with those clients. We now turn to that area of discussion.

HOW DO YOU COMMUNICATE WITH THE SCHOOL DISTRICT'S CLIENTS?

Again the union has a much simpler task, in that it can call meetings at any time and directly communicate with its total membership. In addition, because the union many times has a state union representative sitting in as part of its negotiation team, the union has access to all union contractual activities in the entire state. Many unions in large population areas also establish phone banks during negotiations. The local unions call in their progress during each negotiation session, and any local can call into the area's union negotiation communication media center to receive up-to-date comparative information on the position of every other local district's position.

On the other hand, the board of education and its negotiation team have a much more diverse and complex variety of clients with whom they have to communicate. This complexity can be understood by outlining the four phases of the collective bargaining process during which the board of education and administration may communicate. The four phases are: (1) before negotiations begin, (2) during the process of negotiations, (3) when conflict flares into the public eye and an impasse is declared, and (4) after the master contract is agreed to and ratified by both the union and the board of education.

The following is some action that can be taken in each phase.

(1) *Before contract negotiation begins* it is wise for the board of education to inform the community of the needs identified in the upcoming budget year. The focus should be on program needs, maintenance needs, and capital outlay needs. Obliquely, the message should be given that there is uncertainty over the costs of fringe benefits and employee salaries, as it is a year when a new contract has to be negotiated with the union(s) [14].

(2) *During the process of negotiations* it is generally wise not to provide any information to the media or the public while contract negotiations are moving forward. However, if impasse is reached, it is wise to have a news release that outlines the areas of disagreement between the board of education and the union. It is also important, at this time, to stress the progress that has been made to date.

(3) *During the impasse stages* which usually consist of mediation, fact-finding, and contract arbitration, it is crucial that a status report be given to the public at each stage. These reports should be limited to a factual account of the items in contention between the board of education and the union.

(4) *After the master contract is ratified by the union and the board,* the public has a right to know any significant provisions that were agreed to in the contract. They especially should be given information about the financial cost of the contractual settlement for each year of the contract, if the contract is a multiple year one [15].

SUMMARY

This chapter discussed the involvement of stakeholders, clients, and the larger community. The outcomes of a legislated bargaining process will impact these participants differently, depending on the nature of the union and management relationship, and the quality and amount of the collaboration that exists between the two. The corresponding results of win/win, win/lose, and lose/lose on the public are the production of positive attitudes, decreasing support, or extreme negativism.

The definition of stakeholders was enlarged to include all parent and nonparent community residents and students, as well as civic, business, industrial, and other community organizations, and also district employees and board members. These last stakeholders will respond particularly well to a win/win situation by exhibiting improved morale, efficiency, and effectiveness.

Scenarios were proposed which outlined the contrast between positive and negative collective negotiations. The needs of the clients—climate, academic achievement, teacher expertise, and readiness for job entry—were described. The needs of the community—"product" quality, district integration with the community, and wise financial expenditure, were likewise described.

Client input via expectations was outlined, both the clientele of the union membership and the clientele of the community. Broader-based community and historical information can be gathered to support the normal data and information gathered by both negotiating teams. Such input can be sought from the previous master contractual agreements, through questionnaires or media coverage, or through civic organizations. The board can then provide this information to the negotiating team.

The diversity and complexity of the board's clientele prevents constant, effective communications with those clients during the negotiation process, compared with the more sophisticated network available to the less-restricted union. Four phases of collective bargaining: before negotiations, during negotiations, impasse declaration, and ratification of the master contract were described, and the opportunities for communication with the board's clients were enumerated for each phase of bargaining.

EXERCISES

1. Identify the groups that management can go to for input at the initiation of the bargaining schedule. Record the group name and investigate the access channels to them.

2. Identify the significant groups in your community that need to know as much inside information as is plausible during the negotiations process.

3. Develop a memo to management team members to secure information to be used on any type of personnel contract (teachers, secretaries, etc.) that can be used to develop specific proposals in bargaining.

4. What would be the most feasible way to obtain pre-negotiation input from your community?

5. What communications structures (communications fan-outs) could you put into place to disseminate accurate information to all members of the management team?

6. What communications structures could you initiate to keep the public updated during negotiations?

7. How would you go about presenting important pre-negotiations information to the board of education, and how would you advise the board members to act during the establishment of negotiation guidelines?

REFERENCES

1. Freeman, R. B. and C. Ichniowski. 1988. *When Public Sector Workers Unionize.* Chicago, IL: The University of Chicago Press, p. 41.

2. Barrett, J. T. 1985. *Labor-Management Cooperation in the Public Service: An Idea Whose Time Has Come.* Washington, DC: International Personnel Management Association, p. 30.

3. Barrett, J. T., p. 29.

4. Webster, W. G., Sr. 1985. *Effective Collective Bargaining in Public Education.* Ames, IA: Iowa State University Press, pp. 166–167.

5. Coleman, C. J. 1990. *Managing Labor Relations in the Public Sector.* San Francisco, CA: Jossey-Bass Publishers, pp. 20, 104.

6. Helsby, R. D., J. Tener and J. Lefkowitz, eds. 1985. *The Evolving Process—Collective Negotiations in Public Employment.* Fort Washington, PA: Labor Relations Press, pp. 460–461.

7. Webster, W. G., Sr., pp. 52–53.

8. Webster, W. G., Sr., pp. 44–45, 48.

9. Smith, S. C., D. Ball and D. Liontos. 1990. *Working Together—The Collaborative Style of Bargaining.* Eugene, OR: ERIC Clearinghouse on Educational Management, University of Oregon, pp. 47–48.

10. Guthrie, J. W. and R. J. Reed. 1986. *Education Administration and Policy—Effective Leadership for American Education, Second Edition.* Boston, MA: Allyn and Bacon, pp. 43-44.

11. Keith, S. and R. H. Girling. 1991. *Education, Management, and Participation — New Directions in Educational Administration.* Boston, MA: Allyn and Bacon, pp. 268 – 269.
12. Herman, J. J. 1991. " The Two Faces of Collective Bargaining," *School Business Affairs,* 57(2):10 – 13.
13. Webster, W. G., Sr., p. 73.
14. Webster, W. G., Sr., pp. 121 – 122.
15. Webster, W. G., Sr., p. 76.

PREPARING FOR AND CONDUCTING COLLECTIVE BARGAINING

Section Two consists of four chapters. Chapter 4, *Choosing Your Team and Analyzing Their Team,* deals with the topics related to choosing, organizing, training, and operating with the negotiating team. It also includes a discussion of the advantages of analyzing the other party's team and its members. Chapter 4 ends with a comparison of the difference in behavioral rules that would govern the negotiations when dealing with a win/win environment, rather than dealing with an adversarial negotiating environment.

Chapter 5, *Collecting Background Information prior to Negotiations,* presents a discussion of the various types of background information that should be collected prior to entering into the act of negotiating a new or replacement master contractual agreement between an employees' union and the school district. The information collected includes information about the collective bargaining laws and procedures that govern negotiations in that particular state, financial information, comparative information about other school districts, historical information related to prior negotiations and grievances, and information about needed or desired changes suggested from the existing contract.

Chapter 6, *Preparing to Go to the Bargaining Table,* discusses the areas of drafting at-the-table proposals, anticipating and analyzing the other party's proposals, establishing the strategies and tactics that will be used during negotiations, determining the negotiation guidelines and establishing a pre-negotiations tone. The chapter ends with a discussion of differences that would exist in the preparation for win/win negotiations instead of adversarial negotiations.

Chapter 7, *Doing It: Conduct at and Away from the Table,* discusses the topics of ground rules, methods of exchanging proposals, controlling personality conflicts, selecting the spokesperson, establishing a communications hotline, and timing the negotiations moves. This chapter also discusses projecting multi-year costs, being flexible and creative, setting a tone, posturing and positioning, presenting proposals, analyzing proposals and using quid pro quos, and participating in sidebar bargaining. The chapter ends with a discussion of establishing priorities, cutting deals, drafting counterproposals, keeping score, and reaching closure.

Choosing Your Team and Analyzing Their Team

CHAPTER 4 discusses the following matters. (1) What should be the composition of the collective bargaining team? (2) What roles will the individual team members play? (3) What behavioral rules should govern the behavior of team members at the table and away from the table? (4) What types of pre-negotiations training should be provided to a new team member? (5) What categories of individuals or groups should be made available to support the negotiation team? (6) When should a team member be replaced? (7) What roles can or should be played by nonteam members such as the superintendent, board members, lawyers, business officials, staff, and line administrators? (8) What information should you acquire about the other party's team members, and how will this information be of benefit during the negotiations process? (9) How would the team membership and your procedures differ if you were involved in win/win negotiations rather than adversarial negotiations?

WHY A NEGOTIATION TEAM?

The law in many states is very clear as to the right of employees in public school districts to bargain for wages, hours, and conditions of employment. When such a law is passed, the proper election held, and a legal representative union selected, then the management is notified that there is a willingness to have a negotiated contract put into place. The need to meet to discuss the likelihood of a master contract requires the structure of a team for management.

Like a sports team, the degree of success in goal achievement by a negotiating team will depend upon the degree of skill, the attitude, and the degree of knowledge possessed by the team members. Also, like a sports team, a negotiation team will only be effective and efficient if the individual team members ably fulfill their individual roles, and the team

45

as a whole becomes a positive and high-achieving body. Therefore, selecting a team and determining how it will operate within the negotiating environment is a very important and crucial step in preparing to negotiate a master contractual agreement.

WHAT SHOULD BE THE COMPOSITION OF THE TEAM?

The composition of the negotiating team will vary somewhat according to the type of union group with which the management team is to negotiate. For instance, a school district's management negotiation team might well have different membership and the members may play somewhat different roles if the management negotiation team is dealing with a teacher's union's (AFT or NEA) local affiliate, or if the negotiation team is dealing with the Teamsters, ASCME, AFL, UAW or some other group representing food service employees, custodial or maintenance employees, transportation employees, or some other non-teacher group. The team would also have somewhat different characteristics and the members would probably play different roles if the negotiations were to be conducted in a win/win rather than an adversarial union/management negotiation environment.

One of the more significant tasks that the board of education, the superintendent, and the chief negotiator have is to select the proper team for bargaining at the table with the teacher's or other unions in the school district. It is significant because the team members need to complement each other and enable the chief negotiator to do an efficient job. The chief negotiator can be effective using the skills already possessed, but to be really efficient takes a strong support cadre of personnel who are as dedicated to improving the instructional program as they are to their positions in the district. To be on the team ought to be viewed as an honor ranking as high as any other bestowed upon an administrator.

The number of members on the team will vary with the requirements of each set of negotiations. The general guide is to have as few members as possible, but to include as many members as are required to do the job well. A good target number is six members. If you have too small a team, all the skills needed will probably not be covered, and if the team is too large, communications and actions become overly complicated and burdensome.

Those individuals who are responsible for selecting the board of education's negotiation team should initially choose the membership based upon general selection criteria that have been predetermined. The more important criteria should include:

- persons having a knowledge of the specific laws that control the collective bargaining process in that state
- those who have a knowledge of the history of labor relations in the school district and a knowledge of the current labor/management relations
- persons who have a knowledge of the school board's policies
- persons who have an understanding of the income sources and the expenditure patterns of the school district's budget
- those who know and understand the reasons for the various curricular and co-curricular offerings of the school district
- persons who can control their emotions at the table; good poker players who do not give away their hands
- those who have a lot of patience, since many times this process includes many long and tedious meetings
- persons who care about the quality of education offered students, care about the degree of effort of the taxpaying public, and honestly care about the welfare of the district's employees
- those who possess well-honed listening skills
- persons who can present proposals in a clear, complete, and convincing manner
- those individuals who will subordinate their personal interests to those of the negotiation team when a divergence of views comes about
- persons who are honest, considerate, and ethical

If the negotiation is to take place in a win/win environment, the criterion of being a collaborative decision maker should be added. In win/win, where joint problem solving is the key, a collaborative attitude is a prerequisite [1].

Now that we have outlined general criteria to be used in the selection of negotiation team members, let's discuss the appropriate number of team members and the roles that those members should play. In addition, let's add a few comments on those persons who probably should not serve on the negotiation team, and also add a few comments on the membership and roles of the members if there are negotiations taking place with multiple unions during the same time frame.

The size of the negotiation team is one that can vary depending on the specific character of the current negotiation, and one that can vary if the district is involved in multiple contractual negotiations during the same time period. It is probably not wise to have more than six team members sitting at the negotiations table, although other representatives may be briefly brought to the table for a very specific sharing of knowledge. Alternates should also be appointed in case one of the regular team members is incapacitated or cannot attend some meetings [2].

Significant purposes and tasks for team members could include the following.

- Read critically all proposals of the union.
- Read critically all counters to the management proposals.
- Study the members of the opposing team in order to be understood in confrontational settings.
- Prepare proposals from the subgroup being represented at the table.
- Prepare suggested counters to the opposing team's proposals, with emphasis on the area being represented.
- Do research on assigned topics for documentation to counters or proposals espoused by the CBA.
- Record comments made by "their" opposing team member in discussions at the table.
- Keep their alternate well informed of the work being done in the bargaining process.
- Suggest a caucus at a propitious time to share findings or observations that will assist the CBA.

WHAT ROLES SHOULD EACH TEAM MEMBER PLAY?

Each team member must be a good and accurate observer in the process. The chief negotiator cannot watch all the other team members as they react to the discussion. It is good to assign each team member to observe a specific member of the union team. It is also wise to switch observed members so that there is no tipping of the administrator's hand as to the process the members are pursuing. In any event, the observation of the other team must be done, and individual reports must be made to the chief negotiator in caucuses as she/he frames the counters with the team. Therefore, the observation of the opposite team, the ability to "read" the expressions and subtle nuances of the members' behavior (both verbal and nonverbal) are significant.

Each member ought to be in contact with the group of administrators he/she represents. They must be able to rapidly contact each member of the group, in order that a list of home and work phone numbers are obtained and available for the polling purposes—especially as the process begins to be finalized and the intensive item bargaining begins. Each member ought to be able to speak for his/her group and speak with authority. Perhaps some time at each administrative council meeting should be set aside for this purpose.

In general, the team members and the roles they should cover are as follows.

(1) The *spokesperson* is the most important team member. This is especially true if the negotiations are of an adversarial nature and if there is to be a single spokesperson for the board of education's negotiation team. The role of this person is one of complete control of communication at the table. This person must possess the ability to think on her/his feet, be able to manage conflict and disagreement within the team and between the union and management teams, must possess leadership skills that will cause consensus within the team members, and must share responsibility for the training and overall preparation for upcoming negotiations with the various negotiation team members [3].

(2) The *wordsmith* is another important member of the team. The wordsmith shall carefully prepare the wording of each proposal offered by the management's negotiation team, and the wordsmith shall be responsible for the detailed analysis of every word of every proposal brought to the table by the union's negotiation team [4].

A simple example of the importance of words can be seen when one realizes that the common words "shall" and "will" are mandatory, while the words "could" or "should" are permissive.

(3) The *cost/benefit analyst* is crucial to the team because that individual shall carry the basic responsibility of determining the financial cost of every potential proposal being developed by the management's negotiation team; this person shall also be responsible for determining the financial cost of every at-the-table proposal being made by the union's negotiation team. She/he not only determines the immediate cost, but also projects the financial cost of each proposal into future years [5]. Finally, this person can work with the other management team members to decide whether or not the benefit received through agreement with the proposal exceeds the financial costs involved.

A prime example could be the proposal by the union to lower the pupil-teacher ratio, based on the rationale that each teacher could then be more effective and could give each student more individual attention. While it would be difficult to argue with the desirability of small classroom student size, it could be extremely costly. In fact, if the average class size was twenty-five students and the proposal was to reduce it to twenty students, it is easily seen that numerous new teachers would have to be hired. In fact, this expenditure could well be more than that available to the district for all negotiation purposes [6].

(4) The *recorder* has the responsibility for accurately and comprehensively keeping a written record of every significant discussion or agreement point made at the table by the union, management, or by both parties [7].

(5) The *observer* is responsible for observing the behavior of the union team's members. Since many people telegraph their feelings by nonverbal cues or by tone of voice, the observer may observe that a head nodder always gives away the fact that she/he is agreeing with management's position, or a union team's member may display a very emotional tone of voice when she/he is angry about a statement made or a position taken by management's negotiation team. These cues can be helpful to the spokesperson for the management's negotiation team, because they allow the spokesperson to discern unstated agreements or hidden agendas, or to disrupt the union's spokesperson by triggering anger from one of the members of the union's negotiation team [8].

(6) The *instruction expert* is the one who knows the what and why of the instructional programs being offered in the district, and this expert can alert the management's negotiation team to the impact, positive or negative, of any proposal that the team is considering bringing to the table, as well as the impact on instructional programs of any proposal brought to the table by the union's negotiation team. Obviously, this expert position would be filled by different members of management if one were dealing with food services, transportation, secretarial and clerical personnel, aides, custodial and maintenance personnel, or any variety of union groups with whom management would negotiate [9].

In all probability, it is not wise to have the superintendent of schools or a board member serve on the district's negotiation team. They are persons to whom the team reports and from whom the management's negotiation team will get its guidelines. In any case, if the negotiations are adversarial in nature, there is the potential liability of losing a good superintendent or a good board member through adverse pressure or through political manipulations [10]. It may or may not be wise to have an attorney serve as the team's spokesperson, depending on the expertise possessed by the full-time administrative staff and the personality of the attorney. In any case, even though it is generally not a good idea to have a board member or a superintendent of schools serve on the district's negotiation team, they should be placed on the team if they are the only ones who possess the necessary negotiation skills [11].

The team membership may vary when multiple negotiations with a variety of unions are taking place within the school district during the same time period. In these cases, the board of education's negotiation teams should all have a skilled spokesperson, a wordsmith, a recorder, and an observer, but the expert may vary with each of the board of education's negotiation teams. In addition, the cost/benefit analyst may be used as an advisor to all the teams, rather than being seated as a member of a particular management's negotiating team.

Alternates are important in that they can be good resource persons to whom the chief bargainer turns for nonemotional involvement. By not being at the table, the alternates can be a good resource in times when new thinking is needed for the development of proposals or counters. Alternates can be placed in a group and assigned the task of writing proposals, and, therefore, they will be able to speak from the view of those not at the table and do this with little emotion tied to their comments.

FACTORS THAT IMPACT THE TIMING OF
TEAM SELECTION

There are several and differing influences on the date of appointment of the management team.

(1) The purposes of the bargaining need to be set first. If the contract is to be changed dramatically, the team needs to be in place for at least two months and meet at least eight to ten times before bargaining begins at the table.

(2) If the management team has to prepare proposals, then they need to be organized and discussion must be held based upon a survey of needs. If the team is to develop only counters to the union's proposals, it can be formed literally just before the first session.

(3) Frequently, the two chief negotiators will meet to discuss the upcoming process and set a date to initiate joint at-the-table bargaining. If this is done, the tone will be set, and the magnitude and purpose established. In any event, the team ought to be appointed at least two weeks before the first session.

(4) Contracts often stipulate the date to begin bargaining a new contract. In this case, the judgement of the chief negotiator will prevail, realizing the full impact of the task ahead.

(5) Contracts often stipulate the narrowing down of the numbers of items each side can bargain. This is particularly true, in a larger sense, with annual single contracts. If the wording is correct in the current contract, the alterations needing to be reopened can be done so during the year, so the early starting of bargaining is lessened.

(6) If the contract indicates that only reopeners, and not new proposals, will be entertained, the need for an early formulation of a team is less likely. The number of reopeners will affect the need for early assignment.

(7) Boards annually provide for a meeting schedule. Once known, the superintendent usually has a listing of essential items for each agenda as much as a year ahead of schedule. On one of these lists, the authorization for team selection should be placed.

(8) There will be other work being done by the administrative cadre. This is usually calendared; the chief negotiator may well want to wait until the total termination of this process before making any appointments in the areas upon which scrutiny is being focused this year.

(9) Another factor may be the age or experience of the team members. Some districts appoint a totally new team each time so that all administrators get trained, on the job, to handle confrontation and collaboration in negotiations.

(10) The total effort resulting in the amount of work to be done by the chief negotiator is highly significant. During the time the contract is in effect, the chief negotiator will be making marginal notes in the contract already bargained. Things that go well and those that require adjustment are noted throughout the year to prepare for the next round of negotiations. The chief negotiator will undoubtedly develop some new proposals based upon any application of the grievance procedure. These proposals may be in the form of new

statements to be added to an article in the contract or be prepared as a counter to one that is already spelled out. Summarily, the chief negotiator ought to be ready to assume leadership when the bargaining is slated to start.

(11) Expectations of the superintendent and the board of education need to be considered in terms of when to appoint the team. If the superintendent and board desire large-scale changes in the contract, the chief negotiator needs to ensure success by having the team appointed early.

(12) Lastly, the chief negotiator may wish to appoint the new team as soon as the contract is ratified, which takes away some of the mystery and allows for constant contact as she/he develops new strategies, proposals, or counters. This may be particularly helpful to a group that has not served before. However, a team that is appointed too early may cause some concerns, as the union may place individuals under pressure because they are official team members. There is no harm done in applying several different techniques to see which is best for the district. Be aware, however, that the union changes leadership also, and such change may well call for a different counter strategy by the board and its team.

Now that we have discussed the composition of the collective bargaining team, the roles various team members should play, and the timing of appointing the team, let's turn to the topic of the behavioral rules that should govern the board of education's negotiation team at the table and away from the table.

NEGOTIATION TEAM'S BEHAVIORAL RULES

The rules by which any negotiation team operates depend on the directions given by the official body (the board of education, in the case of the management's negotiation team), which precede the overall guidelines provided to the negotiation team, and to the specific style and role to be played by the negotiation team's chief negotiator and spokesperson [12]. There are three at-the-table choice of rules, depending on the intensity of the negotiation session, the degree of adversarial attitudes, and the experience level of the negotiation team's members. The three choices are: (1) no one speaks at the table but the chief negotiator, (2) all persons are free to speak at any time, and (3) other members besides the chief negotiator can speak at the table, but only if they send the chief negotiator a note asking permission to make a certain comment. If the chief negotiator sees the comment as helping the management's discussion, permission will be granted [13].

With reference to this communication, it is also helpful to consider the shape of the table for bargaining. The chief negotiator needs to be able to make eye contact with his/her team members at any and all times. A straight alignment of chairs will not facilitate this; with practice and judicious chair arrangement, the bargaining team should be able to operate comfortably when the sessions begin.

During caucuses, within a negotiation session, every member is encouraged to give her/his full views and suggestions on all topics being considered. However, between negotiation sessions, only the board's chief negotiator should communicate with the union's chief negotiator. To allow otherwise is to add confusion and complication to an already complicated process.

The chief negotiator ought to encourage the team members to be as nonreactive to issues and items as they can be. The very idea that the nonverbal reading gives away some tone of the discussion is one that needs to be covered in depth. The other behavior that may be desirable is to have the team be prompt in attendance and supportive when issues develop.

If there is truly a win/win attitude during negotiations, all persons on both teams should be able to express an opinion that they hold freely and completely. This open format with complete freedom of expression will serve win/win negotiations well, as the format is for collaborative problem solving with the sole desire to reach a fair and equitable master contractual agreement [14].

With regard to the presence of visitors or observers, the authors have bargained both ways. The difficulty is that the union will maintain the same right to have observers in the room. Whereas one author feels that there is no room for observers in the process, the other feels that it is to the advantage of the bargainers to have a fresh viewpoint expressed in the caucus after an observation. Both authors, however, agree that for the initial or single contract bargaining, there is little or no room for observers. Observers do become less than disinterested in the process, and, like other situations in education, when there is an observer in the room, the chemistry between the chief negotiators and team members is altered. This is particularly true when a visitor is credentialed (such as a superintendent or a board member), and when that person may be involved in a later process. The exposure via observation could affect their means of thinking about the entire contract later. Alternates could attend sessions which also might well affect their potential involvement.

Now that we have discussed the negotiation team's composition and the roles of team members, as well as behavioral rules, we must address the important matter of pre-negotiations training for negotiation team members [15].

PRE-NEGOTIATIONS TRAINING FOR TEAM MEMBERS

If there are negotiation team members who are new to the process, it is crucial that they be given pre-negotiations training. Also, if any significant amount of time has elapsed since the last contract negotiations, it is wise to have some training reviewed for experienced members of the negotiation team.

The types of training that prove most helpful for negotiation team members include: (1) communications, (2) language analysis, (3) review of applicable laws, (4) review of the history of previous negotiations and the history of employee grievances, (5) methods of acquiring helpful comparative data from other school districts, (6) financial status and implications for negotiations, (7) at-the-table behavior, and (8) strategies and tactics to use at the table and outside the negotiation sessions. Let's briefly explore each of the training areas.

- *Communications* training should include the skills of: (1) active listening (listening for emotional tone, not just the spoken word), (2) nonverbal cueing (facial and other mannerisms that telegraph what the person is thinking), (3) paraphrasing (the repeating by the listener of what was said to make certain the meaning is clear), and (4) wait time (not immediately responding, but allowing time to think and react before commenting) [16].
- *Language analysis* training is important, as all members of the negotiation team should be very alert to the actual meaning and the potential for multiple meanings of each word in every article proposed by their team or proposed by the other negotiation team. Again, the use of the words "will" and "shall" (mandatory words) instead of "could" and "should" (permissive words) provides dramatic examples of the importance of training in this area [17].
- *Method of acquiring comparative information* is a training area that

is important for negotiation team members. For the most part, unions—especially teachers' unions—have access to a bank of comparative information on every school district in their region, their state, and the nation. It is incumbent upon management's negotiation team to acquire details of the economic and noneconomic provisions of every master contract from comparative districts within their geographical area, or from those districts to whom they will have to be ultimately compared. Salary structures, fringe benefits, and contractual language are all important. Also, it behooves the management negotiation team to establish a network with those districts who will be involved in negotiations during the same time frame in order to immediately discern the current status of negotiations on each important contractual area being proposed in those districts.

- *Financial status and its implications for negotiations* is another key area of training. Each negotiation team member should fully understand the income and expenditure status of the budget, its historical allocations, and the amount of money available for all purposes, including negotiations [18].

- *At-the-table behavior training* is crucial. If members of a team do not behave in accordance with the pre-decided standards, the at-the-table and the away-from-the-table bargaining can become a comic disaster with very serious consequences for the employees, management, the school district, the community, and most importantly, the students [19].

- *Strategies and tactics* that will be employed and are useful during the negotiations should be discussed and clearly identified. Simulation training for the negotiation team members will assist them in perceiving how various strategies and tactics may or may not be effective during the upcoming negotiations [20]. It may be a good idea to have the previous year's management team come to the table and role-play as the opposition. More caucuses will need to be called during the first actual sessions as the chief negotiator spots something that should be discussed, and will need to be clarified while the observation is fresh in team members' minds.

As an additional consideration there may be different team choices to be made to meet the demands of win/win versus adversarial bargaining. If the situation is deemed to be a no-win situation for management, it is advisable to arrange for those who are not intimidated over conflict to be appointed to the team. There are frequently those in administrative positions who are not highly regarded by the union. They should not be included on the bargaining team if the atmosphere is adversarial.

Let's now turn to a discussion of the categories of individuals and groups that should be made available to support the district's management negotiation team.

SUPPORT GROUPS AND INDIVIDUALS

Although the administrative negotiation team members will be the primary messengers, they often require support from the board of education, the superintendent of schools, the business manager, the director of instruction, the director of food services, the athletic director, the director of library and media service, and other specialized members of the administrative staff. They also require the advice of principals, assistant principals, and department heads [21]. The type of support that is required is of three varying categories. First, they require advice on what should be placed on the table to improve the ability to effectively operate the district; second, they require advice on what should be taken out of the existing master contractual agreement; and third, they require advice on the potential impact on instruction and management of the district that any at-the-table proposal made by the union's negotiation team will have. All administrators need to be considered as significant support cadre members for the chief negotiator and team.

Now, let's turn to a discussion of situations that may justify removing a member of management's negotiation team from active participation in the negotiations process.

REMOVING A NEGOTIATION TEAM'S MEMBER

Removing a member from a negotiation team is a very serious decision, and is one that should not be taken lightly. Removal discredits that person as a viable and valuable member for not only the current negotiations, but it also, in all probability, removes the person from consideration as a member of the negotiation team in the future. This extreme action should only be taken under the following circumstances.

- During long and stressful adversarial negotiations, a member of the team becomes too physically or psychologically exhausted to

continue. In such a case, it is best for the individual and the team to remove the member [22].
- The team member has a serious personality conflict with a key member of the union's negotiation team, and that personality conflict is hindering progress towards reaching a ratified master contractual agreement.
- The team member telegraphs, by nonverbal behavior or voice tones, her/his attitude at the table, and this is a detriment to the poker-like attitude that is required of the team.
- The team member becomes so emotional and/or aggressive that she/he cannot abide by the predetermined behavioral rules established.

Let's next turn to the roles that can or should be played by nonteam members such as: (1) the superintendent of schools, (2) the board of education members, (3) the school attorney, (4) the school district's business manager, and (5) the other staff and line administrators.

ROLES PLAYED BY NONTEAM MEMBERS

Significant controlling or helping roles can be played by the board of education, individual board members, and various nonteam administrators during the process of negotiating a new master contractual agreement with an employees' union. Some of the more important roles by management position are as follows.

- *The board of education,* as a whole, initially provides the overall guidelines that direct the strategic goals of the negotiating team [23]. These guidelines always include financial guidelines, but they sometimes include nonfinancial guidelines as well. In addition, the board of education must react to information and requests from their negotiation team when the team proposes a need to modify the original board of education's guidelines. Finally, the board will have to vote in an officially called board of education meeting to ratify the contract that has previously been ratified by the union. If the district enters the impasse stages of mediation, fact-finding, and arbitration, the board of education must, again, provide guidelines within which the negotiation team must operate [24]. Also since these impasse procedures are many times strung out over a long time period, the board may have to modify its guideline instructions to fit the stage in which the impasse procedures are entered.

- *Individual board members* may also have crucial roles to play [25]. During adversarial bargaining, the president of the board of education or some other board member should be designated as the sole spokesperson for the board when communicating with the media or the general public [26]. This person should also be apprised of the negotiation situation, on a day-to-day basis, through the superintendent of schools.
- *The superintendent of schools* should be available for consultation with the management team's chief negotiator at any time, and she/he should assist the chief negotiator in communications with the board of education members [27].
- *The school attorney* should be available to the negotiation team to read over any language proposed by either negotiation team before the article is TA'd (tentatively agreed to) at the table. The attorney can determine if any of the language puts the district in a position of illegality [28].
- *The business manager,* when sitting as a member of the negotiation team, is a most valuable support resource. The business manager can inform the negotiation team of the amount of money available to settle the contract negotiations, and she/he can price out the cost of all at-the-table proposals by both management and labor [29].
- *Other nonteam administrators* can provide valuable insights to the negotiation team regarding the potential impacts of any proposal made by either the management's team or the union's team on instruction and management in their particular area of specialty and work assignment [30].

Let's turn now to the information that should be collected about the union's team members.

COLLECTING INFORMATION ABOUT THE OTHER TEAM'S MEMBERS

Collecting information about the other team's members is important. It is also important to discover if the control person on the team, who may not necessarily be the local union's spokesperson, is a regional, state, or sometimes even a national official in cases where it is predetermined that the union has established the district as a *target* district (one in which the union wishes to set some precedent).

It is desirable to place members on the team who have not, prior to selection, been too vociferous about the intended outcome of the contract. The management team must also assign one of its members to observe the other team's members and "read" them throughout the negotiations, by noting any changes of expression or displays of sympathy or opposition to any cause or issue presented by either team.

It is important to discover if the team is primarily composed of employees with long years of service to the district, or if it is composed of younger employees. In the case of the teacher's union, it is also important to discover if any of the team members are coaches, music teachers, guidance counselors, or some other identifiable potential control group.

It is also important to discover the specific interests and personalities of the union's team members. Finally, it is important to discover whether or not certain members have previously filed numerous grievances against the district, and it is equally important to discover the specific types of grievances involved [31].

All of this information will help management's negotiation team to deal more effectively with the individuals who comprise the union's team. Management's team members will have a good idea of the specific job categories represented at the table, and they will know about the personalities and interests of the union's team members.

Let's end this team discussion by stating the differences in the procedures utilized if management were to deal with a union that has bought into a total win/win approach to contractual bargaining.

WIN/WIN PROCEDURES

Much of what has been previously said can be modified if management's negotiating team is assured that the union's negotiating team will pursue the current negotiations from a total win/win collaborative approach. In this case, the primary characteristic to be possessed by management's team members is an attitude of cooperation and collaboration in mutual problem solving with members of the union's negotiating team. Also, all team members will be free to speak about any topic being discussed at any time.

In addition, much of the data gathering about comparative districts' contractual provisions can be a shared task, as well as the pricing out of each contractual article [32]. The district's budget should be an open book, and both parties should agree to the total dollars available to settle the contract that is currently being negotiated.

It is also feasible that the negotiation teams will agree to break into subcommittees comprised of members from both teams, who will have the task of arriving at the wording of specific articles and studying the article's impact [33]. Once these tasks are performed, the subcommittee will bring the proposed article back to the total group for at-the-table TA (tentative agreement) and for sign-off by both the union's team and management's team.

Since a great deal of information relating to negotiation teams has been covered, let's turn to a summary of what has previously been covered.

SUMMARY

The composition of the bargaining team, as one possessing skills, attitude, and degree of knowledge, strongly affects the success of negotiations. Choices of team membership are affected by the positive or adversarial nature of the negotiations. Team members should be versed in the law and procedures of bargaining, and should have a collaborative, patient, and calm attitude. Effective interpersonal skills are critical. The optimum size of the team is affected by the need to cover such team roles as spokesperson, wordsmith, cost/benefit analyst, recorder, observer, and instructional expert. The experience demands a skilled chief negotiator and backed up with a viable, symbiotic, supportive cadre of team members.

Behavioral rules must be established within the team, with the focus and control resting in the hands of the chief negotiator. A range of at-the-table intercommunication options is possible, with caucus interchange being much more open. If a win/win attitude prevails, an open format of interaction should be adopted.

Pre-negotiation training is desirable if there has been a gap in team experience or if neophyte members are assigned to the team. The types of training described as most helpful were: communications, language analysis, methods of acquiring comparative information (through research and investigation of comparative districts), financial status and implications, at-the-table behavior, and strategies and tactics.

The roles team members play, in addition to the specifically assigned ones, such as cost/benefit analyst, require an assigned observational match with a union team member, and also require members to stay linked with the team and administration for constant channeling of communication. Consideration should be given to the need for total membership discretion on discussion issues while negotiations are underway, and on the pros and cons regarding observer presence during sessions.

The time frame for team formation was considered in light of a number of factors, including the breadth of desired contractual change, in-place contract requirements, board and administrator calendar and workload demands, and the experience needs of team members. Ample lead time for preparation is important.

Support groups were described as the ''deep'' background resources for the negotiation team, supplying the supportive and specific factual information related to contractual items under consideration. The financial, temporal, and personnel resource impact of potential agreements must be assessed by these content-area experts. The role of such credentialed but nonparticipating individuals as board members, superintendents, and the school attorney was outlined. Dealing with situations when it became necessary to remove a team member was also described.

The chapter concluded with a rationale for the collection of information about the other team's members. The professional profile of the union's teacher team members and information about the interests and previous personnel interactions of them is valuable information. A perspective about the data-gathering procedure and coalition subcommittee formation during win/win negotiations was presented.

EXERCISES

1. Select an imaginary bargaining team and justify your choices by discussing the strengths needed and how these members can complement the entire team.

2. Name a chief negotiator and respond to the criticism of other administrators as to why this person should not be selected.

3. Hold a mini-bargaining session, with roles carefully defined, and see if an audience can identify particular roles.

4. Conduct a mock caucus, following the mini-bargaining session, to involve team members in the debriefing process.

5. Design a pre-negotiations training session for new team members, focusing on one of the types of training described in the chapter.

6. Determine whether adversarial or win/win bargaining (or meet-and-confer sessions) has been the norm in your district, and select two imaginary teams to deal with both situations.

7. Develop some articles to propose at the table. Do this as if you represented management, and also as if you represented the union.

REFERENCES

1. Coleman, C. J. 1990. *Managing Labor Relations in the Public Sector.* San Francisco, CA: Jossey-Bass Publishers, pp. 124−125.

2. Webster, W. G., Sr. 1985. *Effective Collective Bargaining in Public Education.* Ames, IA: Iowa State University Press, p. 144.

3. Webster, W. G., Sr., pp. 139-140.

4. Neal, R. 1980. *Bargaining Tactics−A Reference Manual for Public Sector Labor Negotiations.* Richard G. Neal Associates, p. 28.

5. Neal, R., pp. 26−27.

6. Granof, M. 1973. *How to Cost Your Labor Contract.* Washington, DC: The Bureau of National Affairs, Inc., pp. 20−22.

7. Herman, J. J. 1991. "The Two Faces of Collective Bargaining," *School Business Affairs,* 57(2):10−13.

8. Herman, J. J., 57(2):10−13.

9. Neal, R., p. 34.

10. Webster, W. G., Sr., pp. 24−26.

11. Cloyd, S. 1990. "Involving School Board Members in Negotiations," *School Business Affairs,* 56(12):24−27.

12. Schwerdtfeger, R. D. 1986. "Labor Relations Thrive When You Control Collective Bargaining," *American School Board Journal,* 173(10):41−42.

13. Coleman, C. J., pp. 125−126.

14. Helsby, R. D., J. Tener and J. Lefkowitz, eds. 1985. *The Evolving Process−Collective Negotiations in Public Employment.* Fort Washington, PA: Labor Relations Press, pp. 220−222.

15. Heisel, W. D. 1973. *New Questions and Answers on Public Employee Negotiation.* Washington, DC: International Personnel Management Association, p. 72.

16. Namit, C. 1986. "The Union Has a Communication Strategy−And Your Board Should, Too," *American School Board Journal,* 173(10):30−31.

17. Herman, J. J., 57(2):10−13.

18. Huber, J. and J. Hennies. 1987. "Fix on These Five Guiding Lights and Emerge from the Bargaining Fog," *School Board Journal,* 174(3):31.

19. Coleman, C. J., pp. 127−128.

20. Neal, R., p. 20.

21. Webster, W. G., Sr., pp. 28−29.

22. Neal, R., p. 22.

23. Webster, W. G., Sr., pp. 44−49.

24. Webster, W. G., Sr., pp. 158−159.

25. Schwerdtfeger, R. D., 173(10):41.
26. Cloyd, S., 56(12):24−27.
27. Kennedy, J. D. 1984. ''When Collective Bargaining First Came to Education: A Superintendent's Viewpoint,'' *Government Union Review,* 5(1):26.
28. Herman, J. J., 57(2):10−13.
29. Schwerdtfeger, R. D., 173(10):41.
30. Schwerdtfeger, R. D., 173(10):41.
31. Webster, W. G., Sr., pp. 158−159.
32. Webster, W. G., Sr., pp. 55−56.
33. Neal, R., pp. 182−183.

Collecting Background Information prior to Negotiations

CHAPTER 5 will answer the following questions. (1) What is bargainable? (2) What are the mandated subjects of bargaining? (3) What are the prohibited subjects of bargaining? (4) What are the permissive subjects of bargaining? (5) What data should be collected? (6) What is the role of past practice? (7) What are the at-the-table issues that have not reached closure during prior contract negotiations? (8) What are comparable school districts providing and doing? (9) What can you afford? (10) How do you get suggestions and opinions from those persons in the trenches (principals, supervisors, and other administrators) about problems they are encountering and about existing contract provisions they feel require changes? (11) When and under what conditions do you wish to settle the contract? (12) What are the differences, if any, in the preparation for and the information collected prior to bargaining when planning a win/win strategy instead of an adversarial strategy?

WHAT'S BARGAINABLE?

The first step in collecting information prior to negotiations is to obtain an updated copy of the state law and the rules and regulations adopted by the state's agency appointed to oversee collective bargaining — if any exists. In many states this agency is called the PERB, which stands for the Public Employee Relations Board [1]. With information in hand, particularly related to the topics of the manner of determining bargaining units, the scope of bargaining, impasse procedures, and grievance resolution provisions, it should be clear to the board of education's collective bargaining team which items are bargainable and which conditions have been predetermined by statute or a public governing body. The search of governing laws, and rules and regulations for the state in which the local school district is located should also provide clear information about which items are: (1) mandated subjects of bargaining, (2) permissive subjects of bargaining, and (3) prohibited subjects of bargaining [2].

Most states distinguish among those items that are mandated, permissive and prohibited subjects of collective bargaining [3]. A few examples will clarify the differences among these areas.

- *Mandated subjects* of collective bargaining usually include matters of salary and fringe benefits. Other items will vary from state to state.
- *Prohibited subjects* normally include the right to strike. In some cases, such items as hiring, supervision, job assignment, recruitment, discharge of employees, and evaluation of employees are prohibited.
- *Permitted subjects* include practically anything that can be agreed to by both parties, and which is not contradictory to any existing law. These items vary greatly from state to state to a greater extent than those items that are mandated or prohibited. In the absence of specific inclusion within the state's law governing collective bargaining, the state's public employment relations board's rulings or case law defines the area and range of permitted subjects of collective bargaining. Some items in this category could include class size, agency shop, and/or selection of instructional materials. Proposals and counters are significant here; once something is proposed and left on the table it does not make it bargainable.

Briefly, let's define, at this juncture, the differences among the terms: (1) agency shop, (2) union shop, (3) closed shop, and (4) meet and confer, since three of these categories exist within the states, and one category is prohibited. The specific category under which the local district falls is an important determinant of the strategies and tactics utilized during the negotiation of a new or replacement negotiated master contract.

- *Union shop* refers to a situation wherein teachers or other school district employees are *required to join the majority union organization* that has been recognized by the board and by the National Labor Relations Board or comparable state's governing agency as the exclusive employees' representative, and the employee must remain a member for the term of the collective bargaining agreement(s).
- *Agency shop* refers to a situation wherein all employees are

required to pay a service fee to the union, but they are not required to become members of the union [4]. The fee is intended to cover all the costs of the union when the union is representing the employee in collective bargaining matters.

- *Closed shop* refers to a situation wherein any person wishing to become employed by the school district must become a member of the union prior to being hired. Closed shops are prohibited [5].
- *Meet and confer* refers to those few situations wherein a state permits either collective bargaining or the meet and confer approach, depending on the preferences of the majority of the teachers or other employees within each school district [6].

In most states, either union shop or closed shop provisions dictate the approach used. Again, it is important that the board of education's negotiating team clearly understands which legal positions control the negotiating processes and contents in their local school district.

Now that we have stressed the importance of the specific laws and conditions governing the local collective bargaining process, let's turn to the topic of the data that should be collected prior to beginning negotiations.

✳ WHAT DATA SHOULD BE COLLECTED?

In addition to the legal context within which the collective bargaining shall take place, many other areas of information should be collected prior to beginning negotiations. The major areas of data to be collected and analyzed are: (1) existing personnel policies and practices, (2) existing board policies and the accompanying rules and regulations, (3) financial conditions of both income and expenditures—present and past, (4) past practice in the district, (5) history of grievances and grievance arbitrations, (6) prior at-the-table issues which were not resolved during previous master contract negotiations, (7) history of prior contractual negotiations, (8) comparable school districts' contractual provisions and current negotiating status, and (9) other miscellaneous sources of useful data [7]. Let's begin by investigating existing personnel policies and practices.

Personnel Policies and Practices

Existing personnel policies and practices are important to review prior to negotiations for two basic reasons. First, if management has workable policies, the board of education's negotiating team wants to make certain that nothing is agreed to with the union at the table which will interfere with the operation of the school district under the direction of those personnel policies. Second, these policies can guide the board of education's negotiation team by developing proposed contractual articles that will provide added management decision-making authority in important areas that are not covered by policy [8].

Some of the major personnel policy and practice areas of concern within the framework of collective bargaining are those areas dealing with the recruitment, placement, and evaluation of employees. These activities should be regarded as management rights, which should be held as sole management decision-making areas [9].

Board Policies

Existing board of education policies and the accompanying rules and regulations are also very important documents to be reviewed by management's negotiating team, because these policies provide the philosophical and broad directional operating orders under which the administration runs the district. The major concern, here, is that the management's negotiating team not unknowingly agrees to anything at the table which would interfere with the district's operation under the existing policies and the rules and regulations which supplement and complement those policies [10].

Financial Conditions

Present and past income and expenditures/financial conditions should be studied to determine the sources of the various subcategories of national, state, and local income, the trendlines of the various sources, and the predictability of the various sources in the future. Funding source verification is significant. Many unit members will be paid from funds from different sources (i.e., local, state, and/or federal funds designated as directly applicable only to specific programs, and grants and foundation gifts). Each ''program's'' funding must be categorized by the team so that they know where the money comes from, dates of receipt, and whether the funds are reimbursed monies or budget monies. When studying the expenditures it is important to determine the percent and dollar expenditures of the various accounts within the district. An analysis of the amounts and percentages expended for administration, instruction, fixed charges, and the other budget accounts will display the various current expenditure priorities, and it will also display the trends in the various categories of expenditures over a five-year or longer time period. This information provides an important data base that will assist management's negotiating team in determining what money is available to settle the upcoming master contract [11].

Of course, the key subareas of data involve an analysis of the current and historical salaries, salary schedules, and fringe benefits related to employees. This, coupled with information about the cost-of-living index, the placement of existing employees, the length of the work day, the length of the work year, and estimates of where newly hired employees would be placed, provides the data base most required to enter negotiations with any employee union [12]. The gathering of this information can be distributed across the members of the managerial team.

Next, let's visit the area of past practice. This is an area that may well determine what happens with at-the-table strategies and tactics, and it becomes crucial information if an impasse is reached that terminates with mandated contract arbitration of unresolved issues between the union and management.

Past Practice

Past practice has important implications for future union/management issues. Virtually all activities related to union/management issues can come under the analysis of past practice. Past practice can be discerned by how consistently administrators operate on a day-to-day basis within the policies, rules and regulations, and the existing master union/ management contractual agreements. Any discrepancies between what is in writing and what is done during the operation of the school district can lead to problems. Also, if all administrators do not operate within the letter and intent of the policies, rules, regulations, and master union/management contractual agreements, troublesome precedents can be established. Erosion of the contract or policies by those administrators who choose to ignore, stretch, or misinterpret policy can be devastating to table bargaining. The union can bring up a point they want in the contract and can provide extensive documentation about the past practice of abuse, if there has been even one administrator pursuing a method of operation contrary to policy. These precedential situations become even more demanding if grievance arbitrations have produced rulings for or against specific operational procedures [13].

The flip side of the past practice damage is one in which management (or the union) can break a troublesome past practice by having various administrators operate differently without the union filing a grievance [14]. Past practice can also be broken if various and contradictory rulings on identical or similar items have been rendered by arbitrators during a variety of grievance arbitrations.

In any case, past practice can lead to existing contractual language being challenged (or perhaps even changed) because of past practice. If the language is not changed, it can lead to an impasse, which could ultimately lead to an item in contract arbitration.

History of Grievances

The history of grievances and grievance arbitrations should be studied for the purpose of locating potential trouble spots as one prepares to enter the negotiation phase of collective bargaining. Grievance arbitration is the study of mandated or suggested rulings by an arbitrator when there is disagreement about the specific management actions taken which may or may not violate the actual wording or the intent of the written master contractual agreement. The mandated or suggested rulings depend on the state's laws and regulations, or they depend on what is agreed to within the master contractual agreement that was ratified by the union and the board of education [15].

This differs from contract arbitration, which refers to an outside arbitrator who comes into the school district as a step in an impasse procedure. In this case, the union and management cannot reach agreement on one or more proposed master contract articles, and an arbitrator is hired to come in to resolve the outstanding contractual issues in order that a total master contractual agreement can be reached and ratified. It should be stressed, however, that contractual arbitration can be mandated or permissive, depending on the specific state's laws and regulations governing collective bargaining and/or the specific local agreement to resolve contractual impasses by both the union and management [16].

The seriousness of contract arbitration has already been stressed, but the importance of studying the types and numbers of grievances that are currently on file and those that have been historically filed has not been sufficiently emphasized. In addition, it is even more important to study the history of arbitrators' rulings related to grievances that have been processed through arbitration [17].

Grievances are caused when management exercises its rights to operate the district. When the union feels that management has operated in a manner that is not in accordance with the letter or the intent of the master contractual agreement that has been ratified by both parties, the union can file a grievance [18]. A grievance, depending on the controlling governing conditions in each local school district, can be filed by an individual union member, or the union may file a class grievance when it feels that the grievance relates to a group of union members. The basic rule is that management can demand an employee to comply, and the employee must comply or be considered insubordinate and subject to discipline [19]. The only two exceptions are situations that are considered illegal or immoral.

At the point a grievance is filed, it alleges that management has violated a specific contract article. It then is dealt with as an alleged grievance until it is proven or resolved.

A study of currently existing grievances and the history of union grievances filed against the management of the school district is important because it identifies trouble spots and areas of disagreement that will likely be attended to through contract article proposals at the negotiation table if they are not resolved prior to the beginning of master contract negotiations [20].

History of Unresolved Issues

The history of at-the-table issues that were not resolved during previous master contract negotiations is another important area of data gathering [21]. Previously negotiated master contractual agreements that have been bargained and ratified by both union and management and the strategies and tactics utilized to achieve these agreements provide a baseline of *what is*. Those items that were placed on the table but which were not agreed to by both parties and the strategies and tactics used during the negotiations on those items, provide a potential list of *what could be* placed on the table during the upcoming negotiations [22]. It may be advisable to reserve this area for the chief negotiator, providing she/he was the person responsible for the contract being reopened. If this is the first contract, the job of collecting this data should be distributed among the team members, with the intent to contact neighboring districts for comparable information.

Obviously, both parties will attempt to strengthen the next contract when compared to the one that is terminating. Knowledge of the progression of unresolved issues over prior negotiations which ended with ratified contracts provides a road map, in many cases, to the future [23]. Inadequate research into the issues and the background of these issues will put the bargaining team at a serious disadvantage. Without this research, the management negotiating team will perhaps: (1) put items on the table that are duplications of effort from previous times, (2) introduce or react to items that are never going to be resolved, except through mandatory contract arbitration, (3) reveal a lack of basic knowledge of what has been important in the eyes of the union's negotiating team, and (4) introduce items or react to items that have previously proven to be unnecessary or relatively unimportant.

In some cases, the union's negotiating team or the management's negotiating team introduces new ideas during current negotiations which they know will not be accepted by the other party, but which are then put on record as items to be dealt with during future contract negotiations. This is a technique that is very useful to either party in outlining future at-the-table negotiation agendas [24].

Assuming that there has been discussion of policies, past practices, finance, grievances, and prior negotiations' history, let's turn to the collection of important information from school districts that will serve as a measure of comparability during discussion of provisions at the table.

Provisions of Comparable Schools

Comparable school districts' contractual provisions provide basic data to bring to the table, as these data provide the ammunition to back up the rationales for the offers being made during at-the-table negotiation sessions [25]. These data also become crucial during mediation, arbitration, and fact-finding impasse procedures, as most third parties who serve in these impasse roles will give much weight to the provisions provided by comparable school districts.

Let's explore the types of data that should be collected from comparable school districts. Not only should data be collected about the existing master contract conditions in each of the comparable districts, but data should be gathered about what is being placed on the negotiation table by the union or management if current contractual negotiations are taking place.

The major categories of data should include the following.

- *School district income* from federal, state, local, and other sources. Both the actual dollar amounts and the percent of budget income from each source should be collected [26].

- *School district effort* information is important to collect. Effort can be determined by the amount and percent of the budget raised through local property taxes or by other local tax sources [27].
- *The amount and percentage of the total budget expended for salaries and fringe benefits* for the employees of the various unions and for nonunion employees' various job categories [28].
- *The specific types of fringe benefits* offered members of the various employees' unions, and the cost per employee of each fringe benefit. In this category, some districts provide fringe benefits covering spouses and families, rather than just the specific employee, and it is crucial that this level of detailed information be collected [29].
- *The present pupil enrollment* of the district, with a breakdown by grade level. This detail is important as it is traditionally more expensive to offer secondary programs than to offer elementary programs. Also, related to this matter, there should be an analysis of pupil-teacher ratios for the various grade levels and the various instructional programs offered by the districts [30].
- *The numbers and types of present specialized program offerings* — offerings such as special education categories often have very small class sizes, and teacher aides are also required [31]. Other conditions, such as a student weighting (for example, a weighting of four times the actual number of students being considered for a class in severely mentally retarded or handicapped students) are oftentimes negotiated into a master contractual agreement [32]. In addition, vocational classes, gifted and talented classes, and other specialized program offerings provide important data that should be collected prior to beginning negotiations of a new or replacement master contractual agreement [33].
- *The numbers and types of co-curricular (athletic and other nonclassroom) offerings and the costs related to the same* [34]. The additional salaries and contractual conditions related to the coaches and sponsors of co-curricular offerings are many times a point of deliberation and/or disagreement during the negotiations process.
- *Five-year trends in assessed property valuations within the district* [35]. These data will provide the negotiators with the information that is related to the future potential increase or decrease of the property tax income.
- *The current bonded indebtedness of the district should be carefully reviewed.* The amount of taxes levied to pay off bonds issued by the school district certainly will impact the total taxes available to

settle a future master contract. If there is a large amount of taxes levied to pay off the principal and interest related to bond issues, the probability of increasing the tax rate to support the operational programs of the school district would be very limited at best [36]. Bonded indebtedness cannot be used for salaries; this fact needs to be emphasized.

- *The salary schedules and the array of teacher data on the salary schedules.* These data are important, because if your district is one in which nearly all of the teachers or other employee union groups are at the top of the salary schedule and you are comparing the data with districts who have most of their teaching staff or other employee union group at the beginning steps of the salary schedule, your district will already possess a higher mean (average) salary and will have a larger percentage of the total budget expended for salaries [37]. In addition, if your school district has a step salary schedule, as do most school districts, it will make a difference in the new money that can be allocated to improve the schedule; it will also guide management's negotiating team in devising its proposals to meet the obvious array of teachers or other union employees along the existing salary schedule. For example, if the district has a lot of beginning employees, the money required to move them up steps on the existing salary will be a significant amount, and there will be far less money available to improve the salary schedule, per se. If, on the other hand, most of the employees are at the top of the schedule, the salary schedule can be modified because very little of the available funds will have to go to support movement of the employees up the step increments. In the case of teachers, the same analysis would be true if the district provides a differential for various degree levels or certifications held by employees.

- *The employee work day and work year are also important comparable data to collect.* Obviously, if one district requires a greater number of work hours in the day or a greater number of work days in the year, these data should be factored into the comparisons being made. This also relates to the salary breakdown per day worked comparison among comparable school districts [38].

Now that the standard data collection categories have been discussed, let's turn to other sources of useful information. These may be information sources related to national trends, state trends, or regional trends.

Miscellaneous Other Data

Miscellaneous other sources of useful data may differ from district to district. Some of the categories that might prove helpful, however, could include: (1) data on the number of students, cost of tuition, salaries paid, and fringe benefits provided by private competitive schools in the specific district's area, (2) extent of general support or lack of support for labor unions in the specific community in which the school district is housed, and (3) specific targeted proposal items (such as a "no-layoff" clause) suggested by national, state or regional groups with which the specific local union is affiliated [39].

To end this discussion, it should be stressed that it is not only important to collect these data about contracts that currently exist in comparable school districts, but it is imperative that you establish an information network to gather daily information about the at-the-table give-and-take and the agreements reached by the other school districts who are negotiating master contractual agreements within the same time frame as your local school district. Negotiations are comprised of a series of give-and-take, and of agreements over time. Many of the items being negotiated move slowly, while others move or change overnight. To be lacking updated information on what is taking place in other negotiation venues is to imitate the heavyweight boxer who attempts to win the championship with one hand tied behind his back.

SUMMARY

Determining the current state laws related to bargaining and the scope of possible negotiations is a critical first step in collecting background information. Mandated, prohibited, and permitted subjects were described as different areas of collective bargaining. Key terms were identified: union shop, agency shop, closed shop, and meet and confer, which dictate the approach used in negotiations.

Prior to bargaining, data should be gathered regarding existing personnel policies and practices, existing board policies and accompanying rules and regulations, and present and past income and expenditures. Past practice has important implications for future negotiations in the setting of precedent by management, which may later become an area of negotiation or grievance.

The history of grievance arbitration as a potential (types and numbers of grievances filed) trouble source in negotiations was discussed. Contract arbitration as a step in previous procedures must be considered in data gathering. The history of previously unresolved issues could reveal upcoming overtures in future negotiations.

Comparable school districts' contractual provisions provide basic table data; such major categories as district income, tax effort, budgetary salary expenditure, benefits, enrollment, programs, co-curricular offerings, property valuation trends, current bonded indebtedness, actual salary arrays, and employee work day and year should be collected.

All of this information, gathered collectively and cooperatively by the administration and negotiating team members, must be compiled and organized to provide base data for at-the-table considerations. Provisions must also be made for a continuous update of these data, during negotiations, via an information network.

EXERCISES

1. Investigate the applicable bargaining law in your state, and determine its requirements and specifications. Also, investigate the controlling state's administrative body (PERB or other) and its requirements and specifications.

2. Collect a sample of existing personnel policies and practices in the district, and project which policies might be challenged or renegotiated in upcoming negotiations.

3. Survey your district for any identifiable trends or random policy noncompliance occurrences in past practice.

4. Develop a brief history of grievance and arbitration in your district, and investigate any previous negotiation issues that were unresolved.

5. Using the list of comparable school district data categories, develop a master contract profile fact sheet for three neighboring districts.

REFERENCES

1. Eberts, R. W. and J. A. Stone. 1984. *Unions and Public Schools.* Lexington, MA: D. C. Heath and Company, p. 27.
2. Ross, V. J. and R. MacNaughton. 1982. "Memorize These Bargaining Rules Before You Tackle Negotiations," *American School Board Journal,* 169(3):39.
3. Eberts, R. W. and J. A. Stone, p. 20.
4. Helsby, R. D., J. Tener and J. Lefkowitz, eds. 1985. *The Evolving Process — Col-*

lective Negotiations in Public Employment. Fort Washington, PA: Labor Relations Press, pp. xii – xxxi.

5. Helsby, R. D., J. Tener and J. Lefkowitz, eds., pp. xii – xxxi.
6. Helsby, R. D., J. Tener and J. Lefkowitz, eds., p. 5.
7. Schwerdtfeger, R. D. 1986. ''Labor Relations Thrive When You Control Collective Bargaining,'' *American School Board Journal,* 173(10):41.
8. Seifert, R. 1990. ''Prognosis for Local Bargaining in Health and Education,'' *Personnel Management,* 22(June):54 – 57.
9. Janes, L. 1984. ''Collective Bargaining,'' *NASSP Instructional Leadership Booklet.* Reston, VA: National Association of Secondary School Principals, pp. 22 – 23.
10. Schwerdtfeger, R. D., 173(10):40 – 42.
11. Ross, V. J. and R. MacNaughton, 169(3):39 – 41.
12. Granof, M. 1973. *How to Cost Your Labor Contract.* Washington, DC: The Bureau of National Affairs, Inc., p. 32.
13. Elkouri, F. and E. A. Elkouri. 1973. *How Arbitration Works, Third Edition.* Washington, DC: Bureau of National Affairs, Inc., pp. 389 – 392.
14. Elkouri, F. and E. A. Elkouri, pp. 389 – 392.
15. Lavan, H. 1990. ''Arbitration in the Public Sector: A Current Perspective,'' *Journal of Collective Negotiations,* 19(2):154.
16. Fox, M. J., Jr. and D. Cooner. 1990. ''Arbitration: Preparing for Success,'' *Journal of Collective Negotiations,* 19(4):254.
17. Neal, R. G. 1988. ''At Arbitration Hearings, Justice Favors the Well Prepared,'' *Executive Educator,* 10(11):17 – 18.
18. Trotta, M. S. 1976. *Handling Grievances – A Guide for Management and Labor.* Washington, DC: The Bureau of National Affairs, Inc., p. 2.
19. Paterson, L. T. and R. T. Murphy. 1983. *The Public Administrator's Grievance Arbitration Handbook.* New York, NY: Longman, Inc., 14 – 16.
20. Herman, J. J. 1991. ''The Two Faces of Collective Bargaining,'' *School Business Affairs,* 57(2):11.
21. Herman, J. J., 57(2):11.
22. Webster, W. G., Sr. 1985. *Effective Collective Bargaining in Public Education.* Ames, IA: Iowa State University Press, p. 83.
23. Webster, W. G., Sr., pp. 133 – 135.
24. Webster, W. G., Sr., pp. 152 – 154.
25. Neal, R. 1980. *Bargaining Tactics – A Reference Manual for Public Sector Labor Negotiations.* Richard G. Neal Associates, pp. 19 – 22.
26. Rebore, R. W. 1991. *Personnel Administration in Education – A Management Approach, Third Edition.* Englewood Cliffs, NJ: Prentice-Hall, Inc., p. 260.
27. Candoli, I. C. et al. 1978. *School Business Administration – A Management Approach, Second Edition.* Boston, MA: Allyn and Bacon, Inc., p. 60.
28. Castetter, W. B. 1986. *The Personnel Function in Education.* New York, NY: Macmillan Publishing Company, pp. 455 – 456.
29. Employee Benefit Plan Review. 1990. ''Costs Create Tensions at Bargaining Table,'' *Employee Benefit Plan Review,* 44(11):64 – 66.
30. Gorton, R. A., G. T. Schneider and J. C. Fisher. 1988. *Encyclopedia of School Administration and Supervision.* Phoenix, AZ: Oryx Press, pp. 111 – 112.

31. Eberts, R. W. and J. A. Stone, pp. 32–34.
32. Webb, L. et al. 1987. *Personnel Administration in Education—New Issues and New Needs in Human Resource Management.* Columbus, OH: Merrill Publishing Company, pp. 170–171.
33. Webster, W. G., Sr., p. 119.
34. Webb, L., et al., pp. 195–196.
35. Huber, J. and J. Hennies. 1987. "Fix on These Five Guiding Lights and Emerge from the Bargaining Fog," *School Board Journal,* 174(3):31–32.
36. Webster, W. G., Sr., pp. 123–124.
37. Granof, M., pp. 83–95.
38. Granof, M., pp. 83–95.
39. Herman, J. J., 57(2):11.

Preparing to Go to the Bargaining Table

CHAPTER 6 discusses the following topics: (1) determining how the recognition clause should read, (2) drafting your proposals and counterproposals, (3) determining your fallback positions and your last best offer, (4) preparing quid pro quos, (5) anticipating the other team's proposals and the reaction their team may have to your proposals, (6) studying the existing and prior agreements for directional thrusts, (7) determining what you wish to keep and what you wish to change or eliminate, (8) holding firm on management's rights, (9) establishing your pre-negotiation's tone with employees and with the community, (10) determining throwaway issues, (11) determining the absolutes or strike issues, (12) getting your parameters from the board of education, (13) developing bargaining structures, (14) preparing your bargaining notebook, (15) formulating your bargaining strategy and tactics, and (16) preparing differently for win/win negotiations than for adversarial negotiations. These topics refer to preparing both for the initial bargaining session and for all subsequent negotiating sessions throughout the sometimes lengthy and tedious process of arriving at a ratified master contractual agreement between union and management.

Although it is not directly related to the preparation for at-the-table sessions, the determination of the wording of the clause that recognizes the union as the formal representative of the employees is an important beginning document, and it is most important when written into the initial contract. Let's begin this chapter with this prerequisite topic.

DETERMINING HOW THE RECOGNITION CLAUSE SHOULD READ

Initial recognition of a specific union as the sole representative of an employee group for collective bargaining purposes usually takes place under one of two methods in those states that possess collective bargaining statutes. In the first method, the board of education, feeling that most if not all of the members of the employee group would prefer or vote for a specific union to represent them, may grant exclusive recognition by board of education action. The second method is one wherein the PERB (Public Employees' Relations Board) or whichever body is established to implement the state's collective bargaining law, conducts an election if there is a petition by a group of employees or the employer [1]. Usually, if more than 50 percent of the employees who vote, vote favorably for a specific union, that specific union serves as the official representative of that group of employees for all matters related to the negotiations and for the operational procedures of the master contract between the union and management. The only way to change the specific union that represents the employees is to have a decertification election [2].

In districts that have employees who are members of various unions, it is very important that the recognition clause is crystal clear. If it is ambiguous, many difficulties and much confusion could arise.

A typical recognition clause would read as follows.

> In accordance with the provisions of the 1993 Public Employees' Fair Employment Act of the State of _____, the Board of Education of _____ School District recognizes the _____ union, affiliated with the regional, state, and national _____, as the exclusive representative for all professionally certified personnel, exclusive of those in management positions, for the purposes of collective bargaining as outlined in the Public Employees' Fair Employment Act of 1993.

The wording of the above clearly recognizes a single specified union to be the sole representative of all professionally certified personnel for the purposes outlined in that state's collective bargaining law [3]. By this language, the union is restricted to representing the certified employees to the provisions of the Act of 1993, and the union has no authority to operate outside of the provisions of the Act of 1993.

In addition, the language clearly excludes the union from representing management personnel who also possess professional certification [4]. Obviously, this language also prohibits the union from representing those management employees who may not be required to possess certification. It is very important to exclude management personnel from inclusion with other employee groups whom they may manage.

Next, let's turn to establishing your pre-negotiation tone with the employees of the specific union and with the community at large.

Obviously, the long-term tone between union and management as perceived by the employees who are members of the union and by the community at large, will depend on the long-term day-to-day union/management relationships. If they are adversarial, there will exist a lack of trust between union and management, and the community will probably perceive that their children suffer because of the adversarial relations that exist. On the other hand, if harmonious day-to-day relations exist between the union and management, the members of both groups will possess a high level of trust for the members of the other party, and the community will probably feel that, at the very least, the children are not subject to the aftereffects of poor morale and lack of cooperation among those hired to teach and manage their schools [5].

The period just prior to entering into a specific contractual negotiations process provides an optimal opportunity to attempt to establish a tone that will carry on throughout the contract negotiations process [6]. Below is an example of a correspondence read by the board of education president and adopted by the board of education at a formal board meeting. Following this meeting, the correspondence was distributed to all teachers, to the teacher union officials, and to the media.

This attempt to establish a tone for negotiations was a method used by one of the school districts, where the author served as superintendent of schools. It clearly specifies the intent of a board of education in a school district that traditionally had poor labor/management relations.

Board of Education Approach to
Teacher Contract Negotiations

Theme of Cooperation

It is the desire of the Board of Education to approach teacher contract negotiations in a spirit of cooperation. We believe that our goals for improving the instructional programs in _____ (name of school district) are shared by most teachers. The only way to attain the improvements we desire is to work cooperatively at a professional level.

Our Challenge

There are many myths about what is good for education, and there are constraints which can impede learning. It is clear, however, that all of us in education must unite in common pursuit to overcome the obstacles to successful teaching and learning. This is our challenge.

Some of the undeniable elements of a strong educational system are:

- effective staff development and training
- well-defined objectives for every course of instruction
- a system for evaluating the extent to which instructional programs meet their objectives
- cooperative learning environment
- professional employees who assume assignments where they can be of the greatest help to students
- students engaged in instructional tasks for a high percentage of their time
- students challenged consistent with their abilities
- flexibility of goals and practices to accommodate change and student differences

We need to work together to build these elements into the _____ _____ (name of school district) education system.

Working Principles

The board of education believes in the following working principles and will approach teacher contract negotiations with these as a guidance:

(1) Teachers deserve fair pay and a professional working climate.
(2) Teachers' assignments and student loads should be reasonable.
(3) Teachers' assignments should be made to best use their strengths.
(4) The district should provide and teachers should partake of development and training programs to strengthen and develop teaching skills.
(5) Student learning should be measured and monitored as a means for improvement.
(6) Teachers should be involved in the evaluation of instructional programs and school climate.
(7) Use of technology should be employed to increase the effectiveness of learning and teaching time.
(8) The ratio of benefit to cost of what we do should be maximized.

Once the tone has been established prior to sitting down to negotiate, a collective bargaining notebook should be prepared. This notebook should contain any documents and information that will be helpful as one prepares to enter the formal negotiating sessions.

PREPARING THE BARGAINING NOTEBOOK

The bargaining notebook is a very important reference document that will serve the negotiating team well throughout the entire negotiations process. It should consolidate all of the information that the local bargaining team feels it will require as reference information during the process of negotiations [7]. The major items to be included in all notebooks are:

- a copy of the state's collective bargaining law, and a copy of the collective bargaining implementation rules and regulations promulgated by the state's PERB (Public Employment Relations Board) or the state's body that has been created to manage the state's collective bargaining law
- copies of the current master contract agreement between the union and the school district, and copies of prior master contractual agreements between the union and the school district
- copies of the board of education's policies, and copies of the rules and regulations promulgated to implement those policies
- copies of all grievances and grievance arbitration rulings for the past five years, and copies of any grievances that are currently pending or that are in the process of grievance arbitration
- copies of the minutes of prior years' negotiations, and copies of correspondence between the union and the management negotiation team or the board of education related to the current upcoming negotiations [8]
- copies of adopted budgets for the past five years, which detail income, sources of income, expenditures, and categories of expenditures; also a projection of income and expenditures for the next three years
- copies of financial audits over the past five years; these audits, when compared to the adopted budgets, will indicate any discrepancies and the degree of these discrepancies between the adopted budget, the actual income received, and the actual expenditures made
- information about the union team's members that could prove helpful; key persons will be the union's negotiating team spokesperson and any state or national union representatives who may be part of the team, or who may be influential in terms of the union team's strategies, tactics, or the signing-off regarding contractual articles

- a listing of the current salary schedule and a listing of the number of employees on each vertical (years of service) step or horizontal (degree level for teachers) step of that schedule, that will provide cost information on built-in costs of automatic step schedule changes
- data collected on the historic increases in salary and fringes provided by the district; this information should be compared with the consumer price index for the geographical region's trends over the same time frame; it should also be compared to a rational index of the taxpaying public's ability to pay versus its historical effort made to financially support the school district; such information might well be obtained from a data base or management information system
- historical data on any prior mediation, fact-finding or contract arbitrations that have taken place, and the results of such impasse sessions or rulings [9]
- a listing of each fringe benefit and the cost to the district of each of these fringe benefits; it is also important to find out from the suppliers or to estimate the anticipated cost increase associated with large outlay benefits like health insurance coverages; in this area it is also important to break down the information, where appropriate, into cost data for the individual employee, the individual employee and spouse, and/or for the individual employee and family [10]

A simple scheme will serve this purpose well. Compare present and future benefits by setting up a table of columns with the following titles — "Benefit Title," "Coverage," "Current Cost," and "Estimated Future Cost."

As the negotiations proceed, the following will be added to the notebook:

- guidelines given management's negotiation team by the board of education
- analysis of the current master contractual agreement, of management's operational problems, and of management's desired changes in the existing contract; usually done by having all of the school district's administrators, in a series of meetings, review the existing master contract and offer suggestions for changes that will improve the district's ability to manage the day-to-day instructional and support programs well

- minutes of every negotiation session and any pertinent correspondence between the union and management, or the board of education
- a copy of all proposals and counterproposals offered by either party to the negotiations; each item passed across the table, both from the union and management, needs to be dated, timed, and recorded for later impasse reference
- an analysis of the master contractual agreements of all comparable school districts, and an update on the status of the specifics of negotiations in comparable districts that are undergoing negotiations during the same time frame; it is helpful to record changes proposed or heard from other districts on a separate entry page; each article can be ''logged'' as to the impact the negotiations might have on each item
- information about any directions or suggestions provided by the regional unit, the state's unit, or the national unit with which the local union is aligned
- other information, as determined by the local management's negotiation team, which should be collected and which will prove useful during the process of negotiating a new or renewed master contractual agreement with the union [11]

Once the notebook is prepared, it should be used when meeting with the board of education to obtain those guidelines that the management's negotiating team will follow in the upcoming negotiations. Once these guidelines are issued, they cannot be exceeded by management's negotiating team unless they go back to the board of education and officially receive approval to modify or exceed the original guidelines.

OBTAINING THE BOARD OF EDUCATION'S NEGOTIATION GUIDELINES

If the board of education and the management team anticipate a serious adversarial negotiating environment, it is wise for the board to provide guidelines that would become the *last best offer* of the board under the most adverse circumstances [12]. This worst-case scenario would then give management's negotiating team the greatest amount of flexibility at the table. On the other hand, the board of education, having provided guidelines for its last best offer, can then direct management's negotiating team to get a master contract settlement on more reasonable terms.

Obtaining these worst-case scenario guidelines accomplishes three major purposes. First, it provides management's negotiating team the greatest flexibility in its day-to-day negotiations with the union's negotiating team. Second, it eliminates a lot of the unnecessary and very complex tripartite bargaining: i.e., between and among members of management's negotiating team, between management's negotiating team and the union's negotiating team, and between management's negotiating team and the board of education. Third, it avoids the suffering and untold long-term damage done if there is a serious employees' strike, and the board of education eventually exceeds its own guidelines which were given to its management negotiating team [13]. Why punish the employees, the students, and the community, if the board of education will eventually change its mind under pressure by the local union and union members and officials from the regional, state, and national levels?

Once the board of education guidelines are provided, the administrators of the district have analyzed the current master contractual agreement and provided management's negotiating team with their suggestions, and the bargaining notebook has been prepared, management's negotiating team can study the existing and prior agreements for directional thrusts, and it can prepare the desired structures, strategies, and tactics to be utilized in the upcoming negotiations with the union [14].

DECIDING ON STRUCTURES, STRATEGIES, AND TACTICS

The structural decisions that should be decided prior to entering the actual contract negotiations include decisions such as: (1) Should the team have subcommittee structures [15]? (2) Should the team allow for sidebar (away from the table) discussions [16]? or (3) Should the team have a larger referent group to which they will report progress and receive suggestions [17]? These structural decisions can be modified while negotiations progress, but it is wiser to have them made prior to sitting at the table. Obviously, these decisions may become even more important if negotiations enter the impasse stages of mediation, fact-finding, and/or contract arbitration.

Strategies are the *whats,* and tactics are the *hows.* Strategies deal with broad directional statements, such as, "We can give no more than 5 percent new money for employee salaries and fringes; this new money will be on the base of the current expenditures for these purposes." Obviously, if there are increases in fringe costs from some of the suppliers of benefits, then there will be less than the 5 percent of new money available for improvement in employee salary or fringe benefits structures. On the other hand, there may be a desire to protect or increase control of noneconomic areas, such as the power of administrators to make employee assignments, from contractual obligation or union interference.

The strategies must be broken down into specific measurable objectives in order to be of maximum benefit [18]. Once the specific objectives for each strategic goal have been identified, management's negotiating team can develop specific action programs or tactics to attempt to accomplish the specific objectives and the strategies established. Well-timed, pre-thought, at-the-table concessions provide an example of such a tactic [19]. It is crucial to realize, however, that bargaining strategies, objectives, and tactics are interdependent. Strategies may guide the bargaining team to the development of specific negotiation objectives, and tactics, if successfully employed, should lead to the attainment of strategic outcomes or results.

Some likely bargaining objectives may well include those related to money and those related to decision-making authority [20]. In either case, the objectives must be clearly stated and measurable in order to determine, at some future date, whether or not the specific objective(s) or result(s) desired have been attained. In addition, it is wise to allow flexibility in the objectives to be achieved, or the give-and-take of negotiations will become too rigid [21].

It is wise to state the objectives in three priority categories such as: (1) maximum achievement, (2) realistic achievement, and (3) minimum achievement [22]. The simple example of increased salary provisions from both a union's and a management's point of view could well appear as stated in the following table.

Item: Employees' Salary Increases

	Minimum	Realistic	Maximum
Union	4 percent	5 percent	8 percent
Management	2 percent	4 percent	5 percent

In this example, one can see that the possibility of a settlement exists at somewhere between 4 percent and 5 percent. If the negotiation fell in the win/win environment, this structure would not be necessary, as both parties would share information as to what new money was available [23]; and they would go about the resolution of the final dollar amount by collaborative problem solving.

Some tactics that will be faced or utilized during master contract negotiations may very well include the following.

- *Asking for the moon.* This tactic is based on the assumption that starting big, even though the initial request or offer may be unreasonable, even to the party that proposes it, will serve well when compromises have to be reached in the future [24].
- *Use of public sentiment.* This tactic is utilized in the hope of getting the general populace to agree with the party's positions; and with the hope that the general populace will put pressure on the other party to the negotiations to give in to, or at least come closer to, the position presented by the party [25].
- *Planning for impasse.* This tactic assumes that third parties (mediators, fact finders, and/or contract arbitrators) will provide a settlement closer to the demands of the union, than that which could be achieved by dealing directly at the table with management's negotiation team [26].
- *Use of media releases and letters to the editors.* Newspaper and television coverage of a party's biased report of the status of negotiations can become an effective tactic to arouse the public in support of the union's or management's position. Also, letters by friends of the union or the board of education, although obviously not identified as such, can get the message out. These tactics are frequently used during impasses [27].
- *Hot issues* are sometimes headlined and dramatized to provide a biased perception that all issues are of this nature [28].
- *Promoting popular, high-cost items as noncost items that are good for students.* Such items as reducing class size or pupil-teacher ratios come under this tactical category.
- *Reducing the other parties' expectations.* To accomplish this tactic, the negotiating team has to provide a strong rationale coupled with convincing data that will move the other negotiating team off of its original demand(s) [29].
- *Items for the future.* Since most collective bargaining arrangements are like a good marriage – they go on forever – a useful tactic is to introduce new desired items into current negotiations, expecting

not to achieve those demands during the current negotiations. This, however, does establish a future agenda that can be pushed during subsequent contractual negotiations of replacement master contractual agreements between union and management [30].

- *Presenting proposals equivalent to the best conditions present in master contract agreements of other school districts.* This is a tactic frequently used by unions, especially as the first at-the-table proposal [31].

Now that we have emphasized the importance of strategies, objectives, and tactics, let's turn to the topic of proposals and counterproposals.

PREPARING PROPOSALS AND COUNTERPROPOSALS

There are two rules that should be consistently followed when preparing proposals and counterproposals. First, any and all proposals should be accompanied by a comprehensive and logical rationale, and second, each and every proposal should be supported by comprehensive and convincing data.

It is very wise to prepare alternatives (fall-back proposals), for each of your original at-the-table proposals; this advance preparation will permit you to respond in a reasoned manner without being under the sometimes intense pressure that accompanies the actual negotiation sessions [32]. These alternative proposals may or may not always be used, but it is wise to have them available before starting the initial negotiations, and they are best developed in between sequential at-the-table negotiation sessions.

The actual proposals prepared will be determined by management's negotiating team from information collected previously, including the board of education's guidelines, the administrative staff's analysis and suggestions, and the materials in the bargaining notebook.

The proposals of management's negotiating teams should include all of the following considerations.

- Propose those items you wish to retain in the current union/management master contractual agreement, and those items you wish to eliminate from the current master contractual agreement [33].

- Propose strengthening the management's rights clause in the current master contractual agreement.
- Make at-the-table proposals that will strengthen management's and the board of education's decision-making prerogatives in important instructional and management areas.
- Determine your fall-back proposal positions in advance of the initial negotiating session, and make any required modifications in these fall-back positions between at-the-table negotiating sessions.
- Anticipate the union's proposals and the potential reactions that the union's negotiating team may have to your proposals. Playing the "what if" game can be very valuable when the management team must react quickly under pressure [34].
- Prepare quid pro quo proposals, which basically involve the negotiating team analyzing what they can obtain of equal or greater value than what they would give as a compromise to the other team. This analysis should take place between each and every at-the-table negotiating session.
- Prepare throwaway proposals. These are proposals that are seriously presented, but which are not considered absolutely necessary to secure before reaching a contractual settlement with the other party to the negotiations. These proposals will assist in the give-and-take that accompanies every negotiation.
- Determine absolutes and potential strike items. These positions should be determined by the board of education, with the guidance of management's negotiating team. They might well deal with such items as the right of administrators to evaluate the degree of employee performance, or they might deal with the right of management to make employee assignments, or they might deal with the amount of new dollars that will ultimately be allocated to settle the contract with the employees' union.
- On the other hand, the union will probably have its own list of absolutes or strike items. These may include such matters as the salary schedule being improved to keep up with comparable districts, or an agreement to receive a certain degree of pay for extra duties performed, or the specific conditions under which an employee can be transferred by management [35–37].

With all the details previously discussed, let's turn to the differences that would exist if a management's or a union's negotiating teams were preparing for win/win, rather than adversarial, negotiations.

PREPARING FOR WIN/WIN NEGOTIATIONS

Probably the first major difference would be that in a win/win situation both parties would agree to cooperate in the collection and analysis of the data required to intelligently approach the negotiations of a new master contractual agreement [38]. What has previously been called the *bargaining notebook* would now become a joint data based notebook. In adversarial negotiations, each party would collect its own data (i.e., "ammunition").

The second major difference would become one of deciding upon strategies, objectives, and tactics. In the case of win/win negotiations, the strategy would be one of collaborative decision making; the objectives would become specific measurable desired results agreed to by both the members of the union's negotiating team and management's negotiating team; and the tactics could involve joint media releases, joint progress updates, and subcommittee study committees comprised of membership from both the union and management [39].

The final major difference would become one of an atmosphere in which every individual from either the union or the management would freely speak, recommend, and advise the total unit consisting of both union members and management personnel. In actuality, the labels of "union" and "management" would disappear in favor of one problem-solving team of professionals.

SUMMARY

In preparing to go to the bargaining table, consideration must be given to the specific content of the union recognition clause in order to determine the level of exclusive representation, recognition of multiple unions, and the type of certification election required. A distinction was made regarding the representation of certified management personnel.

The long-term relationship between union and management affects the tone of pre-negotiations, and efforts should be directed toward establishing a positive tone prior to initiating negotiations. A board of education example of such effort was provided.

The development of a notebook containing documents and information was described as a key strategy. This book will serve as a reference throughout the negotiations process. Major items that should be included are: the state collective bargaining law and other pertinent regulations, the current master contractual agreement, board policies, historical grievance mediation and arbitration rulings, prior years' minutes, prior adopted budgets and financial audits, profiles of the union team members, and current and historical salary/benefits schedule information. The notebook is augmented during the process with board guidelines, analysis of desired changes and proposals/counterproposals, current minutes, and comparable-district information. Additionally, the board should provide the negotiating team with the last best offer information in order to maximize flexibility, to achieve agreement, if possible, and to conserve time.

Structures, strategies, and tactics for negotiating should be made in advance, such as the option for subcommittees and sidebar agreements. Broad directional statements underlie strategies, and are broken down into specific objectives, such as those related to money or decision-making authority. These objectives can be categorized and prioritized as maximum, realistic, and minimum. Examples of tactics to support these objectives were given: inflated initial requests, use of public sentiment, planning for impasse, media release use, emphasis of controversial or hot issues, reduction of expectations, "planting" of future issues, and comparable district data contrasts.

Rationales and data must support all of the proposals and counterproposals, and alternative proposals must be available. Consideration must be given to the retention and/or elimination of current agreements, the strengthening of managerial rights, preparation for anticipated union proposals, the development of quid pro quo and throwaway proposals, and the determination of the absolutes, or bottom line.

In a win/win atmosphere, all of the strategies, objectives, and tactics would become collaborative, communication would become joint, and the objectives would be developed by both teams in a professional, problem-solving format.

EXERCISES

1. Identify the union recognition clause, if any, in your district and clarify its meaning.

2. Assuming that negotiations were to begin tomorrow, how would you describe the union/management tone in your district? How would it affect negotiations?

3. Collect samples of data for a bargaining notebook, such as copies

of the state law, the current master contract, and other helpful information.

4. After investigation, how would you characterize the district's history of grievance, arbitrations, and prior negotiations?

5. Obtain a salary/benefits schedule with arrayed employee numbers, and compare it to that of similar neighboring districts. What are the implications for future negotiations?

6. List some desired managerial changes or additions to the master contract; then list some possible union-proposed changes.

7. Which of the strategies and tactics described would be most successful in your district's negotiations?

REFERENCES

1. Kearney, R. C. 1984. *Labor Relations in the Public Sector.* New York, NY: Marcel Dekker, Inc., pp. 66–67.
2. Kearney, R. C., p. 323.
3. Coleman, C. J. 1990. *Managing Labor Relations in the Public Sector,* San Francisco, CA: Jossey-Bass Publishers, pp. 64–65.
4. Helsby, R. D., J. Tener and J. Lefkowitz, eds. 1985. *The Evolving Process—Collective Negotiations in Public Employment.* Fort Washington, PA: Labor Relations Press, pp. 140–141.
5. Bacharach, S. B., J. B. Shedd and S. C. Conley. 1989. "School Management and Teacher Unions: The Capacity for Cooperation in an Age of Reform," *Teachers College Record,* 91(1):97–105.
6. Huber, J. and J. Hennies. 1987. "Fix on These Five Guiding Lights and Emerge from the Bargaining Fog," *School Board Journal,* 174(3):31.
7. Coleman, C. J., p. 127.
8. Webster, W. G., Sr. 1985. *Effective Collective Bargaining in Public Education.* Ames, IA: Iowa State University Press, pp. 133–135.
9. Schwerdtfeger, R. D. 1986. "Labor Relations Thrive When You Control Collective Bargaining," *American School Board Journal,* 173(10):41–44.
10. Davis, W. M. et al. 1990. "Collective Bargaining in 1990: Health Care Cost a Common Issue," *Monthly Labor Review,* 113(1):3–10, 27–29.
11. Kearney, R. C., pp. 106–107.
12. Neal, R. 1980. *Bargaining Tactics—A Reference Manual for Public Sector Labor Negotiations.* Richard G. Neal Associates, p. 220.
13. Ross, V. J. and R. MacNaughton. 1982. "Memorize These Bargaining Rules Before You Tackle Negotiations," *American School Board Journal,* 169(3):39–41.
14. Herman, J. J. 1991. "The Two Faces of Collective Bargaining," *School Business Affairs,* 57(2):11–12.
15. Herman, J. J., 57(2):11–12.
16. Helsby, R. D., J. Tener and J. Lefkowitz, eds., p. 222.

17. Heisel, W. D. 1973. *New Questions and Answers on Public Employee Negotiation.* Washington, DC: International Personnel Management Association, p. 86.
18. Bacharach, S. B. and E. J. Lawler. 1984. *Bargaining—Power, Tactics and Outcomes.* San Francisco, CA: Jossey-Bass Publishers, pp. 42−43.
19. Neal, R., p. 147.
20. Nickoles, K. W. 1990. ''Future Shock: What's Coming to the Bargaining Table,'' *School Business Affairs,* 56(12):36−38.
21. Richardson, R. C. 1985. *Collective Bargaining by Objectives: A Positive Approach,* Englewood Cliffs, NJ: Prentice-Hall, Inc., p. 168.
22. Herman, J. J., 57(2):11.
23. Huber, J. and J. Hennies, 174(3):31.
24. Neal, R., pp. 177−178.
25. Namit, C. 1986. ''The Union Has a Communications Strategy—And Your Board Should, Too,'' *American School Board Journal,* 173(10):30−31.
26. Ross, V. J. and R. MacNaughton, 169(3):39−41.
27. Namit, C., 173(10):30−31.
28. Namit, C., 173(10):30−31.
29. Neal, R., pp. 181−182.
30. Herman, J. J., 57(2):12.
31. Schwerdtfeger, R. D., 173(10):42.
32. Neal, R., pp. 140−141.
33. Webster, W. G., Sr., p. 85.
34. Aaron, B., J. M. Najita and J. L. Stern. 1988. *Public Sector Bargaining.* Washington, DC: Industrial Relations Research Associates, p. 132.
35. Coleman, C. J., p. 127−132.
36. Webster, W. G., Sr., pp. 87−92.
37. Neal, R., pp. 165−168.
38. Coleman, C. J., p. 245.
39. Hendrickson, G. 1990. ''Where Do You Go after You Get to Yes?'' *The Executive Educator,* 12(11):16−17.

Doing It: Conduct at and Away from the Table

CHAPTER 7 discusses all the important details that must be attended to during the period within which contract negotiations are taking place. These details include: (1) establishing ground rules, (2) exchanging proposals, (3) keeping up with the other party's moves, (4) controlling personality conflicts, (5) selecting your at-the-table and away-from-the-table spokesperson(s), (6) establishing a communications hotline, (7) timing your moves, (8) projecting multi-year costs of proposals, (9) being flexible and creative, (10) setting at-the-table tone, (11) carrying out each member's role(s), (12) posturing and positioning, (13) presenting your proposals and demands, (14) analyzing and using quid pro quos, (15) packaging your proposals, (16) participating in the sidebars, (17) analyzing proposals for power and costs, (18) placing yourself in the other party's shoes, (19) prioritizing your proposals and their proposals, (20) drafting counterproposals, (21) observing verbal and nonverbal behavior, (22) identifying the real issues, the giveaways, the musts, and the bargaining chips, (23) cutting deals, (24) working with the other team's members, (25) developing strategies and tactics for each negotiation session, (26) keeping score by analyzing the results immediately following each negotiation session, (27) dividing and conquering, (28) reaching closure on articles and getting TA's (tentative agreements), (29) arriving at total contract at-the-table TA, and (30) emphasizing the differences in at-the-table behavior if the negotiations take place within a win/win environment.

This discussional journey shall begin with the establishment of ground rules. Usually, the first discussion that takes place when the union's negotiating team and management's negotiating team sit down across the bargaining table for the first time is one that establishes the rules within which negotiations will take place.

ESTABLISHING GROUND RULES

At the initial at-the-table meeting of the two negotiating teams, the union's team will propose a set of ground rules for bargaining, and the management's team will propose its own set of ground rules [1]. Bargaining begins in earnest as both teams propose and counter-propose ground rules under which the bargaining will proceed. Sometimes agreement on ground rules may take multiple meetings to reach agreement. Regardless of the number of meetings, agreement on ground rules is ultimately reached, and discussion of the contractual articles begins. These sessions are critical in that they set a tone and determine detail as to rules favoring management and/or labor; hence, the meetings are highly significant in their shaping and in their ultimate impact in the actual bargaining sessions.

Ground rules will vary from school district to school district, and they may even vary within the same district during various replacement contract negotiations. However, most ground rules will include rules similar to the following.

- The place of meetings shall alternate for each session, one meeting being at the administrative offices and the next being at the union's offices [2].
- The time of meeting shall be after normal working hours unless management agrees to pay for the time expended by the union's team members, or the union agrees to pay the district the amount of money equivalent to its team members' pay during the time these members are involved in negotiation sessions [3].
- There will be a time limit on meetings of four hours unless both parties agree to continue beyond four hours [4].
- The union and management will exchange total contract proposals during a specific meeting, and negotiations will be limited to the items submitted in these initial proposals. No additional items are permitted to be added during these contract negotiations [5].
- Both parties shall be allowed to bring resource persons to specific meetings, on the condition that they notify the other party in advance of the intention to bring a resource person to the next negotiating session. Only one resource person at a time can be brought to a specific negotiating session, and the resource person must be able to add information or clarify some substantial aspect of the current negotiation.
- Observers to the negotiations will not be permitted [6].
- There shall be no media releases during the negotiations process unless impasse is reached. During the time of impasse, each party will notify the other party of their intent to issue a media release in

advance of releasing it. These rules are agreed to in the great majority of situations, since history has suggested that releases to the media, observers to the negotiations, and other intrusions on the process appear to lengthen and make more complex the task of reaching contractual agreement [7].

- Both parties shall keep their own minutes of the sessions, unless there is agreement that an official set of minutes shall be accepted. If official minutes are agreeable, both parties generally date and sign the official meeting minutes at the beginning of the next negotiating meeting [8].
- Both parties agree to sign off each article as that article is agreed to, or there is an agreement that there will be no signoff of any article until the total contract document is TA'd (tentatively agreed to). It may be more desirable to discourage individual sign-off of each article; a package sign-off could be a very significant managerial gain [9].
- Other ground rules are accepted as agreed upon by both parties to the negotiation in each school district.

Now that the ground rules have been established, the negotiating teams can get down to exchanging contract proposals. Contracts are broken down into various subsections, called articles, and proposals may include: (1) the introduction of a new article, (2) a modification of an existing article, or (3) the elimination of an existing article.

EXCHANGING CONTRACT PROPOSALS

Procedures for exchanging proposals vary. Sometimes both parties exchange total initial proposals at the same session. Occasionally the union will submit its total set of proposals first, and management will be required to submit its total set of proposals within two weeks, and sometimes the noneconomic and the economic proposals will be submitted at different times [10]. In the cases of splitting the noneconomic and the economic proposals, the economic proposals are usually held until the noneconomic proposals are settled, or an impasse has been reached on them [11]. This impasse may be resolved without the help of a third party, since many times there will be trade-offs between economic and noneconomic proposals as the negotiations proceed [12].

At this juncture, it should be stressed that as proposals and counterproposals are presented and discussed, there is no requirement in the collective bargaining laws that either party has to agree. The only requirement is that both parties negotiate *in good faith*. Good faith implies listening to the proposals of the other party and giving them serious consideration. It also implies that each party continues to meet and negotiate, and that their proposals be honest ones which are based on data and rationale [13].

Initial proposals usually include three types of items: (1) proposals that are absolutely necessary to achieve in order to ratify a contractual agreement, (2) proposals that are meant to be giveaways or bargaining chips, and (3) proposals that are intended to introduce a new item in order to establish an agenda item for future contract negotiation, but which the party does not actually expect to attain agreement on during the current negotiations. One example of each type will help to define the differences among the three proposals.

(1) A *required proposal* by the union would be one to achieve complete board of education paid health coverage for the entire family in a situation where the board of education currently only pays for the individual employee [14].

(2) A *bargaining chip proposal* by management's negotiation team is to have teachers attend a week of staff development workshops each year before the start of the actual student school year, and to do this for substitute teacher wages instead of the normal teacher wage [15].

(3) A *new item proposal* by the union may include adding dental, optical, and auditory care to the health package of fringe benefits. This will be introduced because the trend on comparable districts is beginning to move in the direction of improved health benefits for employees [16].

Now that we have discussed the three major types of proposals, let's examine the scope of proposals that comprise a complete labor/management contractual document. Obviously, the specifics will vary with the category of employees, the type of union, and the specific items included in each school district's master contractual agreement. In general, however, most master contractual agreements will include the following definitive articles.

- Article One—Recognition
- Article Two—Employee and Union Rights

- Article Three—Employment Conditions
- Article Four—Employee Evaluation
- Article Five—Employee Termination
- Article Six—Employee Compensation
- Article Seven—Employee Fringe Benefits
- Article Eight—Employee Leaves
- Article Nine—Grievance Procedure
- Article Ten—Negotiation Schedule and Procedures
- Article Eleven—Duration of the Agreement
- Article Twelve—Management Rights [17]

Now that the types of proposals have been discussed, let's turn to the topic of presenting proposals and the activities and considerations that take place during the negotiating sessions. Both the method and tone of your presentations and the activities of your team during the sessions are important to the success at each at-the-table session.

PRESENTING PROPOSALS

It is crucial that you have a knowledgeable and effective chief negotiator, as this is the person who will make all the initial contract proposals and all counterproposals [18]. The chief negotiator should: (1) know the laws affecting negotiations in the state, (2) know the details of the activities and work performed by the employees and administrators of the school district, and (3) have at hand all the pre-negotiation information collected and arrayed in the bargaining notebook.

Each proposal presented should have a rationale and it should have supporting facts and argumentation. Let's examine an example of both a union proposal and a management proposal.

Example—Union Proposal

Article Sixteen—salary to be modified as follows.
   (1) The initial step of the teacher's salary schedule to be increased from $16,000 to $22,000.
   (2) Each step on the salary schedule to be increased by $200.
   (3) An eleventh step to be added to the current ten-step salary schedule.

(4) The differential between a BA degree and an MA degree to be increased from its current $500 to $1,000.

(5) The differential between an MA degree and a PhD or EdD degree to be increased from $500 to $1,500.

Rationale

There are two excellent reasons for this proposal. First, the district has had difficulty in getting candidates to fill teacher vacancies during this time of a national teacher shortage. Second, the board of education has consistently indicated that it wants excellent employees and that it desires to treat all employees fairly.

Factual Data

In comparing our teachers' salary and salary schedule with the twenty districts that both parties have agreed will be those used for comparative purposes, we find the following. (1) The beginning salaries in all but six districts are at or higher than the level we are requesting in our proposal. (2) Our step increments are anywhere from $50 to $400 lower than twelve of the districts. (3) The average number of steps in the salary schedules of our comparable districts is twelve. (4) The differential between the BA or BS degree and the MA or MS degree average in the comparable districts is $900, with three districts exceeding $1,500. (5) Although only two districts have a salary differential between the MA or MS degree and the PhD or EdD degree, one district allows a differential of $2,500, and the other allows a $4,000 differential. In addition, we feel the board of education should agree with an action that will encourage more teachers to go on for advanced education, which ultimately will accrue to the benefit of the students and the district.

Example — Management Proposal

Article Seven: Fringe benefits to be modified as follows.

Although the board of education pays the complete cost of Green Bills Corporations' hospital and medical insurance, management's negotiating team proposes that: (1) all hospital and medical insurance be bid and the business be given to the lowest bidder, (2) only HMO (Health Maintenance Organization) organizations be asked to bid, and (3) the employee pays for the first $100 of benefits received.

Rationale

The reason for this three part proposal is to provide substantial health coverage for the school district's employees, and to do so at the lowest cost. By achieving the lowest cost, additional money can be allocated to other important employee and school district needs, while maintaining the current level of protection.

Factual Data

In comparing the cost of our health insurance over the years and in comparing our health insurance coverage with other districts, we find:

(1) Our premiums have increased an average of 20 percent per year over the past ten years. This has happened while the additional income received by the district over the same ten-year period has only averaged 4.5 percent.

(2) Districts who have bid their health insurance packages have experienced a reduced premium cost of 5 percent per year.

(3) Districts who have gone strictly to HMOs for their health insurance indicate that they have experienced a yearly savings of 15 percent.

(4) Although we agree that very few employees take advantage of the full coverage paid by the board of education, by causing employees to pay for the first $100 of coverage, those employees who will misuse the policy coverage will be discouraged from further misuse. This also would prevent the possibility of lowering the district's premium cost as our policies' premiums are set on an experienced use basis.

Once initial proposals have been presented, attention is turned to the activities that take place during the at-the-table negotiating sessions. Let's turn now to a discussion of these activities.

ACTIVITIES DURING AT-THE-TABLE NEGOTIATING SESSIONS

Earlier, in Chapter 4, we discussed the roles of the various negotiating teams' members. It is important that the spokesperson control the dialogue; that the recorder keep an accurate account of the happenings of each at-the-table session; that the wordsmith do her/his homework and alert the spokesperson of concerns about the other team's wording of proposals; that the observer cue the spokesperson if any of the other team's members are telegraphing their attitudes towards a specific proposal or comment from the team's spokesperson; and it is important that the finance expert alert the spokesperson to any hidden financial implications in the other party's proposals.

While the team members are performing their roles, it is also important that they work together as a smooth operating whole, wherein all of the players do their roles well, thereby strengthening the entire team and allowing it to be the best it can be [19]. For only as the members help each other and work in tandem, can the team successfully implement their at-the-table strategies and tactics.

Other at-the-table important items to consider include: (1) being flexible and creative, (2) establishing the tone of each session, (3) timing proposal movement, (4) posturing and positioning, (5) dividing and conquering, and (6) controlling personality conflicts.

To a large extent, these moves will not only depend on the activities during the specific at-the-table session, but they will also depend on the power relationship of each party to the negotiations [20]. For example, if taxpayers have consistently refused to vote an increase in the local property tax and state aid to the district has been decreasing over the past five years, it will be extremely difficult for the union's negotiating team to achieve large, if any at all, expenditures related to employees' wages or fringe benefits [21]. On the other hand, if the school district has accumulated an unnecessarily large end-of-year fund balance, it will be very difficult for management's team to have enough power to keep fairly substantial increases in salary and fringe benefits from taking place.

At this point, let's return to the various items listed previously.

- *Being flexible* at the table is a great asset to a negotiating team. Flexibility will many times allow agreement on a contested proposal, by modifying the initial proposal made or counter-proposing a logical modification in the other party's proposal [22]. For instance, in our health insurance example, the proposal may be modified in the following ways: (1) instead of the employee paying the first $100 of benefits, the sum could be reduced to $25, and this would be establishing a future agenda for increased employee contributions, and (2) the proposal to allow only HMOs to bid could be dropped from the original proposal.

- *Being creative* is another means of becoming more effective at the table. For instance, if the union would agree to having each employee contribute $25 toward her/his health insurance costs, the school district would add $50 to another category of employee fringe benefits [23].
- *Controlling personality conflicts* is a skill that must be exercised by the chief negotiator. Controlling involves triggering anger in one of the other party's team members whenever one wants to do so because of the dislike by that member of the chief spokesperson or another member of the negotiating team [24]. It also involves observing her/his own team's members to make certain they are not losing their cool. Finally, it involves the chief negotiator maintaining a calm and collected appearance even when he/she has a serious personality conflict with the other party's chief negotiator.
- *Establishing the tone of each session* is another important skill that will enhance the team's chance for success at the individual negotiating sessions. If the team and its chief negotiator perceive that the other team will not make any movement at the session, the team should establish a tone of courteous listening, intelligent questioning of the other team's comments and proposals, and actions that hide a no-give demeanor [25]. If the team senses that the timing is right for movement, it should establish a tone of flexibility and sincere interest in making progress by give-and-take with the other team's proposals and with its own proposals. The reason for the timing to be right might be because of information that has been obtained indicating where other districts who are in the process of contract negotiations have settled on the item in dispute [26,27].
- *Dividing and conquering* is a useful technique to use when the union team's members represent different interests. For example, in dealing with a teachers' union, one might realize from the pre-negotiation information collected on the union team's members that many of them are at the top of the salary schedule, and 40 percent of the members are coaches. Management's negotiating team may make initial proposals that would not increase the top of the salary schedule, but that would increase the additional salaries paid to coaches by 50 percent. This approach would probably cause serious disagreement among members of the union's negotiating team, and management could use this dissension to come up with an entirely creative proposal in the future. The importance of having

in-depth knowledge about members of the opposition's negotiating team cannot be emphasized sufficiently.

- *Posturing and positioning* are important tactics to be utilized at the table. Posturing implies presenting an artificial position or attitude in negotiations in order to pretend that you feel strongly or take seriously an item that may not actually be one about which you feel strongly or are truly serious. Like a feint by a boxer, posturing is intended to throw the opponent off balance in her/his deliberations [28].

- *Positioning* implies the ability to arrange an order to things. The relative position within the whole, when controlled, adds tactical advantage for the negotiating team when compared to the positioning of the other team. Like the track star who draws the inside lane position for the race, controlling the position of your negotiation team and that of the other party's negotiating team will give one a big advantage during the race for agreement or during each negotiation session. This tactic of positioning can be used as a technique for pairing proposals, for faking proposals, or juxtaposing proposals.

ACTIVITIES AWAY FROM THE BARGAINING TABLE

Now that we have discussed at-the-table activities, let's turn to the events that take place away from the bargaining table. These areas include: (1) packaging proposals, (2) analyzing your proposals and analyzing their proposals by putting yourself in their shoes, (3) prioritizing proposals, (4) drafting counterproposals with an eye towards quid pro quos, (5) participating and cutting deals with between-meetings sidebar discussions, (6) costing proposals for immediate costs and projecting them for multiple year costs from both a financial and power perspective, (7) developing strategies and tactics for each negotiating session, and (8) keeping score by analyzing the results immediately following each session [29].

Packaging Proposals

The collective bargaining process often involves the negotiation of a large number of issues. One way to expedite the negotiations is to package proposals and counterproposals [30]. Packaging involves combining those items that have some relationship into one group, and insisting that all interrelated items be bargained as a unit.

If management were to receive proposals involving: (1) increased sick leave, (2) child care leave, (3) sabbatical leave, (4) paid holidays, (5) life insurance, (6) hospital insurance, (7) medical insurance, (8) accidental death and disability insurance, (9) dental insurance, (10) optical insurance, (11) maternity leave, and (12) salary increases; these items could then be packaged for bargaining purposes.

Management could insist on dealing with all cost and *possible* noncost items as separate packages [31]. In the above case only two items, those of maternity and child care leaves, are noncost items. If, on the other hand, management wanted to package them according to categorical areas and to insist that each category be negotiated as a unit, all leaves would become a package, all insurance would become a package, and salary increases would stand alone [32].

The advantage of packaging is that it provides pressure for the other party to look at a group as a whole, and it allows for reasoned give-and-take within the package. This technique should prove more rational than separate item bargaining, and it should expedite the negotiations process.

Analyzing Proposals by Putting Yourself in the Other Party's Shoes

One of the best ways to analyze your proposals and counterproposals and the other party's proposals and counterproposals is by putting yourself in the other party's shoes. That is, management takes the union's viewpoint and addresses the *what ifs*. (What, if I were the union, would I do to react to management's proposals or counterproposals?) This technique will allow management to anticipate the items that may be approved by the union, and it will also allow management to anticipate areas of disagreement [33]. Of course, the union's negotiating team members will benefit by utilizing the same procedure.

Prioritizing Proposals and Counterproposals

Every proposal or counterproposal made by management is not of equal worth, and every proposal made by the union is not of equal value. It is wise to prioritize the proposals and counterproposals that management presents on some scale such as (1) required, (2) desired, or (3) wishful thinking [34,35]. It is wise to do the same analysis of the union's proposals and counterproposals. Within each rating category, it is also wise to prioritize all items within each category; this procedure will allow you to maximize your strategies, objectives, and tactics on those items that are the most important negotiation proposals.

Drafting Counterproposals for Quid Pro Quo

Drafting counterproposals should be done by each negotiating team, with the wordsmith and the financial resource person taking the lead. The key to drafting counterproposals is making certain that the counterproposal achieves a quid pro quo (that is, the negotiating team will receive equal or greater value than what is given to the other party) [36]. Counterproposals can be limited to a single item, or the negotiating team can propose giving something in one proposal area for receiving something of equal or greater value in another proposal area.

An example of a single-item counterproposal might be one where management offers a better comprehensive health insurance coverage if the employees will pay the first $100 of the premium for coverage. An example of a multiple-item counterproposal might involve agreeing with the union's request for fully board-paid improved comprehensive health insurance in exchange for employees reporting for three days of staff development at substitute pay and the union also agreeing to drop its request for adding a salary step to the existing salary schedule.

Cutting Deals by Sidebars

Sidebars refer to actions taken away from the official negotiation meetings [37]. An example would be the chief negotiators for both management and union meeting at a restaurant with no others present, to see if they can talk about ways to move an item that is stalemated at the official sessions. If a successful compromise is worked out at this meeting, it will then be presented by one chief negotiator at an official negotiating meeting, and both chief negotiators will attempt to get their negotiating teams to agree to the proposal.

Developing Strategies and Tactics for Each Negotiating Session

Not only should overall strategies, objectives, and tactics be determined prior to the initial negotiating session, but they should also be arrived at prior to each collective bargaining session [38]. Negotiations often present an amoeba-like moving target, and that is the primary reason for taking time between negotiation sessions to plan the strategies, objectives, and tactics for the next upcoming negotiation session.

Strategies are the ''whats'' that the team wishes to achieve, the objectives are the specific measurable results to be achieved, and the tactics are the ''hows'' of achieving the strategies and objectives. An example of a management's strategy might be to lessen the escalating cost of health insurance that the board of education pays for employees. A specific objective might be to limit the cost increase to 5 percent over the next three years. The at-the-table tactic might be to offer to provide the union with a much-desired win in another proposal area to achieve the slowdown of cost escalation in the area of health insurance.

Costing Proposals for Power and Financial Impact, and for Immediate and Long-Term Impact

The teacher's union has proposed increases of $500 to each step on the existing $1,000 salary step increment in the schedule, moving the starting salary from its current $20,000 to $22,000, and adding another step to the existing ten-step salary schedule at the master's degree level. The union also wishes to increase the current $1,000 differential between the bachelor's and master's level to $4,000.

Let's examine the current step salary schedule and the placement on that schedule by the current employees. Also, the union's proposals will be placed in parentheses opposite the current salary schedule steps. The example in Table 7.1 is limited to five regular and an added sixth step (instead of the added eleventh step) for the sake of brevity.

The cost increase for future year one if the union's proposal were accepted can be computed as shown in Table 7.2.

Total new money costs for the first future year would equal $1,383,000. In addition, for the subsequent year, the costs would increase dramatically by moving all employees on steps one through four at the bachelor's level and steps one through six on the master's level. As these employees are placed forward one step on the salary schedule, each employee would receive a $1,500 step increment increase in salary, which is built into the schedule. This amounts to 140 teachers each receiving $1,500, or a total built-in increase of $210,000. This does not consider any increase in the basic salary schedule, any addition to the step increments, or any additional steps being added to the schedule for

Table 7.1. Wonderful School District's Current Teachers' Salary Schedule.

Step	No. of Teachers	Bachelor's Degree	No. of Teachers	Master's Degree
1	12	$20,000 ($22,000)	4	$21,000 ($26,000)
2	10	21,000 (23,500)	8	22,000 (27,500)
3	12	22,000 (25,000)	20	23,000 (29,000)
4	2	23,000 (26,500)	32	24,000 (30,500)
5	4	24,000 (28,000)	40	25,000 (32,000)
New	0		18	0 (33,500)

the second year of the master contract's duration. Each year into the future, the built-in cost increases from year one will keep carrying forward [39].

Let's now turn to a noneconomic example of a proposal that will have a long-term impact on the management of the school district. In this example, the transportation union's negotiating team has proposed that all bus routes be bid on the basis of seniority. In analyzing this proposal, management's negotiating team did some ''what if'' thinking. The management team said ''What if a bus driver who had seniority bid to drive a bus with handicapped students, and the driver was too old to assist in their placement on, in, and off the bus?'' The management team said ''What if a bus driver with a lot of seniority, who did not like nor could

Table 7.2.

Step	Current Year	Future Year	Difference
Bachelor's Degree			
1	$ 240,000	$ 264,000	$ 24,000+
2	210,000	235,000	25,000
3	264,000	300,000	36,000
4	46,000	53,000	7,000
5	96,000	112,000	16,000
Master's Degree			
1	84,000	104,000	20,000
2	176,000	220,000	44,000
3	460,000	580,000	120,000
4	768,000	976,000	208,000
5	1,000,000	1,280,000	280,000
New	00	603,000	603,000

handle little children, bid for the kindergarten bus run, and that driver replaced a person who loved small children, and was very gentle and kind to them?'' These what ifs pointed out the long-range damage that could be done to the children and to the reputation of the district within the community at large.

Analyzing the Results of Each Collective Bargaining Session

It is important to analyze the degree to which the negotiating team has achieved its specific session's objectives related to its strategies, and it is also important to analyze the degree of success the negotiating team achieved with the tactics it utilized during the session. This analysis should be conducted as soon after the negotiating sessions end as is practical, since the sooner the analysis is conducted, the better will be the team members' memories of what took place during the session [40]. Also, it is important to keep a running account of the status of negotiations after each session. This procedure will quickly identify for the team where the negotiations have been, the current status of negotiations, and the potential opportunities for future negotiating sessions.

A running diary of the status of proposals during negotiations will prove, along with the bargaining book that was previously prepared, to be a very valuable asset to the negotiating team. Table 7.3 demonstrates this aid.

Once the negotiating team has analyzed the status of each proposal, it should set about establishing means of reaching closure on the articles for which agreement has not yet been reached. As agreement is reached on each proposal and each contractual article, both parties should either TA (tentatively agree) or sign off and date that agreement. This being accomplished, all the TA's can then be reviewed before the entire

Table 7.3. Negotiations' Status Notebook.

Article	Proposed by	Agreed	Compromisable	Objectionable
Recognition	Union			X
Management rights	Management		X	
Employee evaluation	Management	X		

contractual agreement is TA'd, and both parties would then bring the TA'd contractual agreement to their referent group for official ratification [41].

Having dealt with the tentative agreement of contract articles, it is important to briefly indicate the differences that would take place in the conduct of at-the-table and away-from-the-table negotiations if the negotiating climate were a win/win environment rather than an adversarial environment.

WHAT DIFFERENCES WOULD EXIST IF THE NEGOTIATING ENVIRONMENT WERE A WIN/WIN ONE?

The basic differences that would be clearly evident if there were win/win negotiations rather than adversarial negotiations include the following.

- Pre-negotiation preparations would be a joint venture by both the union's and management's negotiating teams [42].
- The negotiating discussions would not be controlled by the chief negotiation spokespersons; rather, all parties would add their comments and suggestions during each and every negotiating session.
- Joint official minutes would probably be utilized.
- There would be no need for sidebar bargaining, as all members of both groups would be privy to all information and to all discussion.
- Subcommittees, comprised of members of both the union's team and management's team, would be used to investigate any area of study, and they would also be utilized to draft proposals that could be presented at the table to the full teams from both the union and management.
- A collaborative problem-solving process would be used, and this would be the greatest and most significant difference from the process used during adversarial negotiations [43].

SUMMARY

The establishment of ground rules is a negotiations process in itself, as both teams will make proposals prior to the actual discussion of contractual articles. Ground rules usually include locations and scheduling for meetings, the specific packaging of proposals, media update agreements, minute keeping, and any tentative agreement arrangements.

Procedures for exchanging proposals range from initial total proposal submission by one or both teams, to the splitting of economic and noneconomic proposals. The specific division of proposals may set the stage for later impasse trade-offs. Good-faith bargaining, implying integrity of intent and accuracy of data, is required at this stage. Initial proposals usually include three types of items—required proposals, bargaining chips, and new items. In general, most master contractual agreements will include such standard articles as: Recognition, Employee and Union Rights, Employment Conditions, Employee Evaluation, Employee Termination, Employee Compensation, Employee Fringe Benefits, Employee Leaves, Grievance Procedure, Negotiation Schedule and Procedures, Duration of the Agreement, and Management Rights.

The presentation of proposals requires a skilled chief negotiator, who is knowledgeable in negotiations law and in the employment details of the district. Examples of such proposals, both union and management, were provided, accompanied by rationales and supporting factual data.

The importance of team members' roles, previously described in Chapter 4 as critical functions in a smoothly running process, is combined with successful at-the-table strategies. (Power relationships intervene as well, particularly as they reflect relative resource strength of the district.) Suggested strategies include flexibility to maximize proposal modification, creativity in proposal modification, and control of personality conflicts. Establishing the tone of each session, sensing optimum timing for proposal give-and-take, and dividing and conquering (to cause union interteam stress), are also effective. Positioning and posturing, to feign attitudes aimed at throwing the opposition off balance and to arrange proposals for maximum advantage by controlling the position of both teams, are additional strategies.

Proposal packaging involves combining similar issues into groups, through categorical or cost/noncost clustering, for example, thus creating negotiation units and allowing for reasoned give-and-take within the package.

Analysis of proposals can be done by assuming the union viewpoint and addressing the what ifs, in order to anticipate counter strategies. Proposals likewise need to be prioritized, and counterproposals must be drafted in order to achieve quid pro quo (equal value). Sidebar agreements are actions taken informally, away from the table, usually addressing stalemated package items.

These and other strategies must be orchestrated, and a game plan determined prior to each negotiation session, bearing in mind that the strategies are what the team wishes to achieve. Objectives are the measurable results, and tactics are the processes to attain them. A cost example was provided to show the financial impact of a salary proposal, and a noncost example of a procedural item was described.

Analysis of each session must be conducted soon after its conclusion, and a running diary or ledger-like account kept to maintain a negotiations status record. Strategies for achieving closure on each of the proposal items can then be planned, and tentative agreement reached and mutual sign-off accomplished.

The occurrence of all this in a win/win climate would likely result in joint venture pre-negotiation preparations, open and free-interchange discussions, joint minutes and subcommittee investigative efforts, and the presence of a collaborative, problem-solving atmosphere.

EXERCISES

1. Describe what you feel would be optimum ground rules for a negotiations session in your district.
2. With regard to past contractual agreements in your district, what proposal items would be most likely to be mandatory, and which might be bargaining chips or new items?
3. Select a management package proposal and create a rationale for it, supporting it with factual data.
4. Select a union package and create a rationale for it, support your package with factual data.
5. Which of the at-the-table tactics described do you feel would be the most effective in your district's negotiations? Which would be the least effective?
6. What would be the best packaging for a proposal in your district? Describe how you would pair, group, and prioritize items for maximum effect.
7. Investigate one previous negotiation's salary proposal, and determine the impact of it on the district's existing salary schedule.
8. Investigate one no-cost or power proposal, and determine its impact on the school district's operation.
9. Explain how you would approach an adversarial bargaining environment.

10. Explain how you would approach a win/win, collaborative bargaining environment.

REFERENCES

1. Kearney, R. C. 1984. *Labor Relations in the Public Sector.* New York, NY: Marcel Dekker, Inc., p. 106.
2. Kearney, R. C., p. 106.
3. Webster, W. G., Sr. 1985. *Effective Collective Bargaining in Public Education.* Ames, IA: Iowa State University Press, p. 149.
4. Herman, J. J. 1991. "The Two Faces of Collective Bargaining," *School Business Affairs,* 57(2):12.
5. Helsby, R. D., J. Tener and J. Lefkowitz, eds. 1985. *The Evolving Process — Collective Negotiations in Public Employment.* Fort Washington, PA: Labor Relations Press, p. 225.
6. Feiock, R. C. and J. P. West. 1990. "Public Presence at Collective Bargaining: Effects on Process and Decisions in Florida," *Journal of Collective Negotiations,* 19(1):69.
7. Namit, C. 1986. "The Union Has a Communications Strategy — And Your Board Should, Too," *American School Board Journal,* 173(10):30 – 31.
8. Neal, R. 1980. *Bargaining Tactics — A Reference Manual for Public Sector Labor Negotiations.* Richard G. Neal Associates, p. 138.
9. Herman, J. J., 57(2):9.
10. Webster, W. G., Sr., pp. 151 – 152.
11. Webster, W. G., Sr., pp. 151 – 152.
12. Webster, W. G., Sr., pp. 151 – 152.
13. Coleman, C. J. 1990. *Managing Labor Relations in the Public Sector.* San Francisco, CA: Jossey-Bass Publishers, p. 119.
14. Kearney, R. C., p. 14.
15. Coleman, C. J., p. 16.
16. Herman, J. J., 57(2):9.
17. Gorton, R. A., G. T. Schneider and J. C. Fisher. 1988. *Encyclopedia of School Administration and Supervision.* Phoenix, AZ: Oryx Press, pp. 62 – 63.
18. Richardson, R. C. 1985. *Collective Bargaining by Objectives: A Positive Approach.* Englewood Cliffs, NJ: Prentice-Hall, Inc., p. 167.
19. Herman, J. J., 57(2):11.
20. Bacharach, S. B. and E. J. Lawler. 1984. *Bargaining — Power, Tactics, and Outcomes.* San Francisco, CA: Jossey-Bass Publishers, pp. 206 – 208.
21. Webster, W. G., Sr., pp. 162 – 163.
22. Ross, V. J. and R. MacNaughton. 1982. "Memorize These Bargaining Rules Before You Tackle Negotiations," *American School Board Journal,* 169(3):40 – 41.
23. Coleman, C. J., pp. 127 – 129.
24. Neal, R., pp. 94 – 96.
25. Herman, J. J., 57(2):11 – 12.
26. Herman, J. J., 57(2):11 – 12.

27. Herman, J. J., 57(2):11 – 12.

28. Webb, L. Dean, J. T. Greer, P. A. Montello and M.S. Norton. 1987. *Personnel Administration in Education – New Issues and New Needs in Human Resource Management.* Columbus, OH: Merrill Publishing Company, pp. 117 – 118.

29. Helsby, R. D., J. Tener and J. Lefkowitz, eds., p. 226.

30. Webster, W. G., Sr., p. 85.

31. Webster, W. G., Sr., p. 85.

32. Webster, W. G., Sr., p. 85.

33. Fisher, R. and W. Ury. 1981. *Getting to Yes – Negotiating Agreement without Giving In.* Boston, MA: Houghton Mifflin, Co., pp. 114 – 128.

34. Kearney, R. C., pp. 106 – 107.

35. Coleman, C. J., pp. 122, 169.

36. Neal, R., p. 167.

37. Kerchner, C. T. 1988. "A New Generation of Teacher Unionism," *Education Digest,* L111(9):52 – 54.

38. Kearney, R. C., pp. 106 – 107.

39. Granof, M. 1973. *How to Cost Your Labor Contract.* Washington, DC: The Bureau of National Affairs, Inc., pp. 2 – 3.

40. Herman, J. J., 57(2):12.

41. Helsby, R. D., J. Tener and J. Lefkowitz, eds., pp. 227 – 228.

42. Venter, B. M. and J. Ramsey. 1990. "Improving Relations: Labor Management Committees in School Districts," *School Business Affairs,* 56(12):21.

43. Nyland, L. 1987. "Win-Win Bargaining Pays Off," *Education Digest,* L111(1): 28 – 29.

FINDING THE TROUBLE SPOTS AND LIVING TOGETHER AFTER COLLECTIVE BARGAINING

Section Three consists of four chapters. Chapter 8, *Reaching Impasse—When Win/Win Has Flown the Coop,* covers information related to mediation, arbitration, and fact-finding.

Chapter 9, *Arriving at Lose/Lose,* discusses preparing for a strike, conduct during a strike, and follow-up after a strike. It also describes the stresses that take place during a strike, and it presents the case for consistent and accurate communications before, during, and after a strike.

Chapter 10, *Finalizing and Communicating the Signed Master Contract,* discusses reaching a tentative agreement, presenting the contract for ratification, giving the other party credit, and printing and publicizing the master contractual agreement that has been negotiated and ratified by both parties.

Chapter 11, *Living with the Contract That Has Been Negotiated— Contract Management,* discusses the topics of communicating and interpreting the contract, training administrators for contract management, setting and breaking precedents, and disciplining for contract violations. This chapter also discusses preparing for and conducting grievances and preparing for and conducting grievance arbitration.

Reaching Impasse—When Win/Win Has Flown the Coop

CHAPTER 8 presents the detailed planning that is required when an impasse is reached and when management and union groups are processed through the impasse resolution methods of mediation, fact-finding, and arbitration. It also provides an example of one state's impasse procedures.

An impasse may be deemed to exist if the union and management fail to reach a total contractual agreement, usually after lengthy negotiations. States vary on impasse procedures; some allow either party to declare impasse and request a mediator from the state's PERB (Public Employment Relations Board) or other state agency that has been designated to oversee the collective bargaining of public agencies in the state. Other states provide a different structure [1].

For example, New York State's Taylor Law defines an impasse as when both parties fail to achieve an agreement at least 120 days prior to the end of the fiscal year of the public employer. In this case, public employers may enter into written agreement with the recognized employees' union about specific measures to end impasses. Such written procedures can include submitting the unresolved issues to impartial arbitration. If there is not such a written agreement between both parties, PERB will appoint a mediator, upon request of either party or by PERB's own motion, to attempt to arrive at a voluntary resolution of items in dispute. If mediation does not end the dispute at least eighty days prior to the end of the fiscal year of the public employer or by such other date determined by PERB to be appropriate, PERB shall appoint a fact-finding board of not more than three members. Finally, if the fact-finding board's recommendations are made public and the impasse is still not resolved, PERB has the power to take whatever steps it deems necessary to resolve the dispute [2].

Another example is that of the State of Iowa's impasse procedures. To quote from *An Introduction to Iowa's Public Employment Relations Act,* which was prepared on the basis of an address by the PERB chairperson:

> PERB (Public Employment Relations Board) has general responsibility for the administration of mediation, fact-finding, interest arbitration, and grievance arbitration. Mediation is provided without cost to the parties and is performed by full-time staff, part-time "ad hoc" mediators, and commissioners of the Federal Mediation and Conciliation Service (FMCS).
>
> The expenses incurred in impasse services other than mediation are shared by the parties. PERB selects the individuals that serve on the fact-finding and arbitration panels. Lists of these individuals are provided the parties from which a selection is made through a striking procedure. Although the following sections deal only with "statutory" impasse procedures, parties may substitute their own mutually-agreed-upon "independent" procedures.
>
> Either party in a dispute may request the services of a mediator. The request must be dated and signed, filed with the Board, and served upon the other parties to the negotiations. Although only ten days are allocated for the mediation process, the Board has determined that the day of the first meeting is the "date of appointment" which commences that time period.
>
> Fact-finding is a compulsory component of the impasse procedures unless the parties mutually agree to eliminate it. In the event mediation efforts are unsuccessful, the statute requires the Board to appoint a fact-finder. Recently, the Board has adopted a policy of allowing the parties to select fact-finders from a list provided by the agency. It is on this basis that the appointment is made by the Board. The fact-finder conducts a hearing and issues findings and recommendations for the parties' consideration. After the fact-finder issues the report, the parties either accept or reject it. If the dispute remains unresolved ten days after hearing, PERB makes the report public.
>
> The advocates of fact-finding argue that it encourages settlement, or at least reduces the issues between the fact-finding and arbitration stage. In Iowa, fact-finding is particularly significant because it becomes a third option for the arbitrator to consider.
>
> Increasingly, states are enacting public laws which require interest arbitration (sometimes called contract arbitration). In Iowa, there is final offer arbitration on an issue by issue basis. If the fact-finder's recommendations are not accepted, either party may request arbitration.
>
> Following a request for arbitration, the parties are required to exchange their final offers on each issue at which they are at impasse. The parties may opt to have one arbitrator or a tripartite arbitration panel hear the

dispute. If the parties cannot agree upon a neutral arbitrator, PERB supplies a list of names from which to make the selection.

The arbitrator is required by statute to consider certain criteria in making his or her award. Included within these criteria are a comparison of wages, hours, and conditions of employment of the involved public employees with other public employees doing comparable work; past contracts between the parties; the employer's power to levy taxes; and the ability of the employer to finance economic adjustments.

The award must be issued within fifteen days of the hearing, unless the parties have otherwise agreed. The arbitrator is prohibited by statute from mediating the dispute. An arbitrator's award is subject to judicial review as agency action under Chapter 17A, *The Code* (1981).

The main function of PERB in grievance arbitration cases is to provide panels of arbitrators upon request. PERB offers staff grievance arbitration services based on an hourly fee rate, shared by the parties and paid to the State. [3]

Other states have different impasse structures. Before the discussion moves to another topic, some specific clarifications should be made.

(1) Interest arbitration (sometimes called contract arbitration) refers to an impasse procedure during the negotiations process. Grievance arbitration, on the other hand, refers to a third party investigating an alleged violation by management of the terms of an existing master contractual agreement as claimed by the union [4].

(2) In some states arbitration precedes fact-finding.

(3) In some states, arbitrators attempt to mediate the resolution, but in all situations, arbitrators or fact finders are not utilized until mediation has been exhausted.

(4) Arbitration and/or fact-finding can be done by a single person serving as an outside party or by a panel serving as an outside body.

(5) The cost for arbitration and/or fact-finding is usually shared equally by both union and management, although it is possible for the other agreed-upon payment structures to be used.

(6) Both fact-finding and arbitration can be compulsory or voluntary, depending on the individual state's laws and rules and regulations, and depending on the agreement between both parties when the state's laws do not restrict the parties to a specific method.

(7) Interest (contract) arbitration, if compulsory or voluntary, can be item-for-item arbitration or total last best offer arbitration. If

arbitration is by the item-by-item method, the arbitrator is free to select the position of either party on each contractual item that remains in dispute, and the arbitrator may rule in favor of one party on some items and in favor of the other party on other items in dispute.

(8) If, however, arbitration is of the last best offer type, the arbitrator must rule in favor of a single party's total last best offer. There can be no decisions on the merits of either party on the individual contractual items in dispute [5].

Now that an overlay of impasse situations has been provided, let's turn to the topic of preparing for impasse. This section will discuss the preparations recommended for each of the impasse situations of mediation, fact-finding, and arbitration.

PREPARING FOR MEDIATION

When you enter this initial impasse stage, it is important that you have kept a complete record of every matter that has been discussed or presented by either party during the negotiations that have taken place to this point [6]. Also, this is where all the pre-negotiations information collected for your bargaining book, the information on the actual status of each article discussed at the table, and the updates of information from comparable districts who are currently involved in negotiations become crucial.

Usually a mediator is assigned by the state's PERB (Public Employment Relations Board), or by some other body that is provided the responsibility for the oversight of public collective bargaining in the state, upon the written request of the local school district's employer or the local school district's union [7]. At this point, it is wise to check on the track record of the mediator to determine the degree of success the person has in resolving disputes.

If, after a few sessions with the assigned mediator, one is not pleased with the mediator's performance, it is wise to request a change of mediators. PERB, however, may or may not grant the request for a change.

The mediator, whose role it is to simply try to resolve the dispute, is not concerned with the values involved in the dispute, nor is the mediator necessarily attempting to get a fair settlement. The mediator's sole role is to obtain a settlement that will be agreed to by both parties in the dispute [8].

The scenario of a hypothetical mediation might very well follow the sequence illustrated as follows.

(1) The mediator contacts the bargaining teams and sets up appointments for her/him to meet with both the union's negotiating team and management's negotiating team.

(2) At the initial mediation meeting, the mediator will meet separately with the union's negotiating team and management's negotiating team. At this meeting, the mediator will review the mediation procedure. Also at this meeting, the mediator will ask each party to stipulate the specific items in dispute, and to clarify the party's current offer on each item. Finally, the mediator will ask for the underlying rationale for the party's position on each item, and she/he will listen to any data that the party feels strengthens the case for the party's current position.

(3) After meeting separately with each party to the dispute, the mediator will conduct a joint meeting of both parties to review the state's collective bargaining law and the applicable rules and regulations as these apply to the impasse procedure entitled mediation. The mediator will also outline the items in dispute and her/his understanding of each party's position on each item. Hopefully, at this session the mediator can get agreement of both parties that the items reviewed are those in dispute, and that the positions of both parties on each disputed item are clear.

(4) At this point, the mediator will generally conduct a series of meetings with the individual parties to the dispute, and she/he will occasionally bring both parties together for meetings. During the meetings with each party, the mediator will explore areas of flexibility, and suggest a variety of compromise solutions. These are exploratory discussions, and they are not binding on either party.

(5) If the mediator feels, after a series of meetings with the union's negotiating team and management's negotiating team, that she/he is in a position to make a proposed settlement, she/he may call both teams together and present a proposal. If the proposal is accepted, it should be signed off by both parties, and the impasse should be resolved. Oftentimes, the mediator may feel it prudent to present additional compromise recommendations, if the original recommendations are rejected by either party or by both parties.

(6) If mediation is unsuccessful after a reasonable period of time, the

mediator or PERB may declare an end to mediation, or either party (or both parties) may terminate the mediation process [9].

With this mediation-sequenced scenario in mind, let's return to the type of preparation the negotiating team should undertake prior to meeting with the mediator. First, the team should clearly identify the items in dispute, and it should prepare the rationale and factual arguments for its position on each contractual item that is in dispute. Second, it should clearly identify areas for which the mediator can be told the team will be flexible, and the degree of this flexibility, and it should identify the areas for which the mediator will be told that there is absolutely no flexibility. Third, the methods of presenting this information to the mediator should be predetermined. Finally, the negotiating team should decide on how much they will tell the mediator about their ultimate position, especially on financial items, when they meet with her/him [10]. This caution refers to the fact that if the entire amount of money available to reach a final settlement is revealed to the mediator and the mediation is not successful, there will be flexibility left for further stages of the impasse process.

Let's review the preparation for mediation of two items in dispute, one being financial and the other being nonfinancial.

A nonfinancial example is one in which the union proposes that management will have to obtain the agreement of the individual employee before that employee can be transferred to another site or another position. In this situation, management would present the following rationale and data.

- Management must retain the right to assign employees, otherwise the entire school district could end in chaos. Specific scenarios would be presented to illustrate this point.
- There is no evidence from comparable school districts that any board of education has ratified a master contractual agreement incorporating such restrictive language.
- The position of management's negotiating team on this item is one of absolute rejection.

A financial example is one in which the union proposes a 10 percent increase in the amount of money allocated to the salary schedule of teachers. Management's response to the mediator includes the following.

- The board of education wants to pay teachers a fair wage, but it cannot afford to increase the salaries of teachers by 10 percent.
- The cost of living index for the district's region is only 4.5 percent, and a 10 percent increase in teachers' salaries is uncalled for at this time.
- Management's negotiating team has offered a 5 percent salary increase, and this offer is one-half of a percentage point in excess of the cost of living increase.
- Management's 5 percent offer will retain the teachers' salary ranking at fourth place, when compared to the area's twenty other districts.
- The public last year voted a two mil increase in property tax for school purposes, and the effort made by the citizens of this community when compared with the taxable base available to it indicates that the district ranks fifth of the twenty-one districts in its financial effort to support its schools.

Assuming that the information shared above by management's negotiating team and the information shared by the union's negotiating team, coupled with the efforts of the mediator, did not end the impasse, the process will move to the fact-finding stage. It should be remembered that this is not the sequence or procedure followed by all districts, and it is not one that is mandated in all states that have passed collective bargaining legislation.

FACT-FINDING

Fact-finding is the step in the impasse resolution process that usually follows an unsuccessful mediation attempt. Sometimes it is carried on by a single fact finder and sometimes it is carried on by a fact-finding panel. Occasionally, the panel is selected by having each party select one member of the fact-finding panel and agreeing on a method of selecting the third member [11].

Although sometimes used as a tactic, it is poor practice for either party to artificially push negotiation into fact-finding with the hope that the fact finder will give them a better deal than could be achieved through at-the-table negotiations with the other party, or through the impasse procedure of mediation [12].

In states where fact-finding is advised, the results of the fact-finding are published if the parties cannot agree. Also, in some states the fact finders' recommendations can include recommendations for settlement, and these can also be published. The publication of the recommendations is intended to put public pressure on either or both parties to settle the disputed areas [13]. In states where fact-finding is binding, this publication step is not required.

During fact-finding, each party presents written documentation and oral arguments that best reflect its case. Witnesses can be called, and the fact finder may legally subpoena witnesses. Fact finders will interrogate these witnesses, and oftentimes a court recorder will be hired to take and transcribe a verbatim transcript. Generally, fact finders will also allow written rebuttals of the opposite party's presentations following the fact finder's hearing; at times, the fact finder will allow the parties to file post fact-finding hearing briefs [14].

In general, fact finders will use a set of criteria upon which to collect facts and on which to make recommendations. A reasonable set of criteria would include: (1) the impact on the education program, (2) equity for both parties, (3) practicality of the issues and of their resolutions, (4) future implications of the settlements, (5) ability of the school district to pay, (6) comparative standards with other school districts, and (7) compromises that assist each party [15].

Don't expect the fact finder to speak to the merits of your position. Her/his recommendations will almost certainly be profoundly influenced by the facts you present and by the effectiveness and relevance of the presentations made on the issues in dispute [16]. Also, remember that if you do not fully understand the fact finder's report, phone her/him to get clarification prior to deciding on a course of action.

The kind of information you should be prepared to give the fact finder will include the following.

- Include a copy of your operating budget and last year's audit.
- Include a list of items that are in contention, and the cost of each of the economic items that are in contention from both the union's demands and management's offers.
- Include gross budgetary increases represented by the union's demands and management's offers.
- Include impact on the tax rate of each of the demands and offers.
- Include impact of anticipated changes in revenues from local, state, and federal sources.
- Include demographic data about the school district and its students;

such data as per pupil expenditures, student enrollment, and the socioeconomic level of the community at large is always helpful to the fact finder.

- Include a statement of the first proposals made by the union and the first counterproposals made by management.
- Include any change of position on the contested items that was made during the mediation process, especially listing those items for which there was tentative agreement.
- Include a clear statement of each party's last best offer on each item in contention [17].

Usually, a fact finder's written report will include sections such as: (1) background information, (2) the criteria used in decision making or in acceptance of the facts submitted by the parties, (3) a listing of all items that are in contention, with the position of both the union and management clearly stated, (4) a summary of all pertinent facts related to each item in contention, and (5) a final section of decisions, findings of facts, and recommendations; this section usually contains the rationale utilized by the fact finder in making her/his recommendations [18].

Assuming that the state in which the school district is located permits the two parties to the negotiations to either accept or reject the fact finder's report, the next step in this state would lead to the impasse process of arbitration. Let's now turn to a discussion of this step in the impasse procedures.

INTEREST OR CONTRACT ARBITRATION

Whether arbitrators or arbitration panels are controlled by PERB or whether the parties to the negotiations apply to the American Arbitration Association for a list of arbitrators, both parties usually can select some names and reject others until agreement is reached [19]. In cases where agreement is not reached, some states permit PERB to select the arbitrator. In all cases, the parties to the negotiations would be wise to contact sources of information about each proposed arbitrator and about rulings that she/he has issued to date, especially her/his rulings on cases involving the specific items that are in contention during the current negotiations [20]. Besides the PERB morgue, a person could search the Bureau of National Affairs' *Labor Arbitration Reports* or the information about arbitrators listed in the Martindale-Hubbell Law Directory, or in the Summary of Labor Arbitration Awards, or any other similar sources of information about arbitrators [21].

Even though arbitration is requested on items in contention, the question of arbitrability of some of the items can be questioned by either party [22]. If the question of arbitrability is raised and a review by the arbitrator of existing contractual language and the state's collective bargaining laws and its supplemental rules and regulations causes the arbitrator to rule that a certain item is not arbitrable, the party who questioned the arbitrability of the item scores a big tactical win. Most times, however, the arbitrator will not be questioned on the arbitrability issue, and when she/he is, the ruling generally is one that states the item is arbitrable. It is becoming more prevalent in contracts that a ruling of arbitrability is made by a court before submitting the case to arbitration. Judges only rule on the arbitrability and not on the case itself.

In many ways, the preparation for the arbitration and the conduct of the arbitration hearing is very similar to the procedures surrounding fact-finding. Again, the arbitration can be voluntary or mandatory, and the hearing can be conducted by a single arbitrator or a panel of arbitrators. In some states, it is permitted that the same person can serve as a mediator and an arbitrator within the same case [23]. In the opinion of the authors, this method truly puts the arbitrator in the position of becoming a super mediator, and it weakens the mediation step in the impasse procedures.

Even though there are many similarities in the preparation for and the conduct of arbitration and fact-finding, let's terminate this discussion on impasse procedures by outlining the steps the party to negotiations should take in preparation for contract arbitration. Also, let's discuss the likely procedures that will be used in conducting the arbitration.

It is important to note that most arbitration cases that are lost by management are due to poor planning and preparation. The steps that should be taken in planning for arbitration are as follows. (1) Pre-deciding on the written data to be presented. These should be mostly identical to those prepared for fact-finding, including the initial information that was included in the fact-finding report if that report favors your party's views. (2) Preparing the oral presentation and deciding on the person(s) who will give the oral presentation [24]. Also, if post-arbitration hearing briefs are permitted by the arbitrator, the briefs should also be carefully planned and expertly prepared.

Now that the parties have prepared for the arbitration, let's briefly outline a scenario of the probable structure of the arbitration hearing.

- The first step will probably involve the introductions of all parties, a short review of the purpose of arbitration, and a review of the items which are in dispute.
- A decision will be made as to whether or not the hearing shall be open or closed. If both parties agree that they wish an open meeting, the arbitrator may or may not agree, and if either party objects to an open hearing, the arbitrator will definitely conduct a closed hearing. Most experts in the field recommend closed hearings.
- If both parties agree to accept testimony of outside parties, the arbitrator will probably rule in favor of this, but if either party disagrees on this item, outside party testimony will probably not be allowed.
- The arbitrator may decide to tape the hearing, or there may be an agreement among the parties that a court recorder be hired to take a verbatim transcript of the hearing. In cases where a transcript is allowed, there should be a prior agreement as to which parties besides the arbitrator are to receive transcripts, and who will pay the expenses of the court recorder and for the preparation and distribution of the transcripts of the hearing.
- Some arbitrators insist that all persons testifying do so under oath.
- Opening statements are presented by both parties. In general, either the union begins or the party who initially requested the arbitration is the first party to present.
- The parties will present their written exhibits and their oral arguments. Sometimes both parties will agree to joint stipulations of the issues being contested, and they will agree to file joint exhibits related to the items stipulated.
- Either party is sometimes permitted to cross-examine the other party's witness, but in all cases, the arbitrator will interrogate the witnesses for clarification and additional detail.
- In some states, the arbitrator is given power to subpoena witnesses or records if information that may be pertinent to the case is not forthcoming.
- Closing arguments will be presented by both parties.
- The arbitrator will end the hearing, and she/he may allow both parties to file post-hearing briefs.
- Within a reasonable period after the hearing, or within a few weeks if a verbatim transcript is required, the arbitrator will make her/his mandates for a settlement known (in situations where arbitration is

mandatory), or the arbitrator will make known her/his recommendations for settlement of the outstanding issues in contention (in situations where arbitration is voluntary).

* If arbitration is mandatory, the issues are resolved and a master contractual agreement is issued. This terminates the negotiations and the impasse procedures [26].

SUMMARY

Impasse may be deemed to exist if the union and management fail to reach a total contractual agreement. State impasse procedures vary in the structures that determine which party, or agency, such as a Public Employment Relations Board, may declare impasse. Examples from New York and Iowa illustrated the language and statutory provisions of impasse. Also addressed were such issues as expenses, mediation participant selection, compulsory fact-finding, contract arbitration, and criteria for awards.

Interest (contract) arbitration, refers to an impasse procedure during negotiations; grievance arbitration refers to allegations of violations of existing contracts. In some states, fact-finding precedes arbitration; in others, the opposite occurs. These procedures may be done by a panel or by an individual, may vary in expense assignment, and can be compulsory or voluntary. Arbitration can also consider settlement item-by-item, or by total last best offer.

Preparing for mediation requires referral to the bargaining book and to updated information on at-the-table items and information about comparable districts. Disputed items should be clarified, and further preparation should be done on proposal rationales, supporting facts, and possible areas of flexibility. The track record of the mediator should be investigated. The procedure itself usually involves separate mediator meetings with the two teams to get a perspective on their proposals, followed by a joint meeting with both parties to review the law and to outline disputed items. A series of individual team meetings follow to allow exploration of flexibility, and a proposed settlement is made. Financial and nonfinancial disputed proposal examples were provided. It should be remembered that the mediator's sole role is to obtain a mutual (not necessarily fair or equitable) settlement.

Fact-finding is the method of impasse resolution that usually follows an unsuccessful mediation attempt. This can be done by an individual, or by a panel of fact finders. Each party presents written documentation and oral arguments for its case, and the fact finders may expand upon that information by subpoena of witnesses or interrogation of witnesses. In general, a set of criteria is used upon which to collect facts and make recommendations. Teams usually provide the fact finders with budget information, proposal items' costs, revenue and demographic data, and a summary of the preceding negotiations process. Sometimes fact-finding is used as a tactic by one party to obtain a better settlement than could be achieved through negotiations. In some states, the results of fact-finding are publicized, particularly if the process is not binding.

Parties to the negotiations usually have the option to select or decline arbitrators. The arbitrability of some items in contention may be questioned. The preparation for interest (contract) arbitration is much the same as that for fact-finding. Care must be given to the preparation of the information and to the presentation of the brief. The procedure (usually closed to the public) itself will usually involve a review of the items in dispute, the submission of any outside party testimony and subsequent cross-examination, the presentation of each party's proposals, maintenance of a transcript of the proceedings, the presentation of closing arguments, and the filing of post-hearing briefs. The arbitrator will, within a reasonable period, decide mandates for settlement, or recommendations for settlement (if arbitration is voluntary).

EXERCISES

1. Investigate the impasse procedures in your state. What is the order of those procedures, and is arbitration compulsory or voluntary?

2. Investigate the record of any fact-finding or mediation processes that involved a district in your state.

3. With reference to the last proposal package prepared by either party in your district, which individual items do you think might have been candidates for flexibility areas during mediation procedures?

4. With reference to the last proposal package prepared by either party in your district, which individual items in dispute might have been factually supported by the testimony of expert witnesses? How would those witnesses have been found?

5. Locate the sources in your state that provide important information about the rulings of individual arbitrators and fact finders.

6. What information would you present at the impasse stages of mediation, fact-finding, and arbitration?

REFERENCES

1. Helsby, R. D., J. Tener and J. Lefkowitz, eds. 1985. *The Evolving Process — Collective Negotiations in Public Employment*. Fort Washington, PA: Labor Relations Press, p. 16.

2. New York State Public Employment Relations Board. 1983 — 1984. *The Taylor Law*. Albany, NY: New York Public Employment Relations Board, pp. 13 — 15.

3. Beamer, J. B. 1985. "An Introduction to the Public Employees Relations Act," address by the Chairman of the Public Employment Relations Board of Iowa. *Public Employment Relations Act*, pp. 13 — 18.

4. Elkouri, F. and E. A. Elkouri. 1973. *How Arbitration Works, Third Edition*. Washington, DC: Bureau of National Affairs, Inc., pp. 44 — 48.

5. Elkouri, F. and E. A. Elkouri, pp. 2 — 8.

6. Webster, W. G., Sr. 1985. *Effective Collective Bargaining in Public Education*. Ames, IA: Iowa State University Press, pp. 250 — 253.

7. Kearney, R. C. 1984. *Labor Relations in the Public Sector*. New York, NY: Marcel Dekker, Inc., pp. 250 — 253.

8. Kearney, R. C., p. 253.

9. Coleman, C. J. 1990. *Managing Labor Relations in the Public Sector*. San Francisco, CA: Jossey-Bass Publishers, pp. 217 — 219.

10. Brock, J. 1982. *Bargaining Beyond Impasse — Joint Resolution of Public Sector Labor Disputes*. Boston, MA: Auburn House Publishing Company, pp. 53 — 54, 71 — 76.

11. Zack, A. 1980. *Understanding Fact-Finding and Arbitration in the Public Sector*. Washington, DC: U.S. Department of Labor, Labor Management Services Administration, p. 2.

12. Neal, R. 1980. *Bargaining Tactics — A Reference Manual for Public Sector Labor Negotiations*. Richard G. Neal Associates, pp. 229 — 230, 232.

13. Kearney, R. C., pp. 255 — 256.

14. Helsby, R. D., J. Tener and J. Lefkowitz, eds., pp. 242 — 243.

15. Webster, W. G., Sr., p. 162.

16. Neal, R., pp. 232 — 233.

17. Webster, W. G., Sr., p. 162.

18. Coleman, C. J., p. 220.

19. Webster, W. G., Sr., pp. 165 — 166.

20. Elsea, S. W., D. A. Dilts and L. J. Haber. 1991. "Factfinders and Arbitrators in Iowa: Are They the Same Neutrals?" *Journal of Collective Negotiations*, 19(1): 61 — 67.

21. Helsby, R. D., J. Tener and J. Lefkowitz, eds., pp. 252 — 253.

22. Zack, A., pp. 58 — 59.

23. Zack, A., p. 3.

24. Zack, A., pp. 39 — 40.

25. Kearney, R. C., pp. 258 — 260.

26. Kearney, R. C., pp. 258 — 260.

Arriving at Lose/Lose

CHAPTER 9 discusses the following topics: (1) preparation for a strike, (2) conduct during the strike, (3) follow-up after the strike, (4) development and execution of the strike plan, (5) selection of a spokesperson(s) to communicate with the community, the board of education, the administration, the employees, and the media, (6) establishment of a "hotline," (7) the hard place: long hours, and the big stress test, and (8) playing "chicken" until the end.

For purposes of demonstration during the chapter, the incident of a teachers' union strike will be used, as teachers comprise the largest and probably the most powerful union group within the local school district. Also, most of the illustrations in this chapter will be presented from a board of education's or management's point of view.

Let's begin by discussing strike preparation. It is important to realize that the worst case scenario in collective bargaining is that of a strike. If a strike exists in a school district, no one wins. At best, a strike is a temporary lose/lose situation, but most often it is a long-term lose/lose situation for everyone involved.

In the case of a teachers' union strike, the students are subjected to an unhappy environment prior to the strike, and they see their teacher role models picketing and behaving in a manner that is not conducive to appropriate modeling behavior. If a state, such as Michigan, prohibits teachers from striking and many teacher strikes still take place without any punishment to the individuals and the union leadership, it also gives some students the thought that if teachers can break the law, they have a similar option to disobey district or classroom rules [1].

Once the parties arrive at the strike stage, propaganda proliferates. Many times the community does not know who is telling the truth, and they lose faith in both parties [2−4]. This community image damage often continues long after the strike is settled.

Finally, the employees are frustrated because they are concerned about their livelihood, concerned about repercussions, and are sometimes not certain where the current situation is heading. Many times, they become emotional. Some employees are forced, because of pressure from other union members, to participate in a strike, picket the school board and administrative office, and do other tasks that are totally opposed to their traditional value system [5].

Once all other efforts to reach agreement during at-the-table negotiation, mediation, fact-finding, and arbitration have failed and the parties are presumed to be definitely headed for a strike, it is crucial that a detailed and comprehensive strike plan be prepared. Without a strike plan, one party is at the total mercy of the tactics of the other party, and sometimes those tactics can become rather severe. Prior to initiating the strike plan and prior to experiencing a strike, management can do much to prepare.

PREPARING FOR A STRIKE

There is only one certain key to surviving a strike, and that key is preparation, preparation, and more preparation. Management cannot over-prepare for an upcoming strike. The best means of preparation include playing ''what if'' scenarios with the board of education, the administrators, and management's negotiating team. In addition, management should establish strategies, objectives, tactics, and countering tactics.

What if scenarios can be developed by recalling the experiences of other districts that have undergone strikes, or, if the district has previously experienced a strike and the union leadership is still in place, many of the union's tactics will be repeated. Prior to actually going on strike the union may have its membership participate in job actions. Some of the what if scenarios for which management should prepare include the following.

- *Sick outs* are when all teachers use sick leave or personal leave, in concert, on the same day in the hopes that a normal school day will be interrupted. Sometimes there will be a staggering usage of this tactic wherein the teachers in one building will all call in sick or take personal leave one day, another building's teacher staff will do this on another day, and so forth [6]. Management's planning responses to this what if scenario could be to: (1) increase the number of substitute teachers that the district normally retains on its payroll, (2) hire some of the normal substitute teachers to a short-term, full-time rotating teaching position, and (3) have all the administrators who are also certified as teachers report to the local schools to do large group instruction or to take the students on field trips with instructional goals. In each case, an action plan should be prepared in advance of the job action, and in the case of the field trip alternative, a lesson plan should be prepared with instructional outcomes stated.

- *Work-to-rule* actions are those whereby teachers are instructed by the union leaders to refuse to perform any duties that are not specifically mandated by the contract [7]. In many cases, this means that teachers will not provide homework, will not meet with students who require help after normal school hours, and will not meet with parents to discuss their child's progress at any time other than normal school hours. About the only responses management can have to these job actions are: (1) to appeal to the professional instincts of the teachers, and (2) to suggest to parents who complain about the teachers' job action that this will be a short and temporary situation, and to state that you are sorry for the inconvenience and lack of normal services caused by this work-to-rule action.

- *Nonfulfillment of coaching and after normal school hours sponsoring activities* is another job action that management might very well face. The students who are involved in these activities will be very vocal; the parents of students who are involved in these activities will become very angry; and in a school district that has football, band, basketball, or some other after-school co-curricular activity as a spectator entertainment that brings pride and recognition to the school and the school district, the general public will become very upset with all parties to the negotiations [8]. Occasionally, coaches or band directors or the sponsors of some other high-visibility co-curricular activity will not march by the union's directives, and if they do so, they will be severely ostracized by the union leadership. They may also very well suffer daily harassment by the other teachers in the school district. Management can do three things that will help in combating this job action scenario. Management can: (1) protect the coaches and sponsors from harm by cancelling all co-curricular activities until after a master contractual agreement is reached. If such action is to be taken, the media and community should be informed of the action recommended by the administration and approved by the board of education, and the community should be informed that the reason for the action was that some coaches and other co-curricular sponsors would continue their after-school duties, but others would not continue. Also, rather than having some students receive the advantage of after-school activities and others not receive them, the board of education should decide to cancel all after-school activities until a master contractual agreement with the teachers' union has been ratified. (2) People who wish to coach or be a co-curricular sponsor but who work for other school districts, or other persons who wish to and are able to coach or sponsor an activity can be hired as replacements. If the board of education authorizes this approach, every new coach or co-curricular sponsor should be told, in advance, of the pressure they will probably receive from members of the school district's teachers' union. (3) In anticipation of a possible job action, the board of education could authorize the administration to prepare and offer written contracts to each coach or co-curricular sponsor that provides the same salary and job assignments as those written into the expiring master contractual agreement, and a clause should be inserted stating that any additional benefits that may accrue to that specific coaching or co-curricular sponsorship will be passed on to the coach or sponsor once the negotiations on the successor master contractual agreement are ratified. This approach will put the situation under contract law, and it will accommodate those coaches and sponsors who wish to continue with the excuse that they cannot violate a signed personal contract.

- In the case of *boycotts of business* establishments or other situations where the school district's board members have an interest [9], about the only thing that can be done is to collect data as to the harm done, and then hire a lawyer to sue the union leaders, individually, for damages. In all probability this technique will not be ultimately successful, but it may cause some concern among the leadership of the union.

- When *picketing* board of education meetings, and, before and after normal school hours, picketing the administration building and the individual school buildings [10] occurs, management had better be prepared to communicate with the media, as the media is definitely going to cover any potential conflict situation [11]. The union's spokesperson will certainly have contacted the media and given the union's side of the story, and management should be prepared with a truthful and clear response. Management, in this situation, should do two things: (1) provide a clear statement of the board of education's current position related to union/management contract negotiations [12], and (2) alert the police department to be on call in case the picketing or the interference with the officially called board of education becomes unpleasant and gets out of hand. It should be clear to the police, however, that their presence on campus should only take place after a call from a specific administrator, as the presence of police oftentimes can incite a riot.

The previous and other job actions will only prove to be successful if the union receives almost unanimous teacher-member compliance. The support of other labor unions, in a school district that has multiple unions, is also important. A school district wherein most of the adults also belong to unions is also an aid to the teachers' union [13]. The timing of the job actions is also important, and the element of surprising management is another area of importance.

Now that we have reviewed the most serious job actions that could be taken by a teachers' union and the possible planned responses of management to each job action, we are still left with a variety of other tactics that are not job actions, for which management will have to plan by playing with what if scenarios. Some of the most likely to be faced tactics and some possible plans that could be enacted by management are the following.

- Union notification to administration that they will be taking a strike vote, or having others spread the word that there might be a strike. If state laws prohibit a strike, the administration, with prior approval of the board of education, could provide a news release, a mailing to each household in the school district, and a copy of both to the union's leadership stating something similar to the following:

Rumor has it that a teachers' strike is looming in our district. Since the state's collective bargaining statute prohibits strikes by public employees, it is our hope and belief that the school district's teachers will not participate in an illegal strike action. However, in order to protect the students and the school district, the board of education has made the decision to start the school year two weeks later than normal next year unless a master contract agreement with the teachers' union has been ratified prior to the beginning of the normal school year. We assure you that students will be provided a full contingent of days of instruction, because the two week late start will be made up by taking an equivalent amount of days from the normal mid-year and spring vacation schedules.

It is important to note that the authors disagree on this particular tactic.

- Writing letters to the editors is another tactic that management is likely to face. In this case, friends of the teachers' union, although not identified as teachers from other districts or relatives of teachers, will write letters indicating that the board of education and the administration are unfair to the teachers. These letters will also indicate that the teachers are merely asking for a decent wage and comparable fringe benefits paid to employees of other organizations, and that many of their union's proposals, such as a reduction in class size, are being proposed to improve the quality of education given the students of the district [14]. Management's most likely response is to have friends of the board of education, who are not identified as such, place similar letters to editors, supporting the board of education's views, in the newspapers that cover the district. These letters should indicate the fairness of the board of education's negotiating team's proposals, and the concern that the board of education has for fairness to the taxpayers and for the welfare of students and the school district's employees.
- Packing board of education meetings occurs when teacher union members from other school districts act as if they are parents in the district or that they are concerned citizens of the district. This is an especially effective technique when the state's sunshine laws call for open meetings and the bylaws of the board call for segments wherein audience or public comment is permitted during each officially called board of education meeting. The board of education's meeting agenda may not have a spot for negotiations-related discussion (most states with sunshine laws permit executive sessions for this purpose), but the audience can certainly ask critical questions or make derogatory statements when called upon by the board chairperson. Also, if the teachers and union members from other school districts are told to report to the site early enough to fill the room so that no room remains for the general public or for supporters of the board of education's position, meeting control shifts to the advantage of the union and its supporters [15].

In all likelihood, the media will be tipped off in advance by the union, and both newspaper and TV media representatives will be present to record the proceedings of the board of education meeting. Management can probably only do two things in this situation. (1) Ask each audience participant to state whether or not they are a resident of the district and whether or not they are a teacher. In most cases, the person will not respond, but the media will at least get some message that then can be pursued after the meetings with the persons who speak at the meeting. (2) Pack the meeting with friends of the board of education's position.

- Having supporters hold coffee klatches sponsored by teachers or by teacher union supporters. The most likely tactic that management can devise in this situation is to attempt to get a person who supports the board of education's position to attend the neighborhood coffee klatch. This person should not readily be identified as a supporter of the board of education's position, and the person should report the content and tenor of the meeting to management. This information will assist management in developing counter-tactics to be used in the future.

Now that we have discussed some of the job actions and some of the tactics that may be used by a teachers' union prior to actually going on strike, and now that we have discussed some of the potential counter-tactics that might be used by the board of education and its administrators, let's turn to the topic of a strike plan. The focus shall continue on a teachers' union and on management's planning.

PREPARING A STRIKE PLAN

Once the possibility of a strike is evident, it is important that a comprehensive strike plan be developed and that this plan not be shared with many people until a strike actually occurs [17]. It would be wise to inform the board of education members and all administrators that a plan has been developed, and that a meeting will be called to share the details of that plan as soon as a strike takes place. It is suggested that the board members and the administrators be told that it is wise to keep the plan confidential to the last minute to avoid accidental leaks to the teachers' union of information about the details of the plan. It is suggested that only three persons have knowledge of the strike plan's details — the board of education president, the superintendent of schools, and the chief negotiator of management's negotiating team.

A copy of an actual strike plan used by a board of education and management personnel in a Michigan school district when an illegal strike was called by a teachers' union is replicated in Appendix H, at the end of the book. This plan was shared at a meeting with board of education members and with all administrative personnel when it was certain that a strike would take place. The identity of the district is purposely concealed. In this case, not only did the State of Michigan in its collective bargaining law prohibit strikes by public employees, but every prior master contractual agreement that was ratified, signed off, and dated by both the union's officials and the board of education included a "no strike" clause as an article.

During any strike situation, administrators and board of education members are under a great deal of stress. Now that we have our strike plans in place, let's discuss the conduct of board of education members and administrators during the strike.

THE HARD PLACE: LONG HOURS, THE BIG STRESS TEST, AND PLAYING CHICKEN UNTIL THE END

During a long and very adversarial strike environment, participants will feel that they are between a rock and a hard place. Long hours will be the order of the day to protect the interest of the district on a twenty-four-hour basis, while many times conducting all day and night meetings with the other party will sap the energy of even the strongest participants. In addition, the stress level of the participants will be greatly increased because of disparaging remarks made by various members of the community and sensationalized reports presented in the media [18].

Finally, both parties will probably participate in a game of chicken (not revealing the final moves) until the last minute before settling the contract. The union will usually want to obtain agreement that any charges against its members or its leaders will be dropped [19], and all salary improvements will be given retroactively [20]. Although the union will undoubtedy attempt to pressure the board and superintendent into a nonreprisal agreement, it is wise to have this decision made ahead of time. After all, illegal acts should not go unpunished; such action would show that the board is selective as to which laws it supports. The roles they must play will be uncomfortable, but that comes with the job. The pressure is somewhat off the board, for with a courageous superintendent making the recommendations, they only have to support or deny support for upholding the law. The superintendent may wish to have the school board attorney frame the recommendations for the board. Charges against the union leaders may have to be made, and its leaders will be involved. The charges (if already made) may be such that they can be dropped, but to expect no reprisal is inappropriate when the law has clearly been violated. As for salary, none must be given retroactively. Any improvements conceded to will be made effective the day the strike ends and normalcy returns.

During this stressful period, it is important that management not portray the participating teachers or the union as villains, because once the strike is settled, the members of the community will still have to be supportive of teachers, administrators, and the board of education if the district is to survive a strike with the least amount of long-term damage [21].

It should be stated that the school district can request injunctive relief, or cease and desist orders from the courts. However, these orders are very seldom issued.

Finally, the strike has ended, the collective bargaining agreement has been presented by the union's leaders to its membership, and it has been ratified. Following this, the district's chief negotiator has presented the TA'd agreement to the board of education with the recommendation that it be ratified. After both parties have ratified it, the master contractual agreement is signed and dated by the officials designated to represent both parties, and the immediate crisis comes to an end.

At both of the meetings to ratify, it is wise for the union leadership and the school district's chief negotiator to give credit to the professionalism and hard work of the leadership on the other side of the table. This is only wise, as it will be the beginning of ending the adversarial relationship between the two parties, and it will bring some credibility to the settlement in the eyes of the general public.

Once the ratification activities and the summary speeches have been made, the district's management has to focus its maximum effort on repairing the damage done within the community and repairing the damage done within the employee group and between the employees and administrators and the board of education. The final discussion in this chapter focuses on the actions following the ending of a strike and the ratification of a master contractual agreement.

ACTIONS FOLLOWING A STRIKE

Once a strike is terminated, the efforts of both sides must focus on repairing the damage done by the strike. Some suggestions for repairing the damage done during a strike include the following.

- Immediately after the master contractual agreement is printed, the chief negotiator and the superintendent of schools should have an all-day meeting with all the administrators of the school district for the purposes of explaining every page of the contract and every detail of the contract. If the intent of any language is unclear, that intent should be clarified at this meeting. A long question and answer period should be planned for the agenda of this meeting. Sometimes the parties desire nebulous language that allows for flexibility in the future dealings. In such a case, the language should not be clarified to any great extent. Also, occasionally there is unfavorable language that has appeared in past contracts and which is carried over into the current contractual agreement; in this case, the rule is to leave it alone if it hasn't caused problems [22].
- If there is unclear language that is of concern to management, a written memorandum should be sent to the union's chief negotiator clarifying management's intent of the language in the specific contract article(s) involved [23]. If the union does not disagree with management's interpretation, management's interpretation shall hold, until it is grieved and adjudicated differently.
- A meeting should be held between the superintendent of schools and the president of the union to see if there are actions that can quickly be taken to start building an environment of trust and respect between the union and management, and between teachers and administrators. Such tactics as having weekly meetings between the superintendent, the chief negotiator, and selected administrative representatives with the union leadership can be held to keep a continuous dialogue going. Also, both the union's leadership and management's leadership can create a series of curricular and other types of study committees comprised of teachers and administrators.
- Management and the union can devise means of publicly recognizing the excellent contributions of individual teachers *and other employees.*
- Management's leadership and the union's leadership can join together with members of visible community groups to assist in community projects. These types of efforts will display to the community members the camaraderie between the school district's administrators, the board of education's members and the unions' leaders, and these efforts will display a willingness for all school district – related parties to participate in activities that will improve the community at large.

- Finally, union and management leadership should encourage all their members to be involved in devising innovative means of recognizing the value of one another's members, and in devising creative ways of redeveloping community support for the school district's schools and for the school district's employees and the board of education [24].

SUMMARY

The worst-case scenario in collective bargaining is that of a strike, which creates an unfortunate and unhappy environment for all members of a school district, including the community. Emotionalism and hostility can mark the experience, and the damage may take years to heal. However, when facing the inevitable, administrators must operate with the intent of damage containment. Preparation is critical; "what if" job action scenarios that must be considered are sick outs, work-to-rule actions, nonfulfillment of after-hour activities, and picketing. Management's responses to these tactics include: substitute teacher and co-curricular sponsor hiring, assignment of administrators to teaching duties, the provision of public relations to assuage the adverse parental/community reaction, and the release of accurate and persuasive information to the media.

Other union tactics include: the spread of a strike rumor, media editorials claiming administrative contract inadequacies or mistreatment of employees, packing board meetings with union-sympathetic citizen input commentary, and holding informal neighborhood meetings to sway public opinion. Management responses to these tactics include: publicizing late-summer contingency plans to delay opening of school, responsive and proactive media editorials, calling for identification of public speakers (who are frequently union activists or nonresident "plants") at board meetings, packing those meetings with supporters of the board's position, and infiltrating, for observational and reporting purposes, the neighborhood meetings.

If a strike is imminent, a comprehensive strike plan should be developed, with details being available to only a few administrators to minimize leakage of tactical details. A copy of an actual strike plan used in a Michigan district outlined recommended critical tactics and strategies. Both an administrative and public hotline must be established for rumor and information clearinghouse purposes. Building administrators must file a daily report on teacher or picket presence.

Questions or visits from the media are to be supervised and reported, and all contacts with union members recorded and reported.

Clear lines of communication to the attorneys, board president, and other governmental agencies must be drawn, with official spokespersons identified. Any services that the district has contracted for or is providing to nonpublic schools must be rearranged, if necessary. Contingency plans must be made to provide for emergency student supervision if employees do not report for work or leave early, and financial/employment arrangements must be made for any necessary layoffs of nonstriking employees and for payroll adjustment of fringe benefits. Security must be provided if all buildings close down completely, and incidents such as unruly picketing must be fully documented. If the strike appears likely to continue for a period of time, then long-term arrangements must be made for downsizing costs and for alternate provision of instruction.

Whatever the outcome of a strike, it is a stressful process, and its conclusion must lay the groundwork for damage repairs to begin. Adequate question and answer—oriented meetings must be held for all administrators, collaborative meetings between the superintendent and union president should focus on planning mutual trust-building activities, individual teacher and administrator contributions should be recognized, and visible effort made for both sides to join with community groups in mutual projects.

EXERCISES

1. As a building administrator, what contingency procedures could you employ in dealing with sick outs, work-to-rule actions, or nonfulfillment of sponsorship activities?
2. Create an emergency administrative plan for notifying key media personnel and community members about a pending strike. What proactive information could be supplied for the editorial pages?
3. Visualize your board of education meeting's format and procedures, and devise a contingency plan to control citizen input and attendance problems.
4. Create a communications chart, indicating lines of connection and authorized official statement sources for your district's administrators.
5. With reference to a particular school in your district, create a

step-by-step emergency plan to supervise students in case of a mid-morning teacher walkout.

6. What would be the most productive ways for teacher/employees and administrators in your district to come together in the ''repair'' process after a strike?

7. Review the strike plan presented in this chapter, and decide whether or not you agree with each item presented.

8. What would you add, delete, or modify to improve the strike plan presented in this chapter?

REFERENCES

1. Doherty, R. E. and W. E. Oberer. 1967. *Teachers, School Boards, and Collective Bargaining: A Changing of the Guard.* Ithaca, NY: New York State School of Industrial and Labor Relations, Cornell University, p. 120.

2. Donley, M. O., Jr. 1976. *Power to the Teacher.* Bloomington, IN: Indiana University Press, p. 109.

3. Webster, W. G., Sr. 1985. *Effective Collective Bargaining in Public Education.* Ames, IA: Iowa State University Press, p. 168.

4. Braun, R. J. 1972. *Teachers and Power — The Story of the American Federation of Teachers.* New York, NY: Simon and Schuster, pp. 107, 112.

5. Kerchner, C. T. 1988. ''A New Generation of Teacher Unionism,'' *Education Digest,* L111(9):52 – 54.

6. Murphy, M. 1990. *Blackboard Unions — The AFT and the NEA 1900 – 1980.* Ithaca, NY: Cornell University Press, p. 226.

7. Doherty, R. E. and W. E. Oberer, p. 100.

8. Doherty, R. E. and W. E. Oberer, p. 100.

9. Webster, W. G., Sr., p. 167.

10. Braun, R. J., pp. 112 – 113.

11. Braun, R. J., pp. 112 – 113.

12. Doherty, R. E. and W. E. Oberer, p. 297.

13. Webster, W. G., Sr., p. 52.

14. Webster, W. G., Sr., pp. 167 – 168.

15. Braun, R. J., pp. 112 – 113.

16. Donley, M. O., Jr., p. 109.

17. Castetter, W. B. 1986. *The Personnel Function in Education.* New York, NY: Macmillan Publishing Company, pp. 170 – 171.

18. Smith, S. C., D. Ball and D. Liontos. 1990. *Working Together — The Collaborative Style of Bargaining.* Eugene, OR: ERIC Clearinghouse on Educational Management, University of Oregon, p. 18.

19. Webster, W. G., Sr., p. 168.

20. Helsby, R. D., J. Tener and J. Lefkowitz, eds. 1985. *The Evolving Process — Col-*

lective Negotiations in Public Employment. Fort Washington, PA: Labor Relations Press, p. 416.

21. Webster, W. G., Sr., p. 168.
22. Webster, W. G., Sr., pp. 134–135.
23. Elkouri, F. and E. A. Elkouri. 1973. *How Arbitration Works, Third Edition.* Washington, DC: Bureau of National Affairs, Inc., pp. 296, 303.
24. Smith, S. C., D. Ball and D. Liontos, pp. 58–59.

Finalizing and Communicating the Signed Master Contract

CHAPTER 10 discusses the topics of: (1) reaching a TA (tentative agreement), (2) presenting the contract for ratification, (3) giving the other party credit, and (4) printing and publicizing the contract document.

The negotiations between the union and management may be of a short duration, or they may be very lengthy and drawn out. The negotiation may be one where the parties to the negotiation settle the contract without assistance from third parties, or it may be one where both parties experienced long and bitter impasse, which caused them to go through the impasse procedures of mediation, fact-finding, and arbitration. Also, the negotiation may be of a serious adversarial nature, or it may have taken place within a collaborative win/win negotiating environment.

Regardless of the length and character of the negotiation, the union's negotiating team and management's negotiating team, sooner or later, end the at-the-table negotiating by TA'ing (tentatively agreeing) to a comprehensive master contract document [1]. At this point, there is a sigh of relief that the negotiation has been concluded, and there is anticipation of the relative difficulty of presenting and recommending the TA'd master contract to the total union membership for a vote and to the board of education for ratification at a formally called board of education meeting [2].

REACHING TENTATIVE AGREEMENT ON A CONTRACT

Let's revert for a moment and paint two-word scenarios of how the TA'ing of the master contract probably came about. The first scenario will outline the steps leading to a TA within a win/win negotiating environment, and the second scenario will outline the steps leading to a TA within a severely adversarial union/management environment.

Win/Win

The path to reaching a TA within a win/win environment regardless of the time expended, is a serious, hardworking, and trusting effort by the members of the union's negotiating team and management's negotiating team [3]. In fact, if one could view the meetings from a window, it would be difficult, if not impossible, to determine which persons at the meeting represented the union and which represented management.

As information is shared, as subgroups (comprised of members of both union and management) present their findings and recommendations to the total body, and as joint minutes are kept which provide the official reference document of prior discussions, the two parties end up agreeing on each contractual article's content and wording [4].

At the point of agreement on each article, both parties may officially vote tentative agreement on the specific article upon which agreement has been reached, or there may merely be a general agreement that the article is in acceptable form and content. In some instances, the chief negotiator for both union and management will officially sign and date each article as tentative agreement is reached on the specific article. On the other hand, the parties may wait until the entire contractual document is in its finalized and agreed-to form before TA'ing the entire master contractual agreement. At this point, the chief negotiator for both parties to the negotiation will definitely sign and date two copies of the TA'd agreement, with one copy kept by the union's negotiating team and the other copy retained by management's negotiating team [5].

Win/Lose

The path to achieving a tentative agreement with a severe adversarial environment will probably be a very long, stressful, negative, and sometimes painful experience. It will usually begin by high ball and low ball proposals being presented (an example would be the union asking for a 20 percent increase in salary each year of a proposed three-year contract, and management responding by proposing a one-year contract and a 1 percent salary increase for that contract year). Also, even though this may be the renewal of a master contractual agreement [6], which is preceded by fifteen years of prior master contractual agreements between the two parties, every single one of the twenty (or possibly as many as fifty) contract articles will have to be re-negotiated, because each article in the master contract has proposed changes – thus reopening negotiations on the entire master contractual agreement.

Since both parties remain very adversarial and antagonistic to one another and since there is a lack of trust of the other party by the members of both the union's negotiating team and management's negotiating team, many long, vociferous, and vituperative negotiating sessions result in very little progress. After months of meetings and a great deal of positioning and posturing in the community and in the media, an impasse is declared. A mediator is assigned by the state's PERB (Public Employment Relations Board) [7].

The mediator meets separately with both parties and discovers that a personality conflict exists between the chief negotiators for the union and management, and practically no agreements have been reached on any contract article [8]. At this point, in one particular case, the mediator considered informing both parties that she/he would not return to assist in resolving the impasse until the parties have narrowed the points of contention to no more than three areas [9]. However, the mediator decided to attempt to assist, even though the entire contract remained in contention.

The mediator, after meeting with both parties, called a joint meeting. During this meeting the mediator informed them of the collective bargaining laws and of the purpose and process of mediation. The mediator also warned both parties that she/he would only continue to meet with them if continuing progress towards settlement was being made [10]. Following this joint meeting, the mediator again met separately with both parties.

When the mediator met with the union's negotiating team, she/he discovered that though the team had initially requested a three-year contract with a 20 percent increase in salary demanded for each year of the contract, they did this with the idea of splitting the difference with the management team. This tactic would, the team hoped, end up with a 10 – 12 percent raise, and the union could prove that it gave up more of its initial request than was given by management if the 10 percent raise was the settlement point [11]. Also, the union identified the proposal of management to increase the rigidity of the employee evaluation procedure as an area where it would absolutely not compromise [12].

When the mediator met with management's negotiating team, she/he discovered that the team didn't really expect to settle the contract for a 1 percent increase in salary, but that it was reacting to the ridiculously high 20 percent per year for each of the three years proposed by the union's team. Also, the mediator discovered that management's negotiating team would also prefer a three-year contract, but the team countered with a one-year contract proposal because the union's team proposed a three-year contract. Management's team felt this approach would give them some flexibility for future trade-offs [13]. Finally, the mediator discovered that management's negotiating team was under a strict board of education guideline that the employee evaluation system and its accompanying language had to be strengthened.

The mediator met many times with both parties in joint sessions, and she/he finally was able to receive some flexibility from both parties in two areas: (1) both the union and management agreed that the length of the contract could be a flexible area for future discussion, and (2) the union reduced its salary increase demand to 15 percent per year for each year of the contract length for which there was agreement, and management increased its salary offer to 3 percent per year for each year of the contract length for which there was agreement. All other matters remained in contention, and the mediator pulled out of the district while indicating to both parties and to PERB that she/he had assisted as much as possible [14].

At this point a fact finder was called in to the district to collect the facts and write a fact finder's report [15]. Since neither party had to accept the fact finder's report and recommendations for settlement, this fact-finding was of the voluntary type.

Upon entry into the school district, the fact finder established a hearing. At this hearing, each party presented its evidence and rationale for its position on each unresolved issue. The fact finder accepted the written documents and recorded the oral presentations, and she/he allowed post-hearing briefs to be filed within two weeks of the hearing. The fact finder also indicated that the written fact-finding report would be issued within one month of receipt of the written post-hearing briefs [16]. Although the fact finder dealt with all issues in contention, we will stay with our three areas as examples of recommendations made by the fact finder in her/his written report. The fact finder recommended the following. (1) A 6 percent raise is to be given for each year of a contract, which would keep the district employees' salary ranking of six out of the twenty-one districts that comprise the comparable districts. (2) A master contract is to be two years in length. (3) The language related to employee evaluation should remain the same as that in the prior master contractual agreement, which had just expired.

Since neither the union or management accepted the fact finder's recommendation, the fact finder published his findings and recommendations in the newspaper that covered the school district. This technique was used at this stage of impasse in order to let the general public know the exact condition of the current negotiations and the recommendations that were made by the fact finder to resolve the items that remained unresolved [17]. This technique was utilized to allow the general public to bring pressure on both parties to settle the contract.

Since neither party accepted the fact finder's recommendation, and the community was vociferously urging both parties to settle and condemning the board members, the administration, and the teachers for not settling their expired union/management master contractual agreement, both parties agreed to contact AAA (American Arbitration Association) for the assistance of an arbitration panel. Both parties agreed that the panel will be selected from the names submitted by the AAA, with the union selecting one member, management selecting the other member, and the third arbitrator being selected by agreement between union and management [18]. However, it was agreed that if no agreement could be reached on the third arbitrator, the other two arbitrators selected could select the third arbitrator.

The AAA submitted a list of potential arbitrators, and both the union's negotiating team and management's negotiating team, who were experienced in negotiations, did research on the prior arbitration rulings of each of the arbitrators who were submitted. After both parties had stricken numerous names from the original list of arbitrators submitted by AAA, the arbitration panel was selected and the arbitration hearing was conducted [19].

Because of the history of bad relations between union and management, the arbitration panel and the parties agreed that a court recorder would be hired and each party would pay one-half of the cost of the recorder and of the five sets of transcripts (one for each member of the arbitration panel, one for the union, and one for management) [20]. Each person who testified at the hearing did so under oath. At the hearing each party reviewed its perception of the history of negotiation to this point, presented written evidence that supported its position on each item in contention, and orally presented the rationale and data defending its position. Cross-examinations were permitted, and the arbitration panel permitted post-hearing briefs [21].

Within four weeks of receipt of the post-hearing briefs and the receipt of the verbatim transcript of the arbitration hearing, the arbitration panel provided its rulings on each master contract item that remained unresolved. At this point, both parties' negotiating teams, tired of the long and unpleasant negotiations, agreed to bring the arbitration panel's recommendations to their referent groups with their recommendations for approval of the recommendations. The union met with its membership and the negotiating team made its case for acceptance, and management's negotiating team recommended that the board of education accept the arbitration panel's recommendation [22]. In each case, the teacher membership and the board of education agreed to the recommendations of the arbitration panel, but they held final ratification approval until they had the entire newly written contract in their hands for an adequate time period prior to a vote for contract ratification.

PRESENTING THE MASTER CONTRACT
FOR RATIFICATION

The union's chief negotiator, the union's president, and the union's negotiating team would do well to plan their strategy and tactics for presentation of the master contractual agreement [23]. This advance planning is important regardless of whether tentative agreement was attained at the negotiating table or through any stage of the impasse procedures [24]. To use the teachers again, as an example, it is important that the union's leadership come out strongly in favor of ratification for if they do not, the contract agreement may be voted down [25].

Depending on the attitude of the union leadership, they will either strongly sell a contract agreement that they feel is the best compromise agreement that they could negotiate during the current negotiations, or they may present the TA'd agreement without recommendation if they feel that they do not want to either recommend or not recommend it, but leave the decision totally in the hands of the general membership [26]. Finally, because of increasing pressure due to public condemnation of both parties or having passed through all of the impasse procedures, the union leadership may agree to bring the recommendations to the total membership, but, behind closed doors, they may recommend that the membership reject the proposed contract and request a strike vote authorization [27].

The strategy and tactics utilized by the union's leadership will vary depending on the outcome they desire when the contract is presented to the total membership. In general, if the leadership wishes ratification, it will not permit dissidents to speak prior to making the sales pitch, and the leadership will limit the time for questions. Also, the leadership will not submit the written TA'd agreement to the membership, as it is easy to quibble over words in a lengthy document; rather they will provide an overview of the gains they have received for the membership and ask for a ratification vote [28,29].

Since the union usually ratifies the TA'd agreement prior to the board of education considering ratification (this procedure is wise because the union leadership may not be willing to sell the agreement and the membership may refuse to ratify it), the management's chief negotiator, the superintendent of schools, and management's negotiating team will await the result of the teacher union's general membership vote before approaching the board of education. Obviously, if the teacher union's general membership refuses to ratify the TA'd contract, it is back to the bargaining table, or back to an impasse procedure; and there is no reason to make a presentation to the board of education.

Assuming, however, that the teacher union's general membership has ratified the contract, the board of education should then be presented with the TA'd agreement, and management's chief negotiator, the superintendent of schools, and management's negotiating team members all strongly support ratification. In the case of the three example items presented earlier, the board would probably be told of the hard fought at-the-table battles and also be told that this is the best agreement they could get during this round of negotiations [30].

On the three specific example items, the board of education members might very well be told the following. (1) The salary increase is well within the district's ability to pay, it keeps the district in its relative salary position in relation to the other comparable districts, and it maintains a salary level that is sufficiently attractive that recruitment of new employees should not become a problem. (2) The two-year contract is better than a one-year contract because it keeps the district out of contract negotiations with all the potential harm that could arise for a two-year period rather than a single year. It also allows expenditure predictability for budget planning purposes for two years into the future. (3) The lack of movement to agree caused the resultant retention of the expiring master contract's language related to the employee evaluation article; this was the best that could be achieved during the current negotiations, but it does establish an emphatic negotiating position and an agenda item for future negotiations. This last item will have to be a very hard sell, since this was a serious demand under the guidelines provided the negotiating team by the board of education.

Immediately after the board of education agrees to ratify the contract in executive session (which is legal for the purposes of discussing negotiations-related items in most states that possess both collective bargaining and sunshine statutes) [31], the board comes out into public session during a legally constituted board of education meeting. At this time, the chief negotiator and the superintendent of schools publicly request ratification by the board of education of this fair compromise, which will become the master contractual agreement to govern union/ management actions for the next two-year period [32]. At this public meeting, much praise is given to members of both negotiating teams for the hard work they expended in arriving at a fair and equitable master contract. Obviously, the media will attend this meeting, and the union's leadership, management's leadership, and the board members should echo the sentiments expressed about the congratulations to both teams for all their efforts and about the pleasure upon reaching a fair and equitable settlement. At this point the contract is moved to the printing stage.

PRINTING AND PUBLICIZING THE CONTRACT

Once both parties have ratified the contract, the actual contract document will be printed and distributed. It is common for the board of education to take responsibility for seeing that the document is typed, carefully proofread, and printed. It is also common for the union and the board of education to equally share the cost of producing the printed contract document.

At this stage a caution is offered. Print the contract in an awkward size, which will prohibit female union members from carrying it around in their purses and male union members from keeping a copy handy in their pants pockets. If the climate continues to be an adversarial one between the union and management, the less ready access that each employee has to the printed master contractual agreement, the less probability there is of many contract grievances being filed.

Once the contract has been printed in all its details, it is important that management's chief negotiator and the superintendent of schools meet with all of the school district's administrators to go over each page and each word of the ratified master contractual agreement [33]. At this meeting, the specific wording will be discussed, the intent of the contract wording will be discussed, and all questions that the administrators may have will be answered. This is an important meeting, because the management of the negotiated master contractual agreement is as important, if not more important, than the act of negotiating the master contractual agreement.

On the other hand, a similar procedure should be followed by the union's chief negotiator and the president of the local union. This meeting should be conducted for the union's stewards, and the dialogue at this meeting should explain the intent of all the contract's wording, and a good deal of time should be spent on answering procedural questions related to the responsibility of the union's stewards under the ratified master contractual agreement [34].

In addition, union leaders, administrative officials, and board of education members should contact the media and/or respond to media queries in a manner that will place the agreement, the employees, the administrators, and the board of education in the best possible light. For once the negotiations are completed, it is important that all parties work hard to repair any damage done between union and management, and it is important that community support be retained at the highest possible level [35].

The best way to achieve both of these results is to make certain that the students of the district are well served instructionally and cared for as valued young people. It should be clear to all parties that schools were not created to provide jobs for teachers and other union and non-unionized employees, for board of education members, or for administrators. The only reason that any school district exists is to educate youngsters, and the quality of that education and the obvious caring concern for students is the best approach to creating a positive school district environment. This is also the best way to obtain and increase community support for the school district, the individual schools, and the people who are employees of the school district.

SUMMARY

The negotiations process, whether lengthy, adversarial, mediated, or win/win and collaborative, usually ends with tentative agreement to a comprehensive master contract document. This recommended contract is then submitted to total union membership and to the board of education for a ratification vote.

Two scenarios can characterize this tentative agreement process. Reaching a TA within a win/win environment is accomplished through a shared effort in an environment of trust. Information is collaboratively collected and analyzed, and joint minutes kept. This collegial process results in an agreement that may be generally approved, or approved article by article, prior to TA'ing the entire master contractual agreement.

Achieving tentative agreement within a severe adversarial environment will most likely be a long and stressful process. Extreme proposal items (high ball and low ball) may be introduced by both sides, and every single one of the existing contract articles may be reopened for negotiation. The bargaining sessions may be marked by discord, personal dissent, and unfavorable media coverage. Impasse may be declared, and a mediator assigned by the PERB may have to direct the parties to narrow the points of contention. Joint and separate meetings with the parties are conducted, during which time the mediator may be able to discover the real threshold of proposal items, and determine the range of flexibility for eventual settlement.

Despite this intervention, contract matters may still remain in contention, and a fact finder may be called to investigate evidence and rationales on each unresolved issue. Recommendations are then made by the fact finder with regard to each area of contention, and, upon the decline of the recommendation package by both parties (the example being one of nonbinding arbitration), the package is publicized by the fact finder to bring public pressure to bear on both sides.

Both parties may then agree to request the assistance of an arbitrator or an arbitration panel. After the selection of arbitrators (involving investigation of their arbitration records by both parties), a hearing is held, and each side reviews its perceptions of the process and presents written and oral evidence to support proposal rationales and data. Cross-examination of witnesses and the submission of post-hearing briefs may be permitted. The arbitration panel provides rulings on each master contract item that remains unresolved, and union ratification and board approval can follow.

The presentation of the master contractual agreement requires strategy on the part of the union leadership, depending on the leaders' assessment of the document. They may strongly recommend ratification (limiting the amount and detail of member input and inquiry), or withhold recommendation without actually condemning the document, leaving the issue up to the membership. In response to public pressure to settle, they may bring a public recommendation for ratification to the total membership, but they may privately recommend rejection and a strike vote authorization.

Usually, it is advisable that the recommendation and union ratification process precede that of the board, in case of nonratification and a return to impasse procedure. Following union ratification, the board is then presented with management's recommendation to approve the agreement, accompanied by detail as to the contract items' cost and noncost impacts. Appropriate media information and management-union visible support should follow the ratification of the contract.

The printing and distribution of the contract is usually shared by the union and management, and meetings are held where management's chief negotiator, the superintendent, and all administrators discuss the contractual intent wording and implementation and procedural detail of the agreement. A similar procedure should be followed by the union's leadership and stewards.

EXERCISES

1. Visualize a win/win negotiation scenario in your district, and describe the group members, subcommittees, informational-search collaborations, and joint media release procedures that could occur during negotiations and ratification procedures.

2. Investigate the public record on any mediated adversarial negotiations session in your district or a neighboring district. Trace the process through the stages of impasse, mediation, fact-finding, and arbitration.

3. Obtain a copy of a master contract from a school district, and review the individual articles. What strategies could have been utilized to sell the items to the board and to the community?

4. Investigate the arbitration process in your state. What is the linkage with the American Arbitration Association?

5. What public channels of information could the union and management use to co-publicize a new contract and what strategies would convince the public that the parties intend to work together collaboratively under the new agreement?

REFERENCES

1. Helsby, R. D., J. Tener and J. Lefkowitz, eds. 1985. *The Evolving Process — Collective Negotiations in Public Employment.* Fort Washington, PA: Labor Relations Press, p. 413.

2. Herman, J. J. 1991. "The Two Faces of Collective Bargaining," *School Business Affairs*, 57(2):12.

3. Nyland, L. 1987. "Win/Win Bargaining Pays Off," *Education Digest*, L111(1): 28–29.

4. Huber, J. and J. Hennies. 1987. "Fix on These Five Guiding Lights and Emerge from the Bargaining Fog," *School Board Journal*, 174(3):31.

5. Herman, J. J., 57(2):12.

6. Neal, R. 1980. *Bargaining Tactics—A Reference Manual for Public Sector Labor Negotiations*. Richard G Neal Associates, pp. 158–159.

7. Brock, J. 1982. *Bargaining Beyond Impasse—Joint Resolution of Public Sector Labor Disputes*. Boston, MA: Auburn House Publishing Company, pp. 13–16.

8. Neal, R., p. 66.

9. Brock, J., pp. 155–156.

10. Helsby, R. D., J. Tener and J. Lefkowitz, eds., pp. 236–238.

11. Neal, R., pp. 158–159.

12. Rynecki, S. B. and J. H. Lindquist. 1988. "Teacher Evaluation and Collective Bargaining—A Management Perspective," *Journal of Law and Education*, 17(3):489–490.

13. Aaron, B., J. M. Najita and J. L. Stern. 1988. *Public Sector Bargaining*. Washington, DC: Industrial Relations Research Associates, p. 148.

14. Webster, W. G., Sr. 1985. *Effective Collective Bargaining in Public Education*. Ames, IA: Iowa State University Press, p. 161.

15. Zack, A. 1980. *Understanding Fact Finding and Arbitration in the Public Sector*. Washington, DC: U.S. Department of Labor, Labor Management Services Administration, pp. 8–13.

16. Zack, A., pp. 50–51, 89–91.

17. Zack, A., pp. 90–91.

18. Elkouri, F. and E. A. Elkouri. 1973. *How Arbitration Works, Third Edition*. Washington, DC: Bureau of National Affairs, Inc., pp. 88–89.

19. Neal, R., pp. 117–118.

20. Neal, R., pp. 217–218.

21. Neal, R. G. 1988. "At Arbitration Hearings, Justice Favors the Well Prepared," *Executive Educator*, 10(11):17.

22. Coleman, C. J. 1990. *Managing Labor Relations in the Public Sector*. San Francisco, CA: Jossey-Bass Publishers, pp. 222–223.

23. Herman, J. J., 57(2):12.

24. Helsby, R. D., J. Tener and J. Lefkowitz, eds., p. 237.

25. Webster, W. G., Sr., p. 25.

26. Maier, M. M. 1987. *City Unions*. New Brunswick, NJ: Rutgers University Press, p. 157.

27. Maier, M. M., p. 157.

28. Helsby, R. D., J. Tener and J. Lefkowitz, eds., pp. 59–60.

29. Eberts, R. W. and J. A. Stone. 1984. *Unions and Public Schools*. Lexington, MA: D. C. Heath and Company, p. 175.

30. Herman, J. J., 57(2):12.

31. Feiock, R. C. and J. P. West. 1990. "Public Presence at Collective Bargaining:

Effects on Process and Decisions in Florida,'' *Journal of Collective Negotiations,* 19(1):69−70.

32. Helsby, R. D., J. Tener and J. Lefkowitz, eds., p. 228.

33. Smith, S. C., D. Ball and D. Liontos. 1990. *Working Together−The Collaborative Style of Bargaining.* Eugene, OR: ERIC Clearinghouse on Educational Management, University of Oregon, p. 59.

34. Brock, J., pp. 80−81.

35. Herman, J. J., 57(2):12−13.

Living with the Contract That Has Been Negotiated—Contract Management

CHAPTER 11 includes discussions on: (1) communicating and interpreting the contract during its operational stage, (2) training the administrators in contract management, (3) setting precedents, (4) breaking precedents, (5) disciplining for contract violations, insubordination or incompetency, (6) disciplining progressively, (7) providing due process, (8) establishing just cause, (9) preparing for grievance arbitration of the active contract (voluntary or mandatory), (10) following grievance procedural steps, (11) paying for the grievance arbitrator and related expenses, (12) providing an example contractual grievance clause, (13) handling employee grievances and union class grievances, (14) judging by the lowest common denominator, (15) observing time limits, (16) preparing a checklist for a grievance arbitration hearing, and (17) following contractual procedures for grievance resolutions. Let's begin by discussing the important topics of communicating and interpreting the contract that has been ratified.

COMMUNICATING AND INTERPRETING THE RATIFIED CONTRACT DURING ITS OPERATIONAL STAGE

Once the contract has been finalized and all articles have been TA'd (tentatively agreed to), management needs to call the entire management team together and go over the contract with the team members to bring about a basic understanding of the document. In some districts this is done with the board and administration in a joint meeting, and in some districts the board needs to review first. Then, with approval, the superintendent and the chief negotiator present the contents to the administrators. The communication comes about between the chief negotiator and the management team as an overview to the document and its implications. It is not, at this unratified stage, a full-scale review of every article and item in the contract.

Many times union and management leaders expend great energy on the negotiation of a new or replacement master contract document, and once the new contract has been ratified, they breathe a sigh of relief and go into a long period of rest and relaxation from the rigors of negotiations. This is a big mistake, for a well-managed contract will prevent grievances from developing, will improve labor/management relations, and will provide a positive labor/management attitude when the parties head into the successor contractual negotiations.

Good contract management is a very important element in the overall collective bargaining agenda, and the first step in good contract management is that of communicating and interpreting the contract [1]. Once the newly negotiated master contractual agreement has been printed and distributed to the employees, administrators, media, and significant community groups, a central authority, such as the chief negotiator or the director of personnel, should meet with all administrators and any media groups or community groups that request further discussion or interpretation of the contract [2]. Of course, the employees' union should do the same with and for its membership.

Interpreting the contract is something different from communicating the contract to the administration. It is done after both sides have ratified the contract. Once ratified, the document must be explained to the managers so there is less room for individual interpretation of the contents.

During a series of meetings with all the school district's administrators, the central authority should review the contract page by page and word by word [3,4]. There should be a lengthy question and answer period, if necessary, where all questions are answered and all interpretations are provided by the central authority. If there are numerous questions about the interpretation of a specific article, it is wise for the central authority, immediately following the face-to-face meeting with the district's administrators, to forward a written memo to all administrators clarifying the article in question. In addition, it should be made clear to every administrator that should a grievance occur or should there be a further question about interpretation, the administrator must, before answering, contact the central authority for the interpretation. This is the only method of consistently ensuring uniform interpretations of the negotiated contract's articles and wording. Some highlights that need to be emphasized are the glossary of terms, an explanation of the background for each item's inclusion, timelines used, applicability of individual interpretation, avoidance of misapplication, and the necessity of following the exact wording. In order to avoid erosion of the contract, any doubt about the meaning of the item or definition of a term calls for the chief negotiator's immediate definition and clarification.

Now that the importance of communicating and interpreting the negotiated master contractual agreement has been stressed, let's focus a little more closely on some of the specific items that should be stressed with the school district's administrators who will be responsible for implementing and interpreting the ratified master contract on a day-to-day basis.

TRAINING THE ADMINISTRATORS IN CONTRACT MANAGEMENT

Training the district's administrators in contract management is not a one-shot event. If the negotiated master contract document is perceived as an instructional document, it should be treated as a training document when the chief negotiator or the director of personnel meets with the district's administrators [5,6]. Everything in the contract document can and usually does impact all aspects of the district's operations. It impacts the budget, decision making, student instruction, personnel policies and procedures, the allocation of time and of personnel, and it many times impacts student relations and public relations [7].

How well the administrators, especially the building principals in the case of teachers who are members of a union, manage the contract at the site level pretty much determines the school climate as it relates to teachers and students. If the contract is administered well, an effective working relationship between the teachers and the principal will be maintained. This effective working relationship will exist while accountability for both teacher and principal actions under the master contractual agreement will be assured. If, however, the administration of the negotiated master contractual agreement is weak, day-to-day relationships will become strained, a proliferation of grievances will probably result, many of the contract's articles will be violated, and numerous unintended precedents will be established that will affect the next round of contract negotiations.

During these training sessions, the areas that should be thoroughly explored, discussed, and interpreted are those that practically every administrator will have a duty to interpret during the term of life of the negotiated master contract. These high-stress areas will definitely include most of the following articles for most employee unions, and they will include all of them for a teachers' union [8].

- union rights
- management rights
- academic freedom
- employee assignments

- employee transfer
- employee evaluation
- unit membership
- grievance process

In addition, school site administrators must be careful not to cause complications in administering the negotiated master contract by:

- attempting to negotiate at the school site level
- resolving grievances without first checking with the district's chief negotiator or the director of personnel
- interpreting a master contract clause that is being questioned by an employee or the union without first checking with the district's chief negotiator or the director of personnel
- giving the impression that they are anti-union or that they are opposed to the terms of the negotiated master contract
- allowing themselves to be intimidated by a strong-willed employee or by a union official from taking action that is called for within the negotiated master contract
- circumventing the school district's policies or the intent of the articles in the negotiated master contract for the purpose of enhancing her/his personal popularity [9]

In addition to the regularly scheduled contractual training sessions, which include the list of cautions to the site-level administrators, management's chief negotiator or the director of personnel should initiate a newsletter that will provide all of the school district's administrators with information about any activity, any change in board of education policy, and any contract interpretation about which union and management disagree and which may impact the day-to-day interpretation of the contract [10]. Only by viewing contract management as a serious and important function [11], and only by perceiving contract management as an ongoing activity during the entire term of life of the negotiated master contract, will the contract be competently and consistently administered. And only by consistently managing the contract, will problems be avoided and positive union/management relations be improved and retained.

Once the training regimen has been well established, management should be constantly on the alert for precedent-setting activities and opportunities for precedent-breaking activities. A permanent place on the administrative agenda should be reserved for a review of any recent actions (grievance or otherwise) which have developed, and a rapid information dispersal system should be made accessible to the chief negotiator. Precedents can certainly influence arbitration decisions if grievances arise, and they can add complexity to the next round of contract negotiations. Also, the chief negotiator must constantly stay in touch with the union officers to make sure the interpretations are agreed upon by the union leadership.

ESTABLISHING AND BREAKING PRECEDENTS

Past practice is a term signifying that a certain action has consistently taken place over a lengthy time period [12]. Past practice can, especially during grievance arbitration, obliterate the wording and intent of the negotiated master contract provision under question if past practice is in opposition to the contract language. Therefore, the establishment of precedential past practices is an area that should be constantly kept under management's microscope as the day-to-day management of the negotiated master contract is continued [13].

Erosion of the existing master contract will take place whenever an administrator deviates from the standards embodied in the contract when she/he manages the master contract document. If the administrator relinquishes her/his authority under the contract in order to be seen as a friend or if the administrator exceeds her/his authority under the contract, erosion of contract begins and contractual problems soon follow this erosion.

To establish a precedent, an administrator only has to make an interpretive decision that is not necessarily covered by the contract, or that exceeds or is in opposition to the contract document. For example, if the contract allows an employee to take one day per year for personal business, and any of the administrators unofficially permits even a single employee to take more than one day of personal business without deducting from the employee a day's pay or disciplining the employee for a contract violation, a precedent has been started [14].

Usually a precedent is created without forethought or malice; it is normally caused by an administrator who doesn't carefully attend to the negotiated master contract, or by an administrator who is deemed lenient in the interpretation of the negotiated master contract [15]. In either case, the damage is done, and the bargained limitation or requirement is of no value, not only in the immediate unit, but throughout the district. It would be better to adhere rigidly to the contract, and through the grievance process bring about an allowable exception that can be done with the firm statement that the allowance is without precedence and is for specific and stipulated reasons. Precedent-setting actions by any of the school district's administrators should be a serious concern to upper level management. For precedence, which is one of the mainstays of our legal system, basically indicates that one must continue the precedential action or decision as actions or decisions are taken in future similar situations. In other words, all administrators are almost always bound by the actions of one of their own — no matter how crass or inconsiderate that action was.

Once a precedent is established, management is usually bound to act in accordance with that precedent [16]. If the precedent is seen as one that is having a harmful effect on the operation of the school district, management may wish to set upon a course to break the precedent. Of course, the union may take the same tactical approaches to breaking a precedent that they feel is harmful to their members or to the union's operation.

Precedents can be broken in three ways. First, during new master contract negotiations, language can be written into the contract (assuming this language remains in the contract that is finally ratified) which has the effect of eliminating the undesirable precedent. Second, management may go about making a variety of different contract interpretations of the same item or it may go about taking a variety of actions applied to the identical situation, and this diversity will, for all intents and purposes, break the precedent because there will be no consistency in the actions or interpretations taken over a reasonable span of time [17]. Third, management may notify the union, in advance of taking action, that it intends to change a standing past practice. This third method is not recommended by the authors.

Next, let's move to a discussion of disciplining an employee for contract violations, insubordination, or incompetency. Usually, any disciplinary action by management immediately brings the union into a confrontational position with management [18]. It should be stressed that the union leadership is compelled to represent their members. In fact, even if they feel management has acted correctly and responsibly, they will represent the employee if the employee requests the union leadership's support [19]. There have been cases where the union leadership has not come to the defense of the employee, and the employee has successfully sued the union leadership for lack of representation [20].

DISCIPLINING EMPLOYEES

If a union employee violates the contract, there must be specific and clear language within the negotiated master contract that completely and irrefutably spells out the means and steps involved in conducting the process of discipline. Incompetency of employee performance, especially in the case of a teacher, is often very difficult to prove, but insubordination or a violation of the specific terms of the negotiated master contract are relatively easy to prove.

The key to successfully disciplining an employee is documentation. Documentation must take place at every step of the disciplinary process, and the documentation must be in writing, with a copy to be placed in the employee's personnel file and a copy given to the employee.

Incompetency refers to the inability of an employee to perform up to the expected standard. For all practical purposes that standard is set at the lowest common denominator. In other words, the employee in question must perform at a level lower than any other employee who is not being disciplined [21]. In many cases of termination procedures initiated by management, the case will eventually be decided by the state's tenure commission. At this hearing, management will present its specifications for termination, prove that the employee has been informed of the specific areas that are to be improved, given assistance in the improvement effort, and given a reasonable time period in which to demonstrate improvement [22]. The union generally will defend the employee, and it will question the objectivity and expertise of the administrators who brought incompetency charges against the employee. Usually, the union will indicate that the administrator(s) bringing charges haven't taught school for many years, and therefore do not truly know good teaching methods. Also, they will claim that since the administrator(s) do not have training in the specific area of expertise of the teacher's assignment, they are not competent to pass judgement of the level of performance of the teacher. Finally, they will present evidence if the lowest common denominator criteria has been violated [23].

The state's tenure commission will oftentimes rule in favor of the employee whenever there is any doubt in the commissioners' minds about the accuracy of management's evidence, the amount of assistance provided, or the amount of time allowed the employee to demonstrate improved performance. On the other hand, if comprehensive and accurate documentation of the termination specifications, the assistance provided, and the time given the employee to improve is provided, management will usually be successful [24].

It goes without saying that termination of an employee for incompetency should be a last resort action, for not only does this employee suffer embarrassment and stress, the employee may lose opportunities for future employment [25]. This situation may drastically and negatively affect the fired employee's entire future life. Management must, nevertheless, do what it has to do, no matter how distasteful the action, to protect the interest of the students and the school district [26]. In the case of teacher incompetency, the decision has to come down in favor of protecting the students, because the only reason school districts exist is to educate the young of the district well.

Insubordination refers to situations in which an employee is asked or ordered to perform a task that does not violate the contract and is not illegal or immoral [27]. If the employee refuses to perform that task after due warning by an administrator of impending discipline for refusal, the employee will be considered insubordinate [28]. Insubordination can be punishable by a variety of means, including termination if the insubordination is considered very serious or if there is a continuing pattern of an employee refusing to perform reasonable tasks. In most cases, firing an employee for serious insubordination will be upheld by any hearing body.

Now that we have reviewed employee discipline for incompetency and insubordination, let's turn to the most frequent cause of employee discipline—that of master contract violations. When a master contract violation occurs, it is management's right to discipline. Subsequently, it is the union's right to grieve management's actions.

Discipline for violation of the master contract involves management taking a specific disciplinary action and informing the employee (and sometimes the union) of the specific contract violation and the specific discipline that is to be administered. At this time the employee or the union, in cases of class grievances (those that involve two or more members of the union in the same grievance situation), will file a grievance against management [29]. This begins the grievance procedure that is spelled out in the master contract document.

A typical master contract grievance procedure will have a series of steps to be followed, and time limits will be included for each step of the procedure. Many grievance procedures will be similar to the example provided in the following section [30].

A TYPICAL MASTER CONTRACT'S GRIEVANCE PROCEDURE

The following four-step grievance procedure shall be available to members of the union for the purpose of resolving concerns that arise out of the interpretation and administration of the ratified collective bargaining master contractual agreement. It is the intent of this procedure to provide for the orderly settlement of alleged grievances in an equitable manner at the lowest possible grievance level.

Definitions

(1) A grievance is a claim by a member of the union that there has been a violation, a misinterpretation, or a misapplication of any specific provision of the collective bargaining master contractual agreement [31].

(2) The grievant shall mean any member of the union or any group of union members, in a class grievance situation, alleging a grievance.

Time Limits and Recording

(1) Each written grievance shall include the name and position of the grievant, the specific article and the section of the master contractual agreement within which the grievance has occurred, the time and place where the alleged event(s) or party allegedly responsible for causing the existence of the said event(s) or condition(s) if known, and a statement of the nature of the grievance and redress sought by the grievant. The written grievance shall be signed and dated by the grievant [32].

(2) The grievance must be taken at step one of the following procedures within five work days following the date that any union member knew or should have known of the act(s) or condition(s) upon which the grievance is based. Time limits at any step of the grievance procedure may be extended only by mutual consent between the

union and the school district's director of personnel. Should the time limits at any step be exceeded by the school district, the grievance may be processed to the next higher step of the procedure, but the grievant must proceed to the next step within the time that would have been allotted had the decision been communicated on the final day of the step. Should the grievant not meet the time limits of the grievance procedure, the grievance will be considered as resolved at the last response, and further appeal shall be barred [33].

(3) All time limits in the procedure refer to scheduled work days [34].

Procedure

(1) Step one: immediate supervisor — Within five days of the alleged grievance, the grievant shall first discuss the alleged grievance with her/his immediate supervisor. The immediate supervisor will respond orally within five days. If the grievant is not satisfied with the oral response, she/he may within five days of being given the oral response, submit the grievance in writing to the immediate supervisor. The immediate supervisor shall respond in writing within five days [35].

(2) Step two: director of personnel — If the grievant does not accept the written determination provided by the immediate supervisor in step one, the grievant must within five days of receipt of that determination, file the alleged grievance with the director of personnel. The director of personnel shall respond in writing within five days [36,37].

(3) Step three: superintendent of schools — If the grievant is not satisfied with the response at step two, she/he may within five days of the receipt of the response, submit the grievance to the superintendent of schools. If the superintendent of schools so determines, she/he may convene a meeting with the grievant, the grievant's immediate supervisor, and the president of the union to review all matters related to the alleged grievance. After reviewing the grievance, the superintendent of schools shall submit a written decision to the grievant within ten days of receipt of the grievance [38].

(4) Step four: grievance arbitration — If the grievant is not satisfied with the response at step three, the grievant and the grievant's union, within five days of the receipt of the response, can request arbitra-

tion of the alleged grievance. The payment of all expenses related to the arbitration shall be borne by the loser in the arbitration, except that the union shall pay the salary and expenses of all its members, and management shall pay the salary and expenses related to its members. In cases where the arbitrator rules partially in favor of both parties, all expenses related to arbitration shall be borne equally by both parties [39].

In following any grievance procedure, the procedure will only work well if the parties to the grievance:

- participate in problem-solving behavior
- involve progressively higher levels of the procedure when the grievance cannot be settled at lower levels
- base actions on factual data
- govern themselves in an ethical and fair manner
- grieve only items that are based on specific contract violations
- attempt to obtain resolution at the lowest possible levels
- result in specific remedies that are fair and equitable [40]

From the standpoint of the union there are two techniques that can be frequently utilized to put pressure on management if the labor/management environment remains an adversarial one. The union can: (1) encourage its members to grieve anything and grieve often, and (2) automatically request arbitration knowing that this will tie up management's time and often be costly to the school district [41].

In order to counter these union tactics, management will attempt to: (1) define limitations on contract grievance in the narrowest sense possible, (2) put very restrictive time limits on filing grievances and in carrying a grievance forward to higher steps of the grievance procedure, (3) deny any request by the union for an extension of the time limits, (4) restrict grievances to individual employees and not allow union or class grievances, and (5) prohibit binding arbitration [42].

Let's step back for a little while from the grievance process itself, and discuss the important matters of progressive discipline, just cause, and due process.

PROGRESSIVE DISCIPLINE, JUST CAUSE, AND DUE PROCESS

Progressive discipline implies that the discipline administered to an employee, with the exception of very serious offenses, must be progressive in nature. That is, the discipline immediately administered cannot be discharge of the employee, but must follow a reasonable and rational sequence of disciplinary actions by the employer [43]. Generally, progressive discipline will follow a series of disciplinary steps similar to those listed in the following.

- As a first step, *an oral warning or reprimand* is given the employee following management's objective investigation of the alleged incident. Of course, this assumes the investigation will provide evidence that the employee's conduct required management to take disciplinary action.
- As a second step, a *written warning or reprimand* is provided. The written reprimand letter or document should include: (1) the specifics of the incident, (2) the reasons for the warning or reprimand, (3) what behavioral changes are expected of the employee, and (4) what disciplinary actions may be administered if the employee continues the undesirable behavior.
- The third step usually will result in the employee being given *time off with pay.*
- The fourth step will usually result in the employee being given *time off without pay.*
- The fifth and final step usually results in the *discharge or termination* of the employee [44].

It should be carefully kept in mind that disciplinary action against an employee should be for corrective purposes, not for punitive purposes [45]. The documentation for any employee's discipline should be accurate and precise. An example of a suspension letter written to an employee for excessive negative actions is provided to emphasize the contents to include in a disciplinary letter.

May 17, 19—

Mr. _____
136 North Street
Anytown, New York 64315-4412

Dear Mr. _____

The established and printed rules of this school district state: "Employees are to be at their assigned work stations and performing their assigned duties at the regular start of the work day." On March 14, 19—, Principal Smith orally warned you about not reporting to work on time, and she indicated that you would receive a written reprimand if your tardiness continued. The reasons for the necessity of all employees reporting to work on time were reviewed with you by Principal Smith.

On March 21, 19—, you again reported late for work and were again given a verbal warning by Principal Smith. She also gave you an additional verbal warning because of your tardiness on March 28, 19—.

On April 6, 19—, Principal Smith gave you a written reprimand for failing to report to work on time in accordance with the work rules of the school district. This action was taken because you had previously reported late for work three times within the period of less than one month. She also indicated at that time that failure to correct your record of tardiness would make you subject to further and possibly more serious disciplinary action.

Since the written reprimand by Principal Smith of April 6, 19—, your work record indicates that you were late for work on the following dates:

April 10, 19— Monday	April 17, 19— Monday
May 6, 19— Friday	May 13, 19— Friday
May 16, 19— Monday	

On each of these dates, Principal Smith was not given an adequate excuse for your reporting late for work.

Since you have apparently not chosen to comply with the school district's normal and published work rules, since you were fully aware of these work rules, and since you apparently have chosen to continue your unacceptable behavior, I am suspending you from work for a two-week period, which shall begin on Monday, May 23, 19—.

Upon returning to work, you will be expected to correct your tardiness and abide by the work rules of the district. Further incidents of tardiness on your part shall result in more severe discipline, including the possible termination of your employment.

Sincerely,

Jim Smooth
Director of Personnel

cc: personnel file

Now that we have elaborated upon the meaning of progressive discipline of an employee, let's turn to the matter of just cause.

Just cause refers to a judgement of whether or not an administrator had just and proper cause to take the action that she/he took against an employee [46]. A typical just cause clause imbedded in a master contractual agreement might well read as: ''No employee shall be subject to corrective discipline, reprimand, discharge, demotion, or deprived of any employee advantages without just cause.''

In simple common language, just cause means that the discipline meted out is justified because of the actions of the employee for which the disciplinary action was taken by an administrator. If the disciplinary action taken was excessive, the school district's administration will probably be ruled against. On the other hand, if the reviewing party feels that the disciplinary action taken was justified by the employee's actions, the school district's administration will probably receive a favorable ruling [47]. In just cause hearings, as in most matters, the documentation defending the action is crucial to achieving a favorable ruling on the matter.

Once a just cause is ratified as a part of a master contract document, this clause will provide the basis upon which an administrator must proceed in corrective discipline, and will be a criterion used in judging the appropriateness of an administrator's actions against an employee during grievance hearings, grievance arbitration, or even during litigation.

Let's now turn to the matter of due process. School district administrators often lose cases because they didn't follow due process guidelines. Sometimes they lose matters even when they did appropriately follow due process, simply because they did not sufficiently document their actions.

Due process refers to a procedure that, when properly implemented, protects the rights of the individual employee [48]. It basically involves a set of criteria that permits a determination of whether or not an employee was treated fairly and whether or not the employee had opportunities to be consistently heard and defended. Due process and just cause are both standards that must be met in dealing with matters of employee discipline.

The following criteria comprise the guidelines for adequate due process being followed by the administrators of a school district in relation to the discipline of the school district's employees.

- The rule, expected conduct, or procedure to be followed was known to the employee, and it was considered reasonable.
- The employee was notified about the expected behavior and about probable disciplinary consequences for failure to comply with the expected behavior.

- There was a fair and objective examination of facts related to the alleged violation by the employee.
- Specific documentation was collected to verify and substantiate the employee's violation, and the employee was given a written copy of the charges.
- The disciplinary action is reasonable and consistent with the nature of the employee's violation, and the employee's previous employment record has been duly considered prior to administering the discipline.
- The employee has been given an opportunity of a hearing on the charges, and the employee has been told of her/his right of counsel and her/his right to call witnesses prior to the disciplinary action being taken. At the hearing the employee can present evidence on her/his behalf, and the employee has the right of cross-examination. The notice of the disciplinary hearing must contain an explanation of all the rules related to the hearing.
- The employee shall be judged by an impartial third party [49].

Now that we have presented the background information on progressive discipline, due process, and just cause, let's return to the major topic of grievances.

PREPARING FOR AND PROCESSING GRIEVANCES

In the grievance articles contained in most negotiated and ratified master contractual agreements there are very specific steps to be followed. Many times this grievance article will even deal with details related to the payment of an arbitrator, court recorder, and other grievance costs if grievance arbitration is included as a step in the grievance process.

In preparing for and processing a grievance hearing, the administrator should collect detailed documentation about the alleged grievance. The specific questions that should be answered as part of the grievance processing should include documentation related to the following.

- Why is this a grievance?
- What specifically is aggrieved?
- Who is involved in the alleged grievance?
- Where did the alleged grievance take place?

- When did the alleged grievance take place?
- What specifically happened during the alleged grievance?
- Were there any witnesses to the alleged grievance? If yes, who were the witnesses?
- What recourse (demand) is the aggrieved employee seeking to resolve the grievance?
- Are there any past practices that may influence the outcome of this grievance [50]?

Once a grievance has been filed by an employee or an employees' union and it has gone to the first level of the grievance procedure, it is then appealed by the employee to other levels of the grievance procedure. Management should develop a checklist to be followed when reviewing an appealed grievance. A simple checklist should cover the following.

- Have I collected all the information available at previous steps of the grievance?
- Have I held a personal conference with the employee who filed the alleged grievance, and have I listened intently to the employee's story?
- If necessary or wise, have I received the union representative's position on the matter?
- Have I taken notes on all the important facts?
- Have I made certain that I am clear on the recourse requested by the employee and/or the employee's union representative?
- Have I reviewed the grievance, the recourse desired, and the pertinent facts with the employee in order that the employee understands these matters, and that the employee understands that I am accurate in the information I have recorded?
- Have I investigated the alleged facts with the employee's immediate administrator who took the action that is being grieved?
- Have I checked the time limits in the negotiated master contract's grievance procedure?
- Am I certain of the grievability of the issue to which I am to respond?
- Have I sought expert advice (legal or other expert) if I felt the need to seek it?
- Have I checked my facts and tentative decision with the school district's director of personnel before rendering a final decision?
- Have I answered the grievance within the time limits, and have I

answered it by clearly stating my understanding of what is being grieved, what recourse is desired, and the reasons for making the decision that I made?
- Have I explained to the employee her/his right to appeal?
- Have I made certain that the action I promised was carried out accurately, completely, and in a timely manner [51]?

If the negotiated master contractual agreement permits the arbitration of grievances as the final step in the grievance procedure, management should prepare a checklist of preparatory steps to be followed by administrators who will be involved in the grievance arbitration hearing [52].

- Study the grievance very carefully, reviewing its history through every step of the grievance procedure.
- Prepare a very clear statement of the issue in dispute, and identify the specific contract article and wording that is involved in the alleged grievance.
- Review the master agreement very carefully, once again, before going to the grievance to assure yourself of the accuracy of the action taken by the administrator and of the possible interpretation of the contract that could be used by the union.
- Assemble all the documents and papers you will need to present your position to the arbitrator, and make certain to have copies available in a well-organized format to hand to the arbitrator at the hearing.
- If the union possesses documents that you feel you require for the hearing, ask the union to provide you with copies or to bring them to the hearing. If they do not, ask the arbitrator to subpoena them.
- Interview all the witnesses you intend to call, and have the school attorney and yourself review all matters until you can make certain that your witnesses thoroughly understand the entire case and that they understand the importance of their own testimony. Coaching witnesses is not only wise, it is a crucial pre-hearing preparation step. Some witnesses, if not coached prior to the actual hearing, may panic and end up hurting your case.
- Develop a written summary of what each witness is supposed to prove. This procedure will assist you in making certain that no important item of testimony is overlooked.
- Study the case carefully from the union's point of view. Play the game of "what if" and prepare to counter any of the union's opposing evidence and/or arguments.

- Conduct a mock hearing, and have other administrators and the school district's attorney look for weak spots and previously overlooked details. Thus, these can be corrected before the actual arbitration hearing takes place. During this mock hearing have some members of your group present the strongest case possible from the union's point of view, and have other members serve as impartial third party mediators. Finally, have the school attorney vigorously cross-examine management's witnesses from the union's point of view.
- Find out as much as you can about the arbitrator, the way she/he conducts hearings, and any prior rulings that she/he has rendered in cases similar to the grievance case that will be arbitrated.
- Following the hearing, ask the arbitrator to render her/his award in a very short time period. If the grievance involves retroactive pay, the amount accumulates daily if the arbitrator ultimately rules in favor of the union's position [53].
- Although not part of the preparation for arbitration, it is important to end this discussion on grievance arbitration by providing very simple guidelines.
- If you win the arbitration, do not brag or flaunt your win in the face of the employee or the union. Remember, this is still your employee, and you will continue to live with the union and its representatives well into the future.

If the administration's action was not upheld in arbitration, make certain that you accept the decision without any thought of getting even with the employee or the union in the future. You win some and you lose some, and experienced unionists and management representatives who deal with the entire collective bargaining process understand and accept this. In fact, experienced hands on both sides of the table usually develop a great deal of respect for one another's skills and fairness over the long haul.

SUMMARY

The operational stage of communicating and interpreting the master contract may seem a lesser endeavor after the task of achieving a collective negotiations agreement, but it is an initial critical step in the administration of the new contract. The dissemination of the tentatively agreed-upon contract to members of the administration is intended to achieve a basic understanding of the contents of the ratified master contractual agreement. Once the contract is ratified by both parties, a more intensive, article-by-article review is recommended to ensure uniform interpretation of the articles and the specific contractual wording. It is a training session for the administrators, and it will assist in setting the tone for an effective working relationship between management and the employees. Particular high-stress areas requiring attention include union rights, management rights, academic freedom, employee assignments, employee transfer, employee evaluation, unit membership, and the grievance process. Clear direction must be given to the members of the administration to guide their day-to-day, detailed implementation of the contract's provisions. Regular communication and updates concerning the contract's implementation should be provided.

The intent of these efforts is to prevent the establishment of unintentional precedents, which can create a single instance or multiple instances of past practice, thus nullifying, for all practical purposes, related contract articles. A precedent may be established which has a harmful effect on the district. Precedents can be broken in two ways: language can be written in ways that eliminate an undesirable precedent, and management may create a diversity of interpretations related to the same action, which breaks the precedent through inconsistency.

Related to the contract implementation are the steps involved in conducting a disciplinary procedure. Violations of the specific terms of the contract may also be classed as incompetency and insubordination. Proving incompetency and insubordination requires documentation, and the union may employ classic defense strategies (such as claiming administrative incompetency in judging teaching performance) to protect the employee.

Progressive administrative discipline underlies these procedures, and usually consists of oral warnings or reprimands, relief from duties with and without pay, and finally termination. The matter of just cause, language that is usually contained in the master contract, is also related to progressive discipline, and refers to the judgement of whether or not an administrator had a right to take a particular action against an employee, and whether or not the discipline taken was reasonable in view of the action taken by the employee. This clause will provide the administrative basis on which corrective discipline proceeds. Due process must also be observed as a standard for administrative procedure throughout the process of employee discipline.

A typical master contract grievance procedure involves definitions, time limits, recording information, and four procedural steps with various levels of appeal (immediate supervisor, director of personnel, etc.). Union grievance tactics in an adversarial climate may include the excessively frequent filing of grievances and the automatic requests for arbitration.

The processing of grievances may be highly detailed in the master contractual agreement. Documentation of an alleged grievance must address such specific areas as the specific nature of the violation, persons, time, and location, identification of witnesses, recourse demanded, and related past practice. Administrators responding to an employee grievance must ensure that due process and careful attention to detail and procedure have been followed, particularly in regard to the requirements of the master contract.

EXERCISES

1. What would be some effective techniques to train administrators on the articles' details and the recommended implementation of a new master contract?
2. Review the variety of administrative practices in your district, and determine which might be the most vulnerable to different interpretation and application, and thus likely to cause a problematic past practice.
3. Outline the steps of an imaginary contract violation (incompetency or insubordination) that would lead to employee termination.
4. Outline the steps of an imaginary progressive discipline situation.
5. Outline the types of data you would present at a grievance arbitration hearing.

REFERENCES

1. Kearney, R. C. 1984. *Labor Relations in the Public Sector.* New York, NY: Marcel Dekker, Inc., p. 281.
2. Kearney, R. C., pp. 283–284.
3. Helsby, R. D., J. Tener and J. Lefkowitz, eds. 1985. *The Evolving Process — Collective Negotiations in Public Employment.* Fort Washington, PA: Labor Relations Press, p. 220.
4. Kearney, R. C., p. 284.
5. Kearney, R. C., p. 285.

6. Webster, W. G., Sr. 1985. *Effective Collective Bargaining in Public Education.* Ames, IA: Iowa State University Press, pp. 190–191.
7. Coleman, C. J. 1990. *Managing Labor Relations in the Public Sector.* San Francisco, CA: Jossey-Bass Publishers, p. 287.
8. Many, T. W. and C. A. Sloan. 1990. "Management and Labor Perceptions of School Collective Bargaining," *Journal of Collective Negotiations,* 19(4): 283–296.
9. Webster, W. G., Sr., pp. 190–191.
10. Smith, S. C., D. Ball and D. Liontos. 1990. *Working Together — The Collaborative Style of Bargaining.* Eugene, OR: ERIC Clearinghouse on Educational Management, University of Oregon, p. 59.
11. Helsby, R. D., J. Tener and J. Lefkowitz, eds., p. 185.
12. Coleman, C. J., pp. 184–185.
13. Kearney, R. C., pp. 284–285.
14. Kearney, R. C., p. 71.
15. Elkouri, F. and E. A. Elkouri. 1973. *How Arbitration Works, Third Edition.* Washington, DC: Bureau of National Affairs, Inc., p. 395.
16. Elkouri, F. and E. A. Elkouri, p. 392.
17. Elkouri, F. and E. A. Elkouri, p. 407.
18. Richardson, R. C. 1985. *Collective Bargaining by Objectives: A Positive Approach.* Englewood Cliffs, NJ: Prentice-Hall, Inc., pp. 212–213.
19. Kearney, R. C., p. 291.
20. Kearney, R. C., p. 291.
21. Kearney, R. C., p. 291.
22. Trotta, M. S. 1976. *Handling Grievances — A Guide for Management and Labor.* Washington, DC: The Bureau of National Affairs, Inc., pp. 24–25.
23. Paterson, L. T. and R. T. Murphy. 1983. *The Public Administrator's Grievance Arbitration Handbook.* New York, NY: Longman, Inc., p. 78.
24. Richardson, R. C., pp. 219–220.
25. Coulson, R. 1981. *The Termination Handbook.* London: Collier MacMillan Publishers, pp. 49–50.
26. Braun, R. J. 1972. *Teachers and Power — The Story of the American Federation of Teachers.* New York, NY: Simon and Schuster, pp. 104–105.
27. Coulson, R., pp. 100–101.
28. Paterson, L. T. and R. T. Murphy, pp. 72–73.
29. Kearney, R. C., pp. 287–289.
30. Webster, W. G., Sr., pp. 195–196.
31. Webster, W. G., Sr., p. 194.
32. Trotta, M. S., pp. 100–101.
33. Trotta, M. S., pp. 98–99.
34. Paterson, L. T. and R. T. Murphy, p. 52.
35. Paterson, L. T. and R. T. Murphy, p. 51.
36. Webster, W. G., Sr., pp. 137–140.
37. Rebore, R. W. 1991. *Personnel Administration in Education — A Management*

Approach, Third Edition. Englewood Cliffs, NJ: Prentice-Hall, Inc., pp. 322−325.

38. Webster, W. G., Sr., p. 196.
39. Webster, W. G., Sr., p. 196.
40. Paterson, L. T. and R. T. Murphy, pp. 4−5.
41. Webster, W. G., Sr., pp. 206−207.
42. Webster, W. G., Sr., pp. 205−206.
43. Coulson, R., pp. 73−74.
44. Coulson, R., p. 122.
45. Justin, J. J. 1969. *How to Manage with a Union − Book Two − The Rules of Collective Bargaining, Grievance Handling, Corrective Discipline, Book One of How to Manage with a Union.* New York, NY: Industrial Relations Workshop Seminars, Inc., pp. 294−295.
46. Paterson, L. T. and R. T. Murphy, pp. 254−255.
47. Trotta, M. S., pp. 58−59.
48. Paterson, L. T. and R. T. Murphy, p. 80.
49. Trotta, M. S., pp. 128−129.
50. Paterson, L. T. and R. T. Murphy, p. 147.

REMEMBERING MISCELLANEOUS ITEMS AND SUMMARIZING

Section Four consists of two chapters. Chapter 12, *Miscellaneous Items,* presents information about union shops and closed shops, power management, reality versus perception, fact versus propaganda, state and local relations with local union affiliates, and the importance of the initial master contractual agreement. It also discusses information leaks, information handling, expedited bargaining, zipper clauses, and limited or focused bargaining. Further, it discusses forces that influence collective bargaining, certifying and decertifying unions, unfair labor practices and bad-faith bargaining. The chapter ends by a discussion of the roles that are played by regional, state, and national unions.

Chapter 13, *Summarizing—The End Piece,* presents a listing of the do's, don'ts, and maybe's of collective bargaining. It also presents information about the benefits and losses suffered by both labor and management. It ends by discussing the benefits and drawbacks of adversarial bargaining and of win/win bargaining, and by elaborating upon the potential impact of school-based (site-based) management on the collective bargaining process.

Miscellaneous Items

CHAPTER 12 discusses a variety of important terms and matters that do not fit nicely into the first eleven chapters of this volume. These discussions begin with the differences between agency shops and closed shops, and they end with the topic of the roles played by regional, state, and national unions in matters of local union business.

AGENCY SHOPS, UNION SHOPS, AND CLOSED SHOPS

An *agency shop* refers to a situation where the employees of a school district are not required to belong to the union that has the exclusive right to represent them in collective bargaining, but the employees are required to pay a service fee to the union [1]. The fee is intended to cover all costs of the union when the union is representing the employee in collective bargaining matters [2]. On rare occasions, union and management have agreed that the individual employee can give the amount of money equal to the service fee to a charity of the employee's choice, rather than paying the money to the union.

The advantage of an agency shop is that it gives employees who do not believe in unionism or who are members of another union, the freedom of choice to refuse to officially join the union that has gained exclusive representational rights [3]. Although the union officials would prefer that all members join their union, it does allow the union to collect fees for its work on behalf of the employees, and it eliminates the possibility of anyone getting a free ride. On the other hand, it does not allow the union to collect full dues, nor does it permit the union to use the agency shop fees for political purposes, such as lobbying legislators [4].

A *closed shop* is one in which all employees have to belong to the union *before* they can be hired by the school district [5]. A closed shop is illegal in most public school situations. The advantages of a closed shop are all in favor of the union that is elected or recognized as the sole representative of the employees (at least of one category of employees, such as teachers) of a school district. It allows the union to collect full dues and to have wide discretion in the use of the money collected [6]. In cases of closed shops, it is often impossible to hire anyone unless the hiring is done through the union hall. Obviously, this tremendously increases the power of the union leaders.

A *union shop* refers to a situation wherein all employees must belong to the union that has been recognized as the sole representative of the employees or at least one category of employees. All employees in that category have to belong to the union, but they do not have to join the union before they are hired [7,8].

TIMING + INFORMATION = POWER MANAGEMENT

The formula for success with the processes involved in collective bargaining depends on the party's possession of complete, accurate, and well-organized information that will convince the other party, the mediator, the fact finder, or the arbitrator that the party's position is the one to accept. This information requirement implies that the persons involved in the processes of collective bargaining: (1) do their homework in great detail and in advance of the need for the information, (2) keep up to date on all changes that are taking place during negotiations in their school districts and in other school districts, and update their information accordingly, and (3) present their information in a clear and convincing manner.

Even though all of the information requirements are met, they are of little use unless they are presented at a time when the chance of success is maximized. To present excellent information in a convincing manner in the early stages of an adversarial negotiation is to waste the information, and doing this prematurely tips off the other party to the negotiations of your information and its intended usage. Also, to provide last best offer type of information to a mediator, when you are fully expecting that the impasse will go beyond the mediation stage, is again to waste the information and prematurely identify your ultimate position(s) [9,10].

REALITY VERSUS PERCEPTION AND FACT VERSUS PROPAGANDA

During a lengthy period of negotiating a new master contractual agreement within an adversarial negotiating environment, it is oftentimes difficult for the members of the union, management, or the public to separate fact from propaganda. It is also oftentimes difficult for the members of both the union's at-the-table negotiating team and management's at-the-table negotiating team to separate reality from perception.

Even though there may be an agreement on a ground rule for the negotiations that no information will be provided by either party to the negotiations until the total package is ratified as a master contractual agreement, a well-used tactic during the times of adversarial bargaining is the leaking of propaganda statements. Some of the typical propaganda tactics would involve such matters as the following [11].

- The board of education is going to reduce the medical insurance.
- The board of education isn't interested in the children because they will not reduce class size.
- The board of education will not agree to any salary increase.
- The board of education's negotiating team is not bargaining in good faith.
- The chief negotiator hates teachers.
- The board of education is purposely acting inappropriately in order to provoke a strike with the hope that it can fire the employees for illegally striking.

The facts related to the above statements could well be as follows.

- Because of the escalating cost of medical insurance, the board has proposed that the employees pay one-fourth of any premium increases.
- The board of education would like to decrease class size, especially at the early elementary level, but it does not have sufficient new monies to accomplish this.
- The management team's negotiating position is that it will not discuss salary increases until all other contractual items in contention are resolved.
- The board of education's negotiating team is bargaining in good faith because it has agreed to meet regularly, it listens intently to the union's proposals, and it offers rational counterproposals. It has not agreed to many items, but that is not a requirement for good-faith bargaining.
- The board of education's chief negotiator is a lawyer whose wife is a teacher in another school district.

- The last thing the board of education wants is a strike, as it knows how a strike makes matters very complex and how it negatively affects all aspects of the school district for many years into the future.

During long, drawn out, and difficult adversarial negotiations, members of the negotiating team often have problems in adjoining reality and their perceptions [12]. This problem results from two situations: (1) when there exists serious animosity between individuals or multiple persons on either negotiating team, or (2) when the proposal, counterproposal activity is voluminous [13]. If either of these situations exist, frustration results and the parties to the at-the-table bargaining have difficulty in determining reality. Obviously, a skewed view of reality by any of the important players complicates matters, and it makes the task of obtaining a TA (tentative agreement) that much more difficult [14]. In negotiations, the members naturally have different feelings about each item, and the emotions that evolve from the underdog attitude of those dealing (often for the first time) with management in a confrontational setting are upsetting.

THEY ARE NEVER ALONE

Although the board of education's negotiating team sits at the table with the local union's negotiating team, its members must be aware that the local employees often are not in complete control of what happens during the negotiations. Some of the influences that may be involved in the local collective bargaining scene when the local is affiliated with the regional, state, and national unions, using the teachers' unions of the AFT (American Federation of Teachers) and the NEA (National Education Association) as examples, are listed in the following.

- The NEA or AFT will make a large data bank of comparative information available to the local district's union officers. These data become powerful argumentational tools during collective bargaining processes.
- The regional coalition of local union leaders may suggest that certain *target districts* be at the forefront of new foot-in-the-door proposals, which, if successfully negotiated, become union demands in all the school districts in the near future.
- The state level will usually provide uniserve directors to service the

local district's union in a variety of ways. These uniserve directors are full-time employees of the state's union.

- Union stewards are usually local union officials who serve as the eyes and ears of the local union in each of the school district's buildings, but they usually are given training at the state level. They also work with the local union's officers through the state level to resolve many of the concerns the local may have about the way the school district's administrators are managing the master contractual agreement that was ratified by both parties.
- During at-the-table negotiations, the uniserve director may very well be the chief negotiator for the local union. If this is not the case, it is almost certain that the uniserve director assigned to that local will be a very influential person in the settlement of the master contractual agreement. In all cases, the uniserve director is a highly trained unionist, and, in addition, the state-level union has training sessions for all local union officers and for the local negotiating team members.
- Regional union members, and in serious conflict situations, state and national union leaders, will be present at the local school district to picket, pack board of education meetings, give media interviews, or conduct other activities intended to put pressure on board of education members, the superintendent of schools, the board of education's chief negotiator, and the negotiating team members to settle the contract in a manner that is favorable to the union's position(s) [15].
- During mediation, fact-finding and/or arbitration, it is certain that the state-level union and perhaps the national level union, will provide: (1) relevant information, (2) consultation and advice, and (3) on-site officials from the state and/or national level(s).
- During grievance resolution sessions and especially during grievance arbitrations, the state-level union might very well have a full-time state union-employed attorney present the union's case. At the very least, the union's attorney or a union uniserve director will be actively involved in the preparation, strategy, and tactics related to the arbitration. This is a wise use of union resources, as the arbitration ruling will establish some precedential direction for the specific local school district into the future, but more importantly, an arbitration ruling against the union on an important matter that might affect numerous school districts is detrimental to the union [16,17].

CONTRACT LANGUAGE IS VERY IMPORTANT

Each word that is memorialized in a ratified master contractual agreement is very important. The wording of each article during negotiations is a technically important matter. Some words, such as "shall" and "will," are words that mandate compliance; whereas words like "may" or "should" allow the party flexible decision-making power when it comes to compliance. If the contract says, for instance, "shall" when it should have said "may," or if the contract language stated "may" when it should have said "shall," many problems could result during the management stage of the contract [18]. Either party could feel that the intent of agreement was being violated, and unless there is a mutual agreement on the interpretation of the specific language at some period after the contract has been ratified, adversarial relations will appear and continue. Such a continuing adversarial relationship during contract management is harmful to both parties, and if the conflict state becomes public, this continuing relationship may cause the general public to lose faith in all the people who are supposed to be operating the district for the childrens' benefit.

Three examples of contractual language will serve to highlight the importance of very specific and clear contractual language.

Example — Class Size

> Both parties agree that the maximum class size for grades one through three shall be twenty pupils. In cases where the individual class reaches twenty-one pupils, the board of education will immediately hire an additional teacher and split the class into two classes.

> Both parties agree that reasonable class sizes are important to the quality of teaching offered the students of Wonderful School District. Therefore, the board of education agrees to attempt to keep the maximum class size for grades one through three at twenty pupils.

> The board of education has the authority to determine class size.

In the first statement, the board of education *must* employ an additional teacher during any time period when any class in grades one through three reaches twenty-one students. This agreement could place the board of education in financial difficulty if it has a tight budget and quite a few classes end up with twenty-one or more students. In fact, if there were merely fifteen such situations and the average teacher salary and fringe benefits equalled $40,000, it is clear that the unanticipated cost increase would amount to a total of $600,000. This could also result in many classes having only eleven to fourteen students. All of this is fine if the board of education assumes that classes in excess of twenty are detrimental to student achievement and if the board of education has the available funds to support such a contractual position without doing harm to other of the district's programs. Once agreed to in the master contractual agreement, it is clear that it is a *mandatory* action that must be taken by the board [19].

The second statement is permissive, even though it provides the directional philosophy that is held by the board of education about the matter of class size. On the other hand, the third statement leaves complete control of class size up to the decision-making power of the board of education.

Further analysis of the three statements indicates that the first statement favors the union, the third statement favors the board of education, and the second statement could well be an agreed-to compromise statement reached during a win/win negotiating atmosphere. Whichever type of statement both parties ratify in a master contractual agreement, it spells out the clear responsibility of both parties in the matter of class size.

IMPORTANCE OF THE FIRST NEGOTIATED MASTER CONTRACTUAL AGREEMENT

The first collective bargaining agreement that is ratified as a master contract is the single most important master contract that the two parties will ever ratify. The initial contract will set the stage for all future contractual negotiations in terms of the specific articles included and in terms of the specific language written into each article [20]. If articles or language included are detrimental to either party to the negotiations or if the language is unclear, it may well take near-crisis situations to eliminate the article or the undesired language during future contract negotiations [21]. In the interim, during the management of the existing contract, adversarial relations may arise within a situation that has historically been one of a win/win employee/administrator atmosphere. This problem could arise simply because of unintended articles, too much power being given to one party, or inappropriate use of unclear and cumbersome contractual language [22].

The most important initial contract articles are: (1) recognition, (2) union rights, and (3) management rights. Also, very important are articles dealing with: (4) class size, (5) leaves, (6) academic freedom, (7) employee evaluation, (8) employee *assignment,* or (9) health insurance. Obviously, any article, in addition to the above, must be carefully analyzed before the contract is ratified, as it is one you will have to live with for a very long time [23].

INFORMATION LEAKS DURING NEGOTIATIONS

During critical stages of the negotiations, it is very important to control leaks of information or of at-the-table positions [24]. During the negotiation process, it is crucial that both negotiating teams go to their referent groups to give them a progress report or to get agreement about a change from the original demands provided by the referent group.

For the chief negotiator and for the negotiating team members this is a very difficult decision that must be made. It not only involves what should be shared with the employees (in the union's negotiating team's case) or with the board of education members (in the management's negotiating team's case), but it involves decisions as to what can be shared and what can be withheld [25]. Sometimes, the immediate negotiations are at such a critical stage that any leak will cause a rupture in the progress made, and in such situations, it might be wise to hide important information from the referent group. This is a most difficult decision for a negotiating team to make, as very few people involved in negotiations feel that their referent group does not have the right to know the stage at which negotiations have arrived or the major areas of concerns [26].

The reason for this dilemma — which could be ethical, political, and pragmatic in nature — is that it is almost certain that all information shared with a referent group will be either purposely or accidentally leaked to the other party, the media, and/or the community at large [27]. This realization is balanced against the legitimate right to know by members of the negotiating team's referent group.

For some reason, a few members of any referent group will feel a need to share information that others do not possess, and this sharing may be to friends, spouses, business acquaintances, neighbors, or members of a like group from other school districts. As these people are provided with this information, they share it with others, and ultimately continuous sharing takes place [28]. If this information sharing impedes progress at the table, makes an already complex situation more complex, or causes problems or negatives at any level, damage will take place and the task and energies of the negotiating parties will be focused on damage control activities rather than on bargaining a final contract that could be ratified.

WHEN AND WHERE SHOULD INFORMATION BE SHARED AND TO WHICH GROUPS

Not only are there difficult decisions to be made by the negotiating teams related to their referent groups, there are continuous decisions that must be made related to the sharing of information. These decisions relate to: (1) what information should be shared, (2) when should the information be shared, and (3) to which groups should the various types of information be shared.

If the parties have agreed to closed negotiations, as is the case in most districts, the only persons who will receive information during the process of negotiations will be the negotiating team's referent group. This closed negotiations agreement is usually violated if the negotiations reach the impasse stage.

Media will receive information during two situations. The first release situation is when both parties agree to a joint progress report on the negotiations during various stages of the negotiating process. The second release situation usually occurs when the negotiations reach an impasse stage. When impasse is reached, the media releases are done separately, and they are usually slanted in a manner that favors the positions of the party releasing the information [29].

The general public is privy to the media releases, but they are generally not informed about the specific proposals or their status during the process of negotiations. Of course, there could be purposeful or accidental leaks to members of the community, but, generally, the public is not given the contractual information until after the master contractual agreement has been ratified by both parties.

It is obvious that the specific information to be released is an important decision milestone, and the timing of that release is also very important [30]. If too much or too little information is released at the wrong time or to the wrong group(s), much damage can be done during the process of negotiating a master contractual agreement.

REOPENERS AND ZIPPER CLAUSES

Reopeners usually refer to a timeline, such as three months prior to the expiration of the existing master contractual agreement, when negotiations are initiated on a successor contract. This timeline is agreed upon to allow both parties to the upcoming negotiations sufficient time, hopefully, to negotiate a successor contract prior to the date of expiration of the current master contractual agreement [31].

A *zipper clause* is language within an existing master contractual agreement that allows re-negotiation of a specific article in the contract while all other contractual conditions remain in effect until the end date of the existing contract. Many times a situation will exist wherein a multiple-year ratified master contractual agreement will contain a zipper clause that allows yearly negotiations of the salary provisions in the existing master contract [32].

In general, a zipper clause is negotiated into a master contract to avoid holding up the ratification of a total contract because of disagreement on a single provision. In the case of salary, the parties may agree to a compromised first year salary provision, but they are reluctant to commit themselves to a salary commitment for future years of the contract. Another situation that may lead both parties to agree to a zipper clause on the salary provisions is one when neither party can predict the degree of increase in the cost of living, and they want to reserve the opportunity to adjust future salary demands to a more certain resource future.

EXPEDITED BARGAINING

Expedited bargaining refers to a situation whereby both parties to the negotiations agree to attempt to achieve a TA (tentative agreement) on a total contract in a very short period of time. Often the time period could be one week or less, and it usually occurs with both negotiating teams meeting at some location removed from the school district's environs. Both parties come very well prepared with information and rationale, and they share both freely and quickly. If successful, it accomplishes many good things, including a feeling of satisfaction and trust between both parties, a parsimonious use of resources by both parties, and it probably signals the beginning of, or the continuation of, a win/win attitude that will permeate all activities of both parties throughout all aspects of the collective bargaining process.

FOCUSED OR LIMITED BARGAINING

This bargaining structure has as its purpose one that is identical to that of expedited bargaining—that of quick and win/win agreement on a master contract. In many cases, limited bargaining, like expedited bargaining, takes place at a motel or at some other off—school district location. In focused or limited bargaining, both parties agree to carry forth into the successor master contractual agreement most items that are currently contained in that agreement, but each party selects two or three areas where formal bargaining will take place.

FORCES THAT INFLUENCE COLLECTIVE BARGAINING

Collective bargaining does not take place in a vacuum. It matters not whether the union's or management's persons are deemed to be the responsible party for collective bargaining; they will have forces that will impact them during the stages of: (1) preparing to negotiate, (2) negotiating at the table, (3) master contract ratification, or (4) contract management. The following forces will influence those responsible for collective bargaining.

- The *public,* because of its attitudes towards taxes; the qualitative degree to which they feel the school district is carrying out its education charge; and its attitude towards teachers, unionism, administrators, the superintendent of schools, and board of education members, will lend its supportive or critical voice to the collective bargaining process.
- *Business and industrial groups* influence collective bargaining because of their supportive or nonsupportive attitude towards the school district, its educational programs, or the taxes that they pay to support the local school district.
- *Political forces* at the local, state, and national levels strongly influence collective bargaining in terms of the legislation they pass and in terms of the amount of funds they supply to the local school district.
- *Judicial agencies and quasi-judicial agencies* influence collective bargaining because of the decisions they render related to collective bargaining and union/management powers and relationships.
- *Governmental agencies* that are located in the local school district

can make a big difference in what happens during collective bargaining. The attitude of other governmental agencies towards the school district, the union, and the management are important. If they are negative, this will cause pressure on the collective bargainers. If they are positive, this will assist the collective bargainers.

- *Media* outlets certainly can influence collective bargaining by the degree to which they issue factual information, the degree to which they issue biased or incorrect information, and the degree to which they produce editorials that reflect the media's leanings.
- *Students* can influence collective bargaining depending on their perceptions of the degree to which they feel they are being treated and serviced well by the teachers and administrators of the district. Once these perceptions are shared with family members, neighbors, and friends, the collective bargaining will be either positively or negatively affected.
- *Parents* influence collective bargaining because of the attitudes they hold related to how well their children are treated and educated, how well they feel they are treated by the school district's functionaries, and how well they feel their taxes are being utilized. As they share their perceptions with nonparent others, they have great influence since the others will give the parents credibility because they currently have children attending the schools.
- *Taxpayers* greatly influence collective bargaining by the degree to which they are willing or unwilling to tax themselves to support the operation of the school district. The attitudes of retired community members who are on a fixed income and taxpayers who have no children of school age are crucial in many districts that have an aging adult population.
- *PERB* (Public Employment Relations Board) influences collective bargaining by the rules they promulgate to carry out the collective bargaining law enacted by the state's legislature. They also influence collective bargaining by the assignment of mediators and arbitrators, and by its compilation of rulings of arbitrators [33].

RECOGNITION CLAUSE

This clause, which usually is the initial clause or article in any printed master contractual agreement, is one that must be very carefully worded.

It specifies which employees the union represents and which it doesn't represent, and it gives sole representation rights to the union in all matters of collective bargaining throughout the length of the ratified master contractual agreement [34]. The contract is binding for its lifetime, but can be challenged by a vote to overthrow the union's legal action requested of the PERB by union members. It is crucial that management and confidential employees are listed as being omitted from the employees that the union can represent.

CERTIFICATION AND DECERTIFICATION ELECTIONS

Although a board of education may accept a specific union as the official representation of a class of employees for the purpose of representation of those employees for all collective bargaining purposes, the union usually has to be selected through a certification election conducted by PERB [35]. New York State's Taylor Law contains the following wording in its section entitled "Determination of Representative Status":

For purposes of resolving disputes concerning representation status, pursuant to section two hundred five or two hundred six of this article, the board or government, as the case may be, shall:

1. define the appropriate employer-employee negotiating unit taking into account the following standards:
   (a) the definition of the unit shall correspond to a community of interest among the employees to be included in the unit;
   (b) the officials of the government at the level of the unit shall have the power to agree, or to make effective recommendations to other administrative authority or the legislative body with respect to, the terms and conditions of employment upon which the employees desire to negotiate; and
   (c) the unit shall be compatible with the joint responsibilities of the public employer and public employees to serve the public.

2. ascertain the public employees' choice of employee organization as their representative (in cases where the parties to a dispute have not agreed on the means to ascertain the choice, if any, of the employees in the unit) on the basis of dues deduction authorizations or other evidences, or, if necessary, by conducting an election.

3. certify or recognize an employee organization upon (a) the determina-

tion that such organization represents that group of public employees it claims to represent, and (b) the affirmation by such organization that it does not assert the right to strike against any government, to assist or participate in such a strike, or to impose an obligation to conduct, assist or participate in such a strike [36].

In most states a decertification election can be requested, and the election will be supervised by PERB if the school district presents evidence that a substantial number of employees in the unit want to decertify or if a substantial number of employees take it upon themselves to petition PERB to supervise a decertification election. Generally, a decertification election can only be called for during a specifically stipulated period close to the end of the master contractual agreement that is in effect. Even if the decertification election is successful, the union previously certified would serve as the sole representative for collective bargaining purposes until the termination date listed in the existing master contractual agreement.

UNFAIR LABOR PRACTICE

Although other matters may be considered unfair labor practices by individual states, normally, an unfair labor practice can be charged against a union when: (1) an employee organization or its agents deliberately interfere with, restrain, or coerce employees in the exercise of the rights granted them under the collective bargaining law, or (2) when the employee organization or its agents does not collectively negotiate in good faith with the public employer [37].

The public employer or its agents can be charged with an unfair labor practice when: (1) it conducts itself in the same manner as the union's unfair practices listed above, (2) it attempts to dominate or interfere with the formation or administration of any employee organization, for the purpose of depriving employees of their rights under the collective bargaining law, (3) it attempts to discriminate against any employee for the purpose of encouraging or discouraging membership in, or participation in the activities of any union, and (4) it refuses to continue the terms of an expired agreement until a new agreement is negotiated.

Sadly, during serious adversarial negotiations, unfair labor practices charges and/or bad-faith bargaining charges are leveled against the other party solely as a tactical move. Usually, when this happens the other party to the negotiations levels counter charges. If the media covers these charges, unnecessary complications result and negative public opinions are often formed.

BAD-FAITH BARGAINING

Bad-faith bargaining refers to a situation wherein either party to the negotiations refuses to attend a reasonable series of meetings, refuses to meet with reasonable frequency, refuses to give serious consideration to the proposals of the other party, or refuses to make reasonable proposals or counterproposals. It should be emphasized, however, that if the above criteria are met, there is no requirement that either party must agree to any proposal [38].

SUMMARY

A number of items and matters that affect collective bargaining require definition. *Agency shop* refers to the arrangement whereby employees may remain nonunion members but are required to pay a fee to the union for representational services. A *closed shop,* usually illegal, is one in which all district employees must belong to the union, even prior to employment. A *union shop* is one in which all employees must belong to the union, but not necessarily before they are hired.

The possession of complete, accurate, and convincing information regarding negotiations must be augmented by its judicious and well-timed use during the negotiating sessions. Separating fact from propaganda during the negotiations process is frequently difficult, due to the leaking of rumors or the release of statements to the media. The NEA or AFT may support the local union's tactics and other strategies, and they can provide the local union with access to: (1) a large nationally based data bank of comparative information, (2) personnel such as uniserve directors (who can serve as chief negotiators), (3) state-level training for local stewards, and (4) regional backup of both information and personnel in case of serious conflict situations.

Contract language is critical in that it defines mandatory terms, or permissive and flexible terms. The first negotiated master contractual agreement is the most important district document ever to be ratified, since it will set the stage for all future contractual negotiations. Key points requiring specific language include class size, leaves, academic freedom, employee evaluation, employee assignment, and benefit packages.

During negotiations, information leaks about tactics, stages of agreement or disagreement, or specific details about article proposals must be minimized, which may require the withholding of information from each side's referent group. Information should be shared with the media through a joint progress report.

Future negotiations may be affected by the establishment of *reopeners,* which set a timeline for successor contracts to be negotiated. A *zipper clause* is language within an existing contract that will allow re-negotiation of a specific article before the end of the existing contract. It is intended to avoid a holdup on items which one party or the other feels should be re-negotiated sooner than the expiration date of the contract. *Expedited bargaining* is a streamlined approach to negotiations, when both teams come well-armed with information and push for a rapid tentative agreement. *Focused or limited bargaining* is similar in that the parties have some prior agreement to hasten the process by carrying forward most of the existing contractual articles, and limiting negotiation to only a few articles.

The forces impacting the negotiations process are many: the public, business and industrial groups, political forces, judicial and quasi-judicial agencies, government agencies, media, students, parents, taxpayers, and the Public Employment Relations Board. The recognition clause is a legal term, indicating which employees the union represents and which it does not, and it gives sole representation rights to the union. Related to this is the legal selection process for that recognition status, done through a certification election conducted by the PERB. A decertification election, requested by membership, removes the union as the sole representative, but this can only be done at the expiration of the existing master contractual agreement.

Unfair labor practices pertain to both union and management. If a union interferes with individual's rights under the bargaining law, or if it does not negotiate in good faith, it may be charged with unfair labor practice. Likewise, the employer may be charged for the same violations, or if the employer attempts to interfere with the organizational rights of the employees. These charges are frequently leveled as a tactical move during adversarial bargaining. *Bad-faith bargaining* occurs when either party refuses to meet, consider, make proposals, offer counterproposals, or neglect or refuse to seriously consider the proposals of the other party to the negotiations.

REFERENCES

1. Aaron, B., J. M. Najita and J. L. Stern. 1988. *Public Sector Bargaining.* Washington, DC: Industrial Relations Research Associates, pp. 220–221.
2. Donley, M. O., Jr. 1976. *Power to the Teacher.* Bloomington, IN: Indiana University Press, pp. 132–133.
3. Donley, M. O., Jr., pp. 132–133.
4. Splitt, D. A. 1991. "How Much Can Unions Charge Nonmembers?" *Executive Educator,* 13(9):18.
5. Helsby, R. D., J. Tener and J. Lefkowitz, eds. 1985. *The Evolving Process—Collective Negotiations in Public Employment.* Fort Washington, PA: Labor Relations Press, p. xxxiii.
6. Coleman, C. J. 1990. *Managing Labor Relations in the Public Sector.* San Francisco, CA: Jossey-Bass Publishers, pp. 220–201.
7. Helsby, R. D., J. Tener and J. Lefkowitz, eds., p. xi.
8. Coleman, C. J., p. 201.
9. Webster, W. G., Sr. 1985. *Effective Collective Bargaining in Public Education.* Ames, IA: Iowa State University Press, pp. 81–86.
10. Neal, R. 1980. *Bargaining Tactics—A Reference Manual for Public Sector Labor Negotiations.* Richard G. Neal Associates, pp. 147–151.
11. Herman, J. J. 1991. "The Two Faces of Collective Bargaining," *School Business Affairs,* 57(2):11–12.
12. Webster, W. G., Sr., pp. 56–57.
13. Webster, W. G., Sr., pp. 150–151.
14. Many, T. W. and C. A. Sloan. 1990. "Management and Labor Perceptions of School Collective Bargaining," *Journal of Collective Negotiations,* 19(4): 283–296.
15. Murphy, M. 1990. *Blackboard Unions—The AFT and the NEA 1900–1980.* Ithaca, NY: Cornell University Press, pp. 270–271.
16. Maier, M. M. 1987. *City Unions.* New Brunswick, NJ: Rutgers University Press, pp. 133–134.
17. Webster, W. G., Sr., p. 170.
18. Castetter, W. B. 1986. *The Effective Function in Education.* New York, NY: Macmillan Publishing Company, pp. 171–172.
19. Castetter, W. B., pp. 171–172.
20. Rebore, R. W. 1991. *Personnel Administration in Education—A Management Approach, Third Edition.* Englewood Cliffs, NJ: Prentice-Hall, Inc., p. 317.
21. Janes, L. 1984. "Collective Bargaining," *NASSP Instructional Leadership Booklet,* pp. 22–23.
22. Janes, L., pp. 22–23.
23. Castetter, W. B., pp. 149–155.
24. Neal, R., p. 153.

25. Neal, R., pp. 73–75.

26. Rebore, R. W., pp. 309–310.

27. Webster, W. G., Sr., p. 76.

28. Webster, W. G., Sr., p. 76.

29. Smith, S. C., D. Ball and D. Liontos. 1990. *Working Together—The Collaborative Style of Bargaining.* Eugene, OR: ERIC Clearinghouse on Educational Management, University of Oregon, pp. 55, 58.

30. Castetter, W. B., pp. 150–151.

31. Webster, W. G., Sr., p. 216.

32. Webster, W. G., Sr., p. 217.

33. Kearney, R. C. 1984. *Labor Relations in the Public Sector.* New York, NY: Marcel Dekker, Inc., pp. 73–74.

34. Helsby, R. D., J. Tener and J. Lefkowitz, eds., pp. 107–108.

35. Kearney, R. C., pp. 50–51.

36. New York State Public Employment Relations Board. 1983–1984. *The Taylor Law.* Albany, NY: New York Public Employment Relations Board, p. 11.

37. Kearney, R. C., p. 332.

38. Neal, R., pp. 203–204.

Summarizing—The End Piece

CHAPTER 13 discusses: (1) the do's of collective bargaining, (2) the maybe's of collective bargaining, (3) the don'ts of collective bargaining, (4) the benefits of collective bargaining for labor and management, (5) the losses for labor and management, (6) the benefits and deficits of adversarial bargaining, (7) the benefits and deficits of win/win bargaining, (8) the school-based management movement and its potential impact on collective bargaining, and (9) a summary of the entire book.

Many years ago there were two farmers who worked adjoining pieces of land. One day they were out plowing the land with their horses and getting the soil ready for the spring planting. They began arguing about who owned the center strip of approximately one-half acre of the land.

Until this day of argumentation, they had always been great friends, and they had even helped one another by loaning horses and physically assisting each other with the planting and harvesting chores. In other words, their working history has been one of *win/win.*

But, for some reason, this day they became embroiled in a heated argument. Tempers flared for weeks, and when they finally began talking again, they ended up playing power games with the purpose of beating the other man out of the contested property. This started the process of *adversarial bargaining.*

Farmer Jim *proposed* that Farmer Ken could keep the contested land if Farmer Ken would give him his prized team of Belgian plow horses. Jim thought to himself: "The Belgians are worth as much or more than the one-half acre of land." Jim realized the value of *quid pro quo* (receiving a value equivalent or greater than the value of what you give). Ken countered by explaining that if he gave up his horses he would have no method of plowing the land, and this would put him and his family in financial disaster. However, Ken *counterproposed* that if Jim would agree that the one-half acre of land belonged to him, he would give Jim one-half of all the vegetables produced on the one-half acre for the next five years.

Jim said he would seriously consider Ken's offer, but that he needed time to think it over and discuss it with his wife. After *caucusing* with his wife, Jim decided that he would reject Ken's offer. He stated that he would have to get something else from Ken for the land, or that Ken would have to give him something in addition to the produce from the one-half acre for the next five years.

After numerous proposals and counterproposals, Ken and Jim agreed that they could not find a way to settle their disagreement. They decided that Farmer Pete, one of their neighbors, was a fair man that both of them respected, and that they would ask Farmer Pete to assist them in reaching an agreement about the contested land, since they had reached an impasse. Farmer Pete served as a *mediator* at this *impasse* stage, but he wasn't able to get Jim and Ken to agree on any settlement of the dispute. Having attempted numerous times to get Jim and Ken to agree, Farmer Pete said that he would not continue to try to get the two men to reach agreement over the disputed one-half acre of land, but he did recommend that Jim and Ken ask Preacher Jack to study the facts in the matter and render a judgement that would be binding on both Jim and Ken.

Jim and Ken took Pete's suggestion, and Preacher Jack agreed to serve as a *fact finder* and as an *arbitrator* to resolve the dispute. Preacher Jack met with both men, and had them agree to the value placed on the land. After looking at the value of other items either party would accept, such as five cows, a trade-off for another piece of land, a certain amount of labor and other trade-off possibilities, Preacher Jack rendered his *fact-finding report*. He determined that since neither party seemed comfortable with any trade-offs for the land, the land would be split in half. The one-quarter acre that adjoined Jim's land would be given to Jim, and the one-quarter acre that adjoined Ken's land would be given to Ken.

Both Ken and Jim felt the preacher's decision was a fair one. However, before Preacher Jack left the two farmers he gave them a good lecture. He stated that the men had been friends for over twenty years and he stressed how they had always helped each other in times of need for all those years, how their wives were good friends, and how their children grew up together. He also told them that they were foolish to let a little piece of land interrupt their friendship for the past seven months, and that if they used common sense, they would realize that their friendship and the friendship of their families was of much more value than the little one-half acre of contested land.

When the preacher left, Jim and Ken began thinking about what the preacher said, and they agreed that their friendship and helping relationship that they had maintained for practically their entire lives was too valuable to lose. They decided to reignite that friendship by having a joint picnic for both of the families after Sunday's church service. They also invited Preacher Jack to join them.

It was towards the end of the picnic that Jim and Ken shook hands, looked each other in the eye and vowed never to be adversaries again. They had learned the value of win/win the hard way, and they weren't about to lose it at any time in the future.

This short fictitious tale spells out in rather simple terms the process of collective bargaining, and the value of a win/win collaborative approach. It also spells out the danger of an adversarial approach to bargaining, and the value of mediation, fact-finding, and arbitration if an impasse is reached during the adversarial bargaining process.

The dual goals of any aspect of collective bargaining are: (1) to arrive at a fair and equitable agreement, and (2) to use a continuing win/win process as the best means of arriving at agreements. Win/win builds respect and caring and honesty and, whenever possible, it is the only way to go.

Now let's turn to the *do's* of collective bargaining. The do's shall be followed by a discussion of the *maybe's* of collective bargaining and the *don'ts* of collective bargaining.

THE DO'S OF COLLECTIVE BARGAINING

If you are involved in any phase of the collective bargaining process, there are some *do's* that will enhance your chance of success. Some of the most important ones include the following.

- Do think win/win and act win/win whenever possible.
- Do your homework, and collect all the data necessary prior to meeting with the other party.
- Do present your position(s) in a clear and simple manner in order to avoid any misunderstanding, and support your position with logic and with factual information.
- Do put yourself in the other party's shoes in order to understand fully where the other party is coming from and the needs of the other party.
- Do listen intently to the other party's position(s), and carefully study the data that the other party presents.
- Do be aware of any outside forces that may be influencing the collective bargaining.

- Do act honestly and ethically.
- Do treat the other party with respect and courtesy.
- Do request assistance such as mediation, fact-finding, and/or arbitration if your differences with the other party cannot be resolved without outside help.
- Do compliment the other party on their hard work leading to the agreement.
- Do commit yourself to working with the other party to initiate win/win (if win/win has not already been initiated), and build upon it for the long-term benefit of both parties, the students, the employees, the administrators, the board of education, and the community at large [1 – 3].

Along with the listing of some do's for collective bargaining, there are also some *maybe's*. These maybe's represent the gray areas that must be decided on a case by case basis by the parties who are involved in collective bargaining.

THE MAYBE'S OF COLLECTIVE BARGAINING

The major maybe's to be considered during any phase of collective bargaining will be varied in number and type, depending on the current phase and state of the collective bargaining process that exists in the school district at a specific point in time. The major maybe's, however, will most certainly include the following.

- Maybe an attorney should serve as the chief negotiator for the negotiating team. The attorney should be very active in the wording of proposals and counters, and should serve as the resident expert in the caucuses with the purpose of offering advice on the legality of what is being proposed by either side.
- Maybe the union should allow a state's uniserve director to serve as the chief negotiator for the negotiating team.
- Maybe the board of education's negotiating team should include some board member representation. Many persons, however, feel that having a board member as part of the composition of the negotiating team is a major mistake.
- Maybe the superintendent should sit in as a member of the board of education's negotiating team.

- Maybe the guidelines given by the board to its negotiating team should low ball – i.e., what it eventually would feel is adequate.
- Maybe the guidelines given the union's negotiating team should high ball – i.e., what the union would eventually feel is a fair settlement.
- Maybe the ground rules agreed to for negotiations should include no publicity, closed sessions, and TA'ing (tentatively agreeing on) each article as it is agreed to by both parties.
- Maybe at the early signs of a possible impasse developing, both parties should request that PERB (Public Employment Relations Board) assigns a mediator to the negotiations.
- Maybe a fact finder should be selected if the mediator is not able to get both parties to agree.
- Maybe an arbitration panel should be selected if the fact finder's recommendations are not accepted, and the public pressure exerted after the fact finder's publication of her/his findings is not sufficient to cause agreement to be reached between the two parties.
- Maybe both parties should choose to make the arbitration panel's rulings mandates for settlement.
- Maybe the union should involve its members in work-to-rule behavior if the contract negotiations reach a critical stage.
- Maybe the board of education's administrators should develop a detailed strike plan, if a strike appears to be a good possibility. It is important that the final strike plan be known only to a very few, and that it best be kept confidential until it is actually put into use.
- Maybe the union should take a strike vote and eventually go on strike if it feels there is no other way to resolve the impasse.
- Maybe cooler and more logical heads can prevail and reach agreement by attempting new offers and using new strategies in the hopes of averting any serious long-term damage to union/management relations well into the future [4,5].

Now that the do's and maybe's of collective bargaining have been explored, one area of discussion remains. The *don'ts* of collective bargaining share equal importance with the do's.

THE DON'TS OF COLLECTIVE BARGAINING

The don'ts may somewhat differ from school district to school district, and they may differ within the same school district at different points in time and during different phases of the collective bargaining process. Be this as it may, there are some universal don'ts that are worthy of emphasis.

- Don't assume that any phase of the collective bargaining process is destined to be adversarial.
- Don't assume that the members of the opposite party have negative intentions, nor that they can't be trusted.
- Don't think of collective bargaining as a battlefield, wherein the other party is the enemy and wherein you must be victorious in all battles.
- Don't ever participate in any collective bargaining phase without doing your homework and being fully prepared.
- Don't look at the negatives, but find the sunshine at the end of the process.
- Don't give up on the other party prematurely.
- Don't be afraid to ask for outside assistance if both parties are stuck in neutral.
- Don't forget that the collective bargaining process is a long-term commitment to fairness and equity in the relations between employees and those who employ them. It is not a quick fix proposition.
- Don't allow any animosities, distrust, or personality conflicts to continue. Resolve them as quickly as possible. Also, develop harmonious long-term relationships between union and management whenever possible [6].

Now that we have briefly outlined the do's, maybe's, and don'ts of collective bargaining, let's turn to the topics of the benefits and losses for both labor and management that are involved in the process of collective bargaining.

THE BENEFITS OF COLLECTIVE BARGAINING FOR LABOR AND MANAGEMENT

It is quite obvious that many state legislatures assumed collective bargaining was beneficial, as most states have passed collective bargaining laws. These laws permit employees in public employment situations, including public school districts, to bargain with their employer over the terms of some of the conditions of their employment, although states differ in the specific items about which they: (1) mandate bargaining, (2) permit bargaining, and (3) prohibit bargaining [7]. A mandated area may be salaries, permitted areas may include class size or teacher load, and a prohibited area may be the right to strike. Regardless of what is permitted, mandated, and/or prohibited, collective bargaining has benefits for both labor and management. Some of these benefits include the following.

- Collective bargaining provides a uniform and continuous means of communication on matters of importance to both employees and their employer.
- Collective bargaining simplifies the number of unions or the numbers of employee-selected leadership personnel that management must contact to resolve issues. This simplification occurs when a specific union is certified, after an election supervised by PERB determines that the majority of the employees in the designated unit desire that specific union to be their sole representative for collective bargaining purposes. It may also, however, have the effect of lessening the number of union leadership personnel that management can contact to resolve issues.
- Collective bargaining causes the two parties to negotiate a master contractual agreement, which spells out *in writing* the contractual details of the relationships between employees and administrators and between the union and management. This contract provides the day-to-day rules that guide the actions of both parties during the time the ratified contract is in effect.
- Collective bargaining allows for third party assistance when a contractual agreement between the two parties reaches the impasse stage.
- Collective bargaining laws prohibit strikes or other actions that are harmful to the public's interest.
- Collectively bargained master contractual agreements contain procedures for resolving grievances that arise during the time frame of the existing master contractual agreement. In many cases, the master contractual agreement will permit an outside third party to assist in resolving grievances when the two parties cannot resolve the grievance themselves.
- Collective bargaining laws prohibit unfair labor practices from being taken by the union or by management.

- Collective bargaining laws, through the rules and regulations promulgated by the PERB, provide a procedure designed to eliminate bad-faith bargaining practices by either party to the negotiations.
- Collective bargaining laws provide the same representational freedom that has long existed in the private employment sector [8].

Not only are there benefits to be derived from collective bargaining for both labor and management, but there are also some drawbacks that occur for both parties. Each individual involved will have to make her/his determination as to whether or not the benefits override the losses, or the losses override the benefits.

THE DRAWBACKS OF COLLECTIVE BARGAINING FOR LABOR AND MANAGEMENT

- Collective bargaining results in some loss of individual freedom for the individual employees. The whole essence of bargaining is groupness and constraints on the mass to bring the picture to the lowest (not highest) common denominator in employee-employer relationships.
- Collective bargaining tends to restrict the flexibility for making decisions related to items that are negotiated into the ratified master contractual agreement. Despite this, it does make for uniform handling of employees and it eliminates patronizing favorites. This is, however, hardly a trade-off for bargaining.
- Collective bargaining often leads to a robot-type situation of day-to-day operating by the book.
- Collective bargaining sometimes causes actions to take place that are not in the interest of the local union, when the local is tied into a unified structure with the union's state and national union officials.
- Collective bargaining sometimes restricts management and the board of education from operating the district in the manner in which it should be operated.
- Collective bargaining, when it becomes extremely adversarial in nature, can destroy excellent employee/administrator relationships for years, can cause a hostile climate in which to educate children and youth, and can result in a loss of emotional and financial support from the community at large [9,10].

THE BENEFITS AND DEFICITS OF
ADVERSARIAL BARGAINING

There is only one benefit to adversarial bargaining—it enables one party to overpower the other party, and thus gain more than it gives. The gains made may not even be defensible, but they certainly will raise havoc with any future labor/management relations. In addition, when the other party reverses the power dimension, it is certain that the other party will take punitive action and get back as much or more than they lost during the last adversarial bargaining of a master contractual agreement [11].

THE BENEFITS AND DEFICITS OF WIN/WIN BARGAINING

If the two parties can collectively bargain and if they can negotiate a master contractual agreement on the basis of collaborative action, within a climate of trust, caring, respect, and mutual problem solving, there really should not be any deficits associated with this win/win approach to collective bargaining. The benefits will accrue to the employees, the administrators, the board of education members, the union and management, and the community at large. But, mostly, they will accrue to the benefit of the students of the school district, for they will attend schools that have an exceptionally positive school climate [12].

SCHOOL-BASED MANAGEMENT AND ITS IMPACT ON
COLLECTIVE BARGAINING

Today, the most popular format for restructuring schools is that of school-based management. The legislatures of the states of Kentucky and Texas have mandated it, as have many local school boards and some superintendents. Some principals and teachers have received permission to attempt it. It matters little if the local school building wishes or doesn't wish to become the center of attention and accountability. The school-based management structure and process is building up a strong head of steam across the United States and Canada. Although this popular reform movement holds much promise for the positive restructuring of schools, it has dramatic potential for impact on the traditional way that collective bargaining has taken place in school districts [13].

In reality, many of the areas that are included in traditional ratified master contractual agreements become the business of a third party – that of the school-based management committees, comprised of teachers, parents, and the individual school building's principal. Even though the State of Kentucky does not have a collective bargaining law, many of the school districts have included some of the items contained in the Kentucky Reform Act of the 1990s in the decision-making power of the local school building's school-based management committee. A cursory glance through the major portions of the act related to school-based (sometimes called school-site in many locations) management, as outlined in Chapter 2, will illustrate the potential impact on the traditional collective bargaining decision-making structure.

Now that we have discussed the do's, maybe's, and don'ts of collective bargaining; the benefits and the drawbacks for both labor and management; the benefits and the drawbacks of adversarial and win/win collective bargaining; and the potential impact of school-based management on the traditional format of collective bargaining, it is clearly time to bring this book to closure. Closure will be accomplished by briefly summarizing all that has been covered in preceding pages [14].

A FINAL SUMMARY

Collective bargaining is a dynamic, important, and very serious process. Preparing for it, doing it, and living with its results will determine, in many aspects and to a large degree, the organizational structure that will exist in a school district and in the day-to-day procedures to be followed. Because of the impact on the school district's structure and procedures, the results of collective bargaining will have a significant effect on the climate and culture of the school district. In addition, the way it is conducted by union and management and the results achieved by it can strongly influence the attitudes of students, parents, taxpayers, and the citizenry of the school district. It is extremely important, and it must be handled carefully and wisely by all parties involved in it.

The innovation of school-based or site-based management, which promotes the direct involvement of employees and citizens in management decisions related to the individual school buildings, has been a main focus. If the school district allows school-based management teams to have authority over the selection of employees, the structure of the school day, and some budgetary areas, both union and management must take these matters seriously when managing or re-negotiating a master contract. Business-as-usual approaches will not suffice; the environment has changed substantially, and the tenor of collective negotiations will be profoundly altered.

In the introduction, the reader was promised a how-to-do-it road map that would present practical details on all the important aspects of collective bargaining at the local school district level. It proposed to set the stage by discussing how administrators and employees live and work together in the school district environment. Subsequent chapters detailed all of the strategies, tasks, events, and influences that bear on the collective bargaining process, from the initial certification election of a union through the preparation for, negotiation of, and administration of a union/management collective bargaining agreement. The book focused on administrators, teachers, and nonteaching employees, and on union and management groups who participate in the dynamic, emotional, and intellectually stimulating and draining process called collective bargaining. It also focused on win/win, win/lose, and lose/lose situations that affect the individuals and groups who work within the school district and that subsequently affect those who are served by the employees of the school district.

It is likely that every school district will have to endure win/lose or even lose/lose negotiations at one time or another. When such confrontational periods conclude, it is important to bury the bad feelings and look to the future of the district together. Never forget that teachers and administrators are all part of the same team, dedicated to educating the children and youth of their districts. No one will be well served if the school is allowed to become a battlefield, or if personal enmity is allowed to transcend the primary goal of education.

It is the authors' hope and belief that as groups continue to mature in this dramatic process of collective bargaining, they will recognize the power and benefits of a win/win approach. Through win/win, employees and administrators can come together with a realistic view of the district's resources and a realistic view of employees' needs, to produce the best overall educational plan possible. The collaborative atmosphere of win/win will permeate the district, improving the reputation of the schools and making all citizens more willing to contribute to the betterment of the children. Remember that the only reason schools exist is to educate children and youth — and if the students lose, no one wins.

REFERENCES

1. Nyland, L. 1987. "Win/Win Bargaining Pays Off," *Education Digest*, L111(1): 28–29.
2. Maddux, R. B. 1988. *Successful Negotiation—Effective "Win/Win" Strategies and Tactics*. Los Altos, CA: Crisp Publications, Inc.
3. Thompson, B. L. 1991. "Negotiation Training: Win/Win or What?" *Training*, 28(6):31–35.
4. Smith, S. C., D. Ball and D. Liontos. 1990. *Working Together—The Collaborative Style of Bargaining*. Eugene, OR: ERIC Clearinghouse on Educational Management, University of Oregon, pp. 58–59.
5. Barrett, J. T. 1985. *Labor-Management Cooperation in the Public Service: An Idea Whose Time Has Come*. Washington, DC: International Personnel Management Association, pp. 29–30.
6. Neal, R. 1980. *Bargaining Tactics—A Reference Manual for Public Sector Labor Negotiations*. Richard G. Neal Associates, pp. 39, 115, 193, 197.
7. Helsby, R. D., J. Tener and J. Lefkowitz, eds. 1985. *The Evolving Process—Collective Negotiations in Public Employment*. Fort Washington, PA: Labor Relations Press, pp. 5–12.
8. Coleman, C. J. 1990. *Managing Labor Relations in the Public Sector*. San Francisco, CA: Jossey-Bass Publishers, p. 32.
9. Castetter, W. B. 1986. *The Personnel Function in Education*. New York, NY: Macmillan Publishing Company, pp. 137–138.
10. Richardson, R. C. 1985. *Collective Bargaining by Objectives: A Positive Approach*. Englewood Cliffs, NJ: Prentice-Hall, Inc., p. 251.
11. Smith, S. C., D. Ball and D. Liontos., pp. 18–19.
12. Smith, S. C., D. Ball and D. Liontos., p. 12.
13. Nickoles, K. W. 1990. "Future Shock: What's Coming to the Bargaining Table," *School Business Affairs*, 56(12):36–38.
14. Miller, M. H., K. Noland and J. Schaaf. 1990. *A Guide to the Kentucky Education Reform Act*. Frankfort, KY: Legislative Research Commission, p. 6.

Selected Examples of Four States' Collective Bargaining Laws' Section on Representation

FROM MARYLAND

6-402. Employees may join organization; membership restrictions.

(a) *Employees may form and join organization* — Public school employees may form, join, and participate in the activities of employee organizations of their own choice for the purpose of being represented on all matters that relate to salaries, wages, hours, and other working conditions.

(b) *Membership restriction and dismissal* — An employee organization may establish reasonable:

(1) Restrictions as to who may join
(2) Provisions for the dismissal of individuals from the membership

6-403. Employees may refuse to join employee organizations. In most situations, this is bargainable and not part of the law. This is a good service to the nonunion teachers.

FROM MASSACHUSETTS

Chapter 150E — Labor relations: public employees (only as it impacts education).

''Employee'' any person in the executive or judicial branch of a governmental unit employed by a public employer except elected officials, appointed officials, members of any board or commission, representatives of any public employer, including the heads, directors and executive and administrative officers of departments and agencies of any public employer, and other managerial employees or confidential employees, and. . . . Employees shall be designated as managerial employees only if they (a) participate to a substantial degree in formulating or determining policy, or (b) assist to a substantial degree in the

213

preparation for or the conduct of collective bargaining on behalf of a public employer, or (c) have a substantial responsibility involving the exercise of independent judgment of an appellate responsibility not initially in effect in the administration of a collective bargaining agreement or in personnel administration. Employees shall be designated as confidential employees only if they directly assist and act in a confidential capacity to a person or persons otherwise excluded from coverage under this chapter.

FROM MISSOURI

105.500 Definitions—Unless the context otherwise requires, the following words and phrases mean:

(1) "Appropriate unit" means a unit of employees . . . or in a function of a public body which establishes a clear and identifiable community of interest among the employees concerned.

FROM OREGON

Collective Bargaining

(1) "Appropriate bargaining unit" means the unit designated by the board to be appropriate for the purpose of collective bargaining.

Example Provisions from Local School Districts' Master Contracts Related to Insubordination, Incompetency, Contract Management, and Grievance Procedures

POLICY FOR INSUBORDINATION, INCOMPETENCY, OR CONTRACT MISMANAGEMENT BY MANAGEMENT PERSONNEL

Management personnel shall be those who are not allowed to be members of the employee union for those subordinate to the level of the administrator.

When a proved situation arises that the management person has violated a responsibility called for in her/his personal contract, the superintendent shall hear the administrator and the person bringing charges against her/him.

The administrator can bring to the hearing any witness she/he shall determine to be appropriate to the resolution of the situation. The person bringing the charges must present hard evidence that the infraction did in fact take place. The use of witnesses shall be expected and reasonable.

GRIEVANCE PROCEDURE

A. A ''Grievance'' is a claim, based upon a teacher's or group of teachers' belief that there has been a violation, misinterpretation, or misapplication of any provision of this Agreement. The ''Grievance Procedure'' shall not apply to any matter which is prescribed by law, State Regulation, over which the Board is without power to act. No Board prerogative shall be made the subject of a grievance. A grievance may be filed by the Association only when the grievance applies to more than one building and a group of teachers with a common complaint have requested such action.

B. Procedure: Since it is important that grievances be processed as rapidly as possible, the number of days indicated at each Step

215

should be considered as maximum and every effort will be made to expedite the process. The time limits specified may, however, be extended by mutual agreement.

In the event a grievance is filed on or after 1 June, which, if left unresolved until the beginning of the following school year, could result in irreparable harm to a party in interest, the time limits set forth herein shall be reduced so that the grievance procedure may be exhausted prior to the end of the school term, or as soon thereafter as is practicable.

1. *Level One* — A teacher with a grievance shall first discuss it with her/his immediate supervisor or principal, within ten (10) school days from the time of the incident over which the teacher is aggrieved or has reasonable knowledge of the incident. At her/his option, the teacher may invite an Association representative to be present while the grievance is discussed. Every effort shall be made to resolve the grievance informally. If the grievance is not resolved, the matter shall be reduced to writing by the grievant and submitted to the same principal/supervisor. The grievance must be reduced to writing, on the proper grievance form, two (2) school days from the time of the discussion between the grievant and her/his supervisor. Within two (2) school days after presentation of the written grievance, the principal/supervisor shall give her/his answer in writing to the grievance. The Association shall receive a copy.

2. *Level Two* — In the event that the aggrieved person is not satisfied with the disposition of her/his grievance at Level One, or in the event that no decision has been rendered within two (2) school days after the presentation of the grievance, she/he may file the grievance in writing with the Association or its representative within five (5) school days after the decision at Level One, or lack of, at Level One.

   The Association shall make a judgement on the merits of the grievance. If the Association decides that the grievance lacks merit, or that the decision at Level One is not in the best interests of the educational system, it shall notify the teacher and the principal, and the matter insofar as the Association is concerned, is terminated.

   If the Association decides, in its opinion, the grievance has merit, it shall refer such grievance in writing to the Superintendent, or such person as the Superintendent may designate, within five (5) school days after receipt of the grievance from the grievant. Copies shall also go to the Superintendent or her/his designate, the appropriate Director and the Principal/Supervisor.

Within five (5) school days after the Superintendent or designate receives a grievance, she/he shall meet with the aggrieved teacher and a representative or representatives (maximum—5) of the Association, in an effort to resolve her/his grievance. If the grievance is transmitted directly to the Superintendent or designate (omitting Level One), she/he shall meet with the Association within five (5) school days. The decision on the grievance shall be rendered in writing within five (5) school days after such hearing; copies sent to the aggrieved, the Association, the principal/supervisor, the appropriate Director and the Superintendent.

3. *Level Three*—If the Grievance is not settled at Level Two, it may be referred in writing to the Board of Education within five (5) school days after receipt of the decision in Level Two. The Board shall hold a hearing, or designate one or more of its members to hold a hearing, or otherwise investigate the grievance, or prescribe such other procedures as it may deem appropriate for consideration of the grievance. The Association shall have an opportunity to present its view at this level within twenty (20) days to the Board, or its representative, as it may authorize. Within twenty-five (25) school days after receipt of the grievance, the Board shall render a decision on the grievance and present it in writing to the aggrieved teacher, the Association, the Principal/Supervisor, the appropriate Director and the Superintendent.

4. *Level Four*

   (a) If the grievance is not settled at Level Three, the Association may, within ten (10) school days, after the receipt of the Board's decision at Level Three, request that the grievance be submitted to arbitration. The request for submission to arbitration shall be made by written notice to the Board.

   (b) Within (10) school days after the date of a written request for arbitration, a committee of the Board, or its designated representative, and the Association, may agree upon a mutually acceptable arbitrator. If the parties are unable to agree upon an arbitrator, within the ten (10) day period herein provided, either the Board or the Association may, within twenty (20) school days after the date of the written request for arbitration, request the American Arbitration Association to submit a list of qualified arbitrators. The arbitrator shall then be selected according to the rules of the American Arbitration Association.

(c) The arbitrator shall hear the grievance in dispute and shall render her/his decision in writing within thirty (30) days from the close of the hearing. The arbitrator's decision shall be submitted in writing and shall set forth her/his findings and conclusions with respect to the issue submitted to arbitration. The arbitrator shall confine her/his decision to the particular case submitted to her/him. Both parties agree to be bound by the award of the arbitrator and agree that judgement thereon may be entered in any court of competent jurisdiction.

(d) The arbitrator shall have no authority except to pass upon alleged violations of the express provisions of this Agreement and to determine disputes involving the application or interpretation of this Agreement.

The arbitrator shall construe this Agreement in a manner which does not interfere with the exercise of the Board's rights and responsibilities, except to the extent that such rights and responsibilities may be expressly limited by the terms of this Agreement.

(e) The arbitrator shall have no power or authority to add to, subtract from, or modify any of the terms of this Agreement and shall not substitute her/his judgement for that of the Board where the Board is given discretion by the terms of this Agreement. The arbitrator shall not render any decision which would require or permit an action in violation of the Michigan School Laws. The termination of probationary teachers shall not be subject to arbitration.

(f) The arbitrator's fees and expenses shall be shared equally by the Board and the Association. The expenses and compensation of any witness or participants in the arbitration shall be paid by the party calling such witness or requesting such participant.

(g) A complaint or dispute involving the discharge or demotion of a teacher on continuing tenure shall not be subject to the grievance and arbitration procedure, but shall be presented, heard, and resolved pursuant to the provisions of Act 4, Public Acts of Michigan, 1937 (Ed. Sess.), as amended (Tenure of Teachers Act).

(h) All arbitration hearings shall be held in the school district.

C. Rights of Teachers to Representation

1. Members of the Association involved in the Association business shall continue to enjoy the good faith and professional treatment they have enjoyed in the past.

2. The Association shall have the right to be present and to state its view at all stages of this grievance procedure. Either party at any level may be represented by counsel, but reasonable notice shall be given the other party in advance, if counsel is to be present.

3. Nothing contained herein shall be construed to prevent any individual teacher from presenting a grievance and having the grievance adjusted at Level One, without intervention of the Association, if the adjustment is not consistent with the terms of this Agreement, provided that the Association has been given the opportunity to be present at such adjustment.

D. Miscellaneous

1. Levels Two and Three of this Grievance Procedure may be passed to the next level for any reason as determined by the Board, or its representative (e.g., no authority to make the judgement, a decision has been rendered in a similar previous decision). However, a hearing must be held at one of the above levels.

2. It is assumed that grievance problems will be handled at a time other than when the teacher is at work, and that members of the Association will be present to process grievances promptly. In the event this is not possible due to conflict in schedules (unwillingness of witnesses to testify after hours), or for other reasons, the grievance will be processed during the working day, and the Association for the teacher (if the Association will not be present) will pay the cost of its member and witnesses, and the Board will pay its witnesses. If Level Four is imposed, all costs

will be shared equally by the Association and the Board (if there are any costs).

3. If more than one teacher has a similar complaint, which has been individually discussed as provided in Level One, the Association may file a grievance to be commenced at Level Two, in lieu of individual grievances.

4. Failure at any level of this procedure to communicate the decision of a grievance within the specified time limit shall permit the Association to proceed to the next Level of the procedure.

5. Failure to file the grievance in writing, as specified in Level One, or to forward as specified in Levels Two, Three, or Four, shall mean the grievance is waived.

6. If the employee elects to be represented, she/he must still be present at any Level of the grievance procedure, where her/his grievance is to be discussed, except that she/he need not be present where it is mutually agreed that no facts are in dispute, and that the sole question is the interpretation of this Agreement.

7. The filing of a grievance shall in no way interfere with the right of the Board to proceed in carrying out its management responsibilities, subject to the final decision of the grievance.

8. The Association is prohibited from processing a grievance on behalf of an employee or group of employees without her/his (their) consent.

9. Grievance decisions with individual employees which appear in conflict with this Agreement may be grieved by the Association beginning with Level Two.

10. All documents, communications, and records dealing with the processing of a grievance shall be filed separately from the building personnel files of the participant.

Examples of Cost and Power Analyses of Master Contract Proposals

AS proposals are presented by either party (union or management) to the collective bargaining process, it is crucial that each proposal is analyzed for its costs and its power relationships. The cost analysis is especially crucial if a multiple-year contract agreement is to be ratified.

Three examples will illustrate the importance of these analyses of proposals.

EXAMPLE ONE

The union's negotiating team proposes changing the health insurance paid by the school district to coverage of spouse and to full family coverage from single employee coverage. Since it is anticipated that the master contract will eventually be ratified, the cost impact will be as follows.

Analysis

(1) Current base year's cost per single employee	$1,450
(2) Added cost per spouse = + $950	$2,400
(3) Added cost per full family = + $1,450	$2,900
(4) Average increase in premium over the past five (5) years = 18%	
(5) Anticipated number of single employees – 1,000	
(6) Anticipated number of spousal coverage – 800	
(7) Anticipated number of full family employees – 800	

(1) Current base year's cost:	$1,450,000
(2) Future year one's cost	$3,976,600

Base year	$1,450,000
Spouse $950 × 800	760,000
Full family $1450 × 800	1,160,000
Total base	3,370,000
Anticipated yearly 18% premium increase	× 18
Premium increase	606,600
Total	3,976,600

(3) Year two's cost: $4,692,388
    (18% premium increase × $3,976,600 = $715,788)
    ($3,976,600 + $715,788)

(4) Year three's increase: $5,537,018
    (18% premium increase × $4,692,388 = $844,630)
    ($4,692,388 + $844,630)

Note the tremendous escalation of costs to the district if the board of education ratifies a three-year master contract that includes this additional employee health benefit. The benefit request is a reasonable one, but the cost may be prohibitive.

EXAMPLE TWO

The board of education's collective bargaining team proposes that all teachers be required to attend one week of staff development activities prior to the beginning of school for the students. During this week, the board's team proposes that the teachers will be paid the substitute teachers' daily rate of forty dollars ($40) rather than their daily contracted salary rate.

Analysis

(1) *Power* is in favor of the board of education in that it, in essence, is *requiring* an extra week of work at a reduced pay rate.

(2) *Cost to board* for 400 teachers = $80,000
    (400 × $40 = $16,000 × 5 days)

(3) *Cost to teachers* for 400 teachers = $376,000
    The average teacher salary computed on a daily basis is $228 and they will work for $40. This is a loss per day of $188.
    ($188 × 400 teachers = $75,200 × 5 days)

EXAMPLE THREE

The union proposes that no board policy or administrative rules and regulations shall be adopted or promulgated without the union first having received the proposed policy or rules and regulations at least one calendar month prior to adoption. Also, the union will be given the opportunity for a hearing, if it so chooses, on the matter prior to adoption at a legally constituted board meeting.

Analysis

If this proposal is accepted as part of a ratified master contractual agreement, the union is gaining significant power in that it obtains a review procedure prior to any important board of education policy or rules and regulations action. It also gains a public hearing that can be utilized to strategize a negative media event opposing the policy or rules and regulations if the union chooses to be in opposition.

The board of education loses power and it has nothing to gain from agreeing to this proposal.

A Format for Analyzing Fringe Benefits and the Costs of Master Contract Articles

THE first thing needed is a series of several grids on which up-to-date information is posted so that each cell becomes a cost item based upon the number that is reflected therein. Here is an example of a ''scatter grid'' for a public school district showing the total number of employees that would be impacted by the settlement. The example below is for your study and understanding so that you can prepare a similar grid showing the number of teachers in each cell represented by the number of years of teaching credit (in the district), down the column and across the columns showing the degree status your district honors for pay.

No. Teachers	BA	+15	+30	MA	+15	+30	EdS	EdD
1	12			6	1			
2	15	10	5	6	11			
3	5	20	21	11	11			
4			25	7	7			
5	2	3	26	22	10	5	1	6

You can also use this same grid for the cost of various leave days during the prior year of school. By substituting the numbers in the cell with the facts of cost for subs, you can also cost-out the days being used and number being requested. The grid on days *not* taught will be extremely valuable for the management team. It shows the number of teachers that used each of the columns for leave during the year.

No. Days	Funeral	Sick	Personal	Pregnancy	Misc.
1	12	3,532	121	11	15
2	45	2,128	265	35	26
3	5	1,120	11	11	26

No. Days	Funeral	Sick	Personal	Pregnancy	Misc.
4	5	189		7	8
5	1	102		20	5

When more than five consecutive days are used for any purpose, a tally must be kept and then rows added to the grid as the numbers are finalized. This grid already shows that the regular teachers were absent from the classroom for 142 funeral days, 12,414 sick days, 684 personal days, 242 pregnancy days (short term), 202 miscellaneous days including court appearances, etc. (Don't forget your sabbatical costs should be added to this grid, also.)

Using this grid, the cost of an increase can be computed rather easily on a computer by merely plugging in the increase costs (by cell) and using the number of teachers as the multiplier for the product to be printed in a like grid. The totals will show you where the costs are highest for your counterproposals.

A separate grid needs to be developed by the fringe benefit office so that the same type of information will be available for costing the fringe benefits.

Type Coverage	Single	Spouse	Family	Other
BCBS	462	322	621	
Major medical	12	106		
Dental	2	60	0	
Life	0	20	121	11
Optical	25	7	7	

In this grid, you will use the cost of Blue Cross/Blue Shield for a single member times the 462 persons and the product would go into the cell as follows $$$$$$/462 and follow this same scheme in each cell of the grid. When a proposal is made, the new product would go into the cell. There will be some shifting of costs so only the column's total will make the right data for a decision to be made.

Survey of Collective Bargaining Positions by Washington, D.C. and All the States in the United States

STATES WHERE THERE IS NO BARGAINING LAW

Alabama	Nebraska
Arizona	North Carolina
Arkansas	Rhode Island
Colorado	South Carolina
Georgia	Texas
Kentucky	Utah
Louisiana	Virginia
Mississippi	West Virginia
Missouri	Wyoming

STATES WHERE LEGISLATIVE ACTION WAS CONSIDERED DURING 1989 OR 1990

Louisiana has bills presented annually to allow collective bargaining as there are currently six parishes (counties) that do formal bargaining, and as there is no law denying, nor none permitting this action.

North Dakota is considering extending law to *binding arbitration.*

South Dakota considers changes annually.

West Virginia, as late as 1989, defeated a bill to allow public sector (educators) bargaining rights.

STATES THAT HAVE ENACTED COLLECTIVE BARGAINING LAWS

Alaska	Nevada
California	New Hampshire
Connecticut	New Jersey
Delaware	New Mexico

Florida
Hawaii
Idaho
Illinois
Indiana
Iowa
Kansas
Maine
Maryland
Massachusetts
Michigan
Minnesota
Montana

New York
North Dakota
Ohio
Oklahoma
Oregon
Pennsylvania
South Dakota
Tennessee
Vermont
Washington
Washington, D.C.
Wisconsin

NAMES OF COLLECTIVE BARGAINING LAWS, DATE ENACTED, CONTROLLING ADMINISTRATIVE BOARD

Names of Bargaining Laws		Date	Controlling Board
Alaska	dr. 180, SCA 1990	1990	Labor Relations Agency
California	Educ. Emps. Relations Act	1975	Pub. Emp. Relations Board
Connecticut	Teacher Negotiation Act	1961 [1]	
Delaware	Pub. Emps. Relation Act	1982	Pub. Emp. Rels. Bd.
Florida	Chapter 447 Florida Statutes	1974	Pub. Emp. Rels. Comm.
Hawaii	Ch. 89[2]	1970	HI Labor Rels. Bd.
Idaho	Statute FL 1971, Ch. 103	1970	Local Board of Trustees of School District
Illinois	IL Ed. Lab Rels. Act	1984	IL Ed. Labor Rel. Bd.
Indiana	Public Law 217	1973	Ed. Emps. Rels. Bd.
Iowa	IA Public Ed. Rels. Act	1975	Pub. Emp. Rels. Bd.

[1]CT—Educational Employees Relations Act.
[2]HI—Hawaii Revised Statutes Collective Bargaining in Public Employment.

Names of Bargaining Laws		Date	Controlling Board
Kansas	Certificate Laws of 1970 Ch. 2,84	1970	Secretary of Human Res.
Maine	Municipal Emps. Labor Rels. Act	1974	ME Labor Rels. Bd.
Maryland	Annotated code; Art. 778, 160	1969	Local Board of Trustees of School District
Massachusetts	An act related to collective bargaining by publ. employees—Chap. 150E	1973	Labor Rels. Commission
Michigan	Publ. Emps. Relations Act	1965	MI Emp. Rels. Comm.
Minnesota	MS-179-A[3]	1975	Unknown
Montana	Chapter 441	1973	Board of Personnel Appeals
Nevada	Relations between gov't. and pub. emps. NRS 288	1969	Local Gov't. Employees Mgt. Rels. Board
New Hampshire	Chap. 273-A[4]	1975	Pub. Emp. Labor Rels. Bd.
New Jersey	Employee-Employer Rels. Act 34:13A-1 et seq.	1941	NJ Pub. Emp. Rels. Bd.
New Mexico	3A-1 et. seq.		
New York	Ch. 392 of Laws of 1967	1967	Pub. Emp. Rels. Bd.
N. Dakota	15-38.1[5]	1979	Educ. Fact-Finding Comm.
Ohio	FB 133	1984	State Employment Rels. Board

---

[3]MN—Public Relations Labor Relations Act.
[4]NH—Public Relations Labor Relations Act.
[5]ND—Teachers Representation and Negotiations.

Names of Bargaining Laws		Date	Controlling Board
Oklahoma	Negotiations between school employees and districts	1978	None
Oregon	Pub. Emp. Collective Bargaining Act	1969	Educ. Relations Bd.
Pennsylvania	PA Pub. Emp. Rels. Act	1970	PA Labor Rels. Bd.
S. Dakota	Ch. 88 of Laws of 1969	1969	Div. of Labor and Mgmt. Dept. of Labor
Tennessee	Ed. Prof'l. Negotiation Act	1978	None
Vermont	16V.S.A. Ch. 57[6]	1969	Labor Rels. Bd.
Washington	Educ'l. Emp. Relations Act	1975	Pub. Emp. Rels. Comm.
Wisconsin	Chap. 111.70[7]	1959	WI Emp. Rels. Comm.
Washington D.C.	D.C. Gov't. Comprehensive Merit Personnel Act	1978	Pub. Emp. Rels. Bd.

[6]VT—Labor Relations for Teachers.
[7]WI—Public Employees Collective Bargaining Law.

An Example of One State's Impasse Procedures—Iowa's Public Employment Relations Act

20.19 IMPASSE PROCEDURES – AGREEMENT OF PARTIES

As the first step in the performance of their duty to bargain, the public employer and the employee organization shall endeavor to agree upon impasse procedures. Such agreement shall provide for implementation of these impasse procedures not later than one hundred twenty days prior to the certified budget submission date of the public employer. If the parties fail to agree upon impasse procedures under the provisions of this section, the impasse procedures provided in sections 20.20 to 20.22 shall apply [C75,77,79,81,20.19].

20.20 MEDIATION

In the absence of an impasse agreement between the parties or the failure of either party to utilize its procedures, one hundred twenty days prior to the certified budget submission date, the board shall, upon the request of either party, appoint an impartial and disinterested person to act as mediator. It shall be the function of the mediator to bring the parties together to effectuate a settlement of the dispute, but the mediator may not compel the parties to agree [C75,77,79,81,20.20].

Referred to in 20.19.

20.21 FACT-FINDING

If the impasse persists ten days after the mediator has been appointed, the board shall appoint a fact finder representative of the public, from a list of qualified persons maintained by the board. The fact finder shall conduct a hearing, may administer oaths, and may request the board to issue subpoenas. The fact finder shall make written findings of facts and recommendations for resolution of the dispute and, not later than fifteen days from the day of appointment, shall serve such findings on the public employer and the certified employee organization.

The public employer and the certified employee organization shall immediately accept the fact finder's recommendation or shall within five days submit the fact finder's recommendations to the governing body and members of the certified employee organization for acceptance or rejection. If the dispute continues ten days after the report is submitted, the report shall be made public by the board [C75,77, 79,81,20.21].

Referred to in 20.19.

20.22 BINDING ARBITRATION

1. If an impasse persists after the findings of fact and recommendations are made public by the fact finder, the parties may continue to negotiate or, the board shall have the power, upon request of either party, to arrange for arbitration, which shall be binding. The request for arbitration shall be in writing and a copy of the request shall be served upon the other party.

2. Each party shall submit to the board with four days of request a final offer on the impasse items with proof of service of a copy upon the other party. Each party shall also submit a copy of a draft of the proposed collective bargaining agreement to the extent to which agreement has been reached and the name of its selected arbitrator. The parties may continue to negotiate all offers until an agreement is reached or a decision rendered by the panel of arbitrators.

   As an alternative procedure, the two parties may agree to submit the dispute to a single arbitrator. If the parties cannot agree on the arbitrator within four days, the selection shall be made pursuant to Subsection 5. The full costs of arbitration under this provision shall be shared equally by the parties to the dispute.

3. The submission of the impasse items to the arbitrators shall be limited to those issues that had been considered by the fact finder and upon which the parties have not reached agreement. With respect to each such item, the arbitration board award shall be restricted to the final offers on each impasse item submitted by the parties to the arbitration board or to the recommendation of the fact finder on each impasse item.

4. The panel of arbitrators shall consist of three members appointed in the following manner:

   a. One member shall be appointed by the public employer.
   b. One member shall be appointed by the employee organization.
   c. One member shall be appointed mutually by the members appointed by the public employer and the employee organization. The last number appointed shall be the chairperson of the panel of arbitrators. No member appointed shall be an employee of the parties.
   d. The public employer and employee organization shall each pay the fees and expenses incurred by the arbitrator each selected. The fee and expenses of the chairperson of the panel and all other costs of arbitration shall be shared equally.

5. If the third member has not been selected within four days of notification as provided in Subsection 2, a list of three arbitrators shall be submitted to the parties by the board. The two arbitrators selected by the public employer and the employee organization shall determine by lot which arbitrator shall remove the first name from the list submitted by the board. The arbitrator having the right to remove the first name shall do so within two days and the second arbitrator shall have one additional day to remove one of the two remaining names. The person whose name remains shall become the chairperson of the panel of arbitrators and shall call a meeting within ten days at a location designated by the chairperson.

6. If a vacancy should occur on the panel of arbitrators, the selection for replacement of such member shall be in the same manner and within the same time limits as the original member was chosen. No final selection under Subsection 9 shall be made by the board until the vacancy has been filled.

7. The panel of arbitrators shall at no time engage in an effort to mediate or otherwise settle the dispute in any manner other than that prescribed in this section.

8. From the time of appointment until such time as the panel of arbitrators makes its final determination, there shall be no discussion concerning recommendations for settlement of the dispute by the members of the panel of arbitrators with parties other than those who are direct parties to the dispute. The panel of arbitrators may conduct formal or informal hearings to discuss offers submitted by both parties.

9. The panel of arbitrators shall consider, in addition to any other relevant factors, the following factors:

   a. Past collective bargaining contracts between the parties including the bargaining that led up to such contracts.
   b. Comparison of wages, hours and conditions of employment of the involved public employees with those of other public employees doing comparable work, giving consideration to factors peculiar to the area and the classifications involved.
   c. The interests and welfare of the public, the ability of the public employer to finance economic adjustments and the effect of such adjustments on the normal standard of services.
   d. The power of the public employer to levy taxes and appropriate funds for the conduct of its operations.

10. The chairperson of the panel of arbitrators may hold hearings and administer oaths, examine witnesses and documents, take testimony and receive evidence, issue subpoenas to compel the attendance of witnesses and the production of records, and delegate such powers to other members of the panel of arbitrators. The chairperson of the panel of arbitrators may petition the district court at the seat of government or of the county in which any hearing is held to enforce the order of the chairpersons compelling the attendance of witnesses and the production of records.

11. A majority of the panel of arbitrators shall select within fifteen days after its final meeting the most reasonable offer, in its judgement, of the final offers on each impasse item submitted by the parties, or the recommendations of the fact finder on each impasse item.

12. The selections by the panel of arbitrators and items agreed upon by the public employer and the employee organization, shall be deemed to be the collective bargaining agreement between the parties.

13. The determination of the panel of arbitrators shall be by majority vote and shall be final and binding subject to the provisions of Section 20.17, Subsection 6. The panel of arbitrators shall give written explanation for its selection and inform the parties of its decision [C75,77,79,81,20.22].

Referred to in 20.19.

Main Points of Kentucky's Reform Act of 1990 Related to School-Based Decision Making (SBDM)

1. By 1/1/91 all school boards shall adopt policy to promote SBDM, and modify existing policies if necessary.
2. By 6/30/91 each school district shall have a minimum of one school in SBDM. If none (two-thirds of the faculty) vote to volunteer, the superintendent selects one. By 7/1/96 all schools in Kentucky shall implement SBDM. There are exceptions to this requirement; districts with only one school do not have to participate, and schools meeting their goals may be exempt.
3. Each participating school shall form a school council comprised of two parents, three teachers and the principal. Parents cannot be related to any school employee.
4. The council's responsibilities include:

   a. Establishing school policy in accordance with the goals of the Reform Act of 1990, and with local school board goals and policy.
   b. The principal shall be the primary administrator and instructional leader.
   c. All certified staff members ''may'' be participants in committees and a majority of each committee shall ''elect'' a chair to serve a one year term.
   d. Within available funds, the council ''shall'' determine the number of persons to be employed in each job classification at the school, and it can make personnel decisions on vacancies. It cannot recommend transfer or dismissal.
   e. The council ''shall'' determine which instructional materials and student support services shall be provided in the school.
   f. From a list of applicants recommended by the superintendent, the principal ''shall'' select personnel to fill vacancies after consultation with the school council.
   g. To fill a principal vacancy, the school council ''shall'' select

from among those persons recommended by the superintendent, and the superintendent "shall" provide additional applicants upon request.

5. The council shall adopt policies to be implemented by the principal in these additional areas:

   a. Determination of curriculum, including needs assessment, curriculum development, alignment with state standards, technology utilization, and program appraisal within the local school board's policy.
   b. Assignment of "all" instructional and non-instructional staff time.
   c. Assignment of students to classes and programs.
   d. Determine the schedule of the school day and week, subject to the beginning and ending times and the school calendar set by the board of education.
   e. Determine the use of school space during the school day.
   f. Plan and resolve issues regarding instructional practices.
   g. Select and implement discipline and classroom management techniques, including the roles of students, parents, teachers, counselors and principals.
   h. Select extracurricular programs and determine policies relating to student participation based on academic and attendance requirements, program evaluations and supervision.

6. The school board "shall" make liability insurance available to all members of the school council when they are performing their council related duties.

Confidential Contingency Plan for Use during a Strike

1. A special confidential ''hotline'' is established by which you can report any strike activities that are taking place at your site, and from which you can receive the latest status report from management's central strike control. The phone number is (906) 432-1161 (fictitious phone number).

2. From this date forward, administrators hearing rumors or possessing pertinent information should immediately report the same to the superintendent of schools. The superintendent shall immediately share this information with the school district's chief negotiator, and the superintendent shall make a judgement as to whether or not to share this information with the board of education president (or with the board member selected as the primary communication contact person for the board of education). The board president will then decide whether or not to share this information with other board members, and the chief negotiator will decide whether or not any specific administrators will be informed—this decision by the chief negotiator will be on a ''need to know'' basis.

3. Parents, students, community members, or employees who phone with questions or comments are to be told that a public hotline has been established by the board which will be connected to a recorder that will provide the latest updated information on the situation and on the progress to date. Also, please ask them not to attempt to phone board members or administrators, because these personnel have great responsibilities to carry out during this time of crisis. Finally, assure them that the hotline messages will be updated at least once per day and sooner if that is required. This public hotline number is (906) 321-0567 (fictitious phone number).

4. Daily during the strike, each administrator is to be prepared to comply with the following regimen.

a. Hand deliver a daily report on the form outlined below to the office of the superintendent of schools by 5:00 P.M. daily.

DAILY STRIKE REPORT

School _____   Date _____

9:00 A.M. Report

Number of *employees* present _____

Number of students present (report only if we attempt to continue student instruction during the strike) _____

Do you have pickets? _____   How many? _____

Any unusual union activity (explain)? _____

1:30 P.M. Report

Number of *employees* present _____

Number of students present _____

Do you have pickets? _____   How many? _____

Any unusual union activity (explain)? _____

4:00 P.M. Report

Number of *employees* present _____

Number of students present _____

Do you have pickets? _____   How many? _____

Any unusual union activity (explain)? _____

Reported by (administrator's signature):

_____

b. Prepare for a brief 4:30 P.M. meeting daily in the superintendent's office.

5. Also, during the strike, it should be understood that:

a. Any questions from the media are to be referred to the district's chief negotiator and spokesperson, and the chief negotiator will automatically be forwarding appropriate releases to the media covering our school district.

b. Any media representative wishing to visit within any school building shall be accompanied by the building principal or by the administrator in charge of the building at the point of the requested visit. This requirement is put in place to have an eyewitness to what the media representative sees, and to check the accuracy of the media representative's report. It also is being put into place, since frequently the presence of a media representative will be cause for heightened union activity.

c. Any communication with teachers or with the teachers' union representatives is to be handled *in writing solely by the district's chief negotiator.*

d. Any contact with attorneys shall be by the district's chief negotiator or the superintendent of schools.

e. All communication with the board of education president or with board of education members shall be through the superintendent of schools, or from the superintendent of schools to the board president where the board president will communicate with the other board of education members.

f. All communication with other governmental agencies, including the police and other school districts, shall be through the negotiator after the chief negotiator has reviewed the communications with the superintendent of schools.

g. Nonpublic school officials shall be contacted by the superintendent of schools, and the superintendent of schools shall make any necessary decision as to future transportation and other traditional services provided by the school district to the nonpublic schools in the school district. The same procedures will prevail in regards to the special education and vocational education students who are transferred into or out of our school district for their instruction.

h. The *only spokespersons* for the school district are the district's chief negotiator and the superintendent of schools, and the board members have agreed that their *sole spokesperson* shall be the president of the school board.

i. Do not discuss any matters related to negotiations or the strike with any teacher or nonadministrator, regardless of friendship or respect patterns that you may have with those individuals.

6. Principals and other administrators must understand that:

a. Since we start school earlier for secondary school students, if teachers do not show for work on the first day, call the transportation office to arrange for secondary students to be returned home, after receiving permission to do so by the superintendent. The superintendent can reach the radio stations and cancel elementary school classes, and also cancel school for the remainder of the day. This is the procedure for the second day of the school year as well. An announcement will be made at that point if school is being cancelled until further notice.

b. If teachers walk out during the day, call the central office for assistance until students are picked up by the bus. Secretaries, aides, administrators, and other available nonteacher personnel will be sent to your buildings. PTA presidents and PTA members will be contacted only if sufficient supervision is not available by utilizing the school district's employees.

c. All teachers, teacher aides, cafeteria workers, and transportation employees who report for work shall be paid for the initial two days. Thereafter, they shall be notified in writing by the individual building's principals (for teachers, aides, and cafeteria workers), and by the director of transportation service (for transportation employees) that they are laid off until further notice. This is not intended to be a punitive step, but the money that will be saved will be required when the school days missed are made up later. Also, explain to these dedicated employees that we can't afford to pay them if there is no work for them to do at this time.

d. All fringe benefits of striking employees shall be continued only upon payment of the costs by the individual employee. The assistant superintendent for business affairs will forward a letter, which is also signed by the superintendent of schools and the president of the board of education, to each striking employee, so informing them.

e. If custodial or other employees absent themselves in support of the teachers' union, all buildings shall be completely closed down. The assistant superintendent for business shall be authorized to hire off-duty police or other appropriate individuals to maintain security on a twenty-four hour basis, if this action is deemed necessary. If necessary, administrators shall devise a plan to cover all buildings with administrators for day, afternoon, and evening shifts.

f. If the strike continues beyond the second day, an administrators' meeting shall be conducted to deal with how to provide interim instruction, and with means of cutting all overhead and other costs to a minimum level. All administrators should give prior thought to this need area.

g. All after-school activities, except for a complete shutdown, shall take place as scheduled when the individual building's principal and the director of co-curricular activities are assured of proper supervision and normal arrangements.

7. Further, during the strike:

a. Paychecks for previous work completed shall be distributed through the buildings in accordance with normal procedures.

b. Pickets are to be permitted *only outside* of school buildings. If pickets attempt to enter the building or otherwise become unruly, immediately call the superintendent or the chief negotiator and he/she will decide whether or not to have the assistant superintendent for business call the police for assistance.

c. Daily, file an incident report in the format listed below.

INCIDENT REPORT

Building _____

Reporter _____   Date _____

The following is an account of all activities that took place at this building today. It includes pertinent information regarding any unusual incidents that occurred and any information available describing strangers on school building grounds. Also, it includes the names of those persons involved in the incidents, and a statement of any threats received or vandalism observed or discovered. Please use the camera that you were issued to take photos of the people involved or the damage incurred.

Time of incident _____

Activity_____
_____
_____
_____

8. During the strike, principals should:

a. Maintain a complete log (names, addresses, phone numbers, and topics) of any person making contact with the administrator.

    b. Report any unusual incident that takes place. The principals should take a photo or videotape to document the incident.

9. The assistant superintendent for operations shall inform the director of transportation, the director of custodial and maintenance services, and the director of food services of the arrangements that specifically apply to their operational areas.

10. Greater and in-depth planning shall be shared at a meeting immediately following the initiation of the first day of the strike. Before administrators are asked to attend a central meeting, there will be a replacement assigned to their facility.

Absolutes are those bargaining proposals from which the negotiators will not retreat.

Academic Freedom means the scholarly right of teachers to teach and behave professionally according to their own determination of instructional and professional appropriateness.

Accidental Death and Disability Insurance is a fringe benefit intended to provide emergency insurance coverage for employees who experience a fatal or catastrophic accident.

Administration is one of three basic means of operation in management. It is the skill to direct others in the accomplishment of the institution's goals.

Administrator is a person employed to take day-to-day responsibility for the operation of a unit, such as a school building, or of a program, such as special education.

Adversarial Bargaining happens when both sides continually make attempts to gain power from the other side. It can occur because of conflicting personalities of the chief negotiators, because of tight money in economically strapped times, or because of inside or outside pressure to settle or not to settle a contract.

AFL American Federation of Labor.

Agency Shop refers to a situation wherein all employees are required to pay a service fee to the union, but they are not required to become members of the union. The fee is intended to cover all the costs of the union when the union is representing the employees in collective bargaining matters.

American Arbitration Association is a professional group that will supply a list of arbitrators for both parties.

American Federation of Teachers (AFT) an AFL-CIO international union; its membership is mostly urban. It represents the professional, economic, and social concerns of teachers, as well as other public employees.

Arbitrability refers to the negotiable status of individual contract items; arbitrability may be questioned by either party. If the question of arbitrability is raised and a review by the arbitrator of existing contractual language and the state's collective bargaining laws and its supplemental rules and regulations causes the arbitrator to rule that a certain item is not arbitrable, the party who questioned the arbitrability of the item scores a big tactical win. Most times, however, the arbitrator will not be questioned on the arbitrability issue; and when she/he is, the ruling generally is one that states the item is arbitrable.

Arbitration is a voluntary (when both sides agree) or compulsory (is the law in some states) method designed to settle disputes, whereby an outside agent (impartial third party) reads documentation presented, conducts a hearing, and renders a decision as to the final settlement of a contract. The decision is usually final and binding.

Arbitrator is an impartial third party to whom parties in dispute present their differences for decision.

Assessed Property Valuations are data that provide negotiators with information that is related to the taxable value of the property that exists in the school district, and its future potential to increase or decrease the income from a district's property tax.

Association of State, County, and Municipal Employees (ASCME) is an employee organization that draws membership from the ranks of mainly classified district employees.

Authority is the expressed right to complete tasks assigned by upper levels of management.

Bad-Faith Bargaining refers to a situation wherein either party to the negotiations refuses to attend a reasonable series of meetings, refuses to meet with reasonable frequency, refuses to give serious consideration to the proposals of the other party, or refuses to make reasonable proposals or counterproposals.

Bargaining Chip Proposals are meant to be giveaways or bargaining chips.

Bargaining Notebook is a compilation of data consolidating all of the information that the local bargaining team requires as reference information during the process of negotiations. Major items include copies of the state's bargaining law, the current master contractual agreement, financial status, etc.

Bargaining Process is a set of meetings, caucuses, and document preparations for proposals and counterproposals, which will be completed when both teams agree to each proposal, and receive approval of the proposed contractual agreement by both of their respective referent groups.

Bargaining Team refers to those members who are selected or elected to represent the union or the management during the process of negotiating a collective bargaining master contractual agreement.

Bargaining Units are employee groups recognized by employers, or designated by an authorized agency, as the organization for conducting collective negotiations.

Bargaining Rules are those rules by which any negotiation team operates, depending on the directions given by the official body (board of education, in the case of the management's negotiation team), which precedes the overall guidelines provided to the negotiation team, and to the specific style and role to be played by the negotiation team's chief negotiator and spokesperson.

Belief is something accepted as true or accurately perceived as being true.

Board of Education is the policy-setting local body that carries legal responsibility to the official decisions related to the education of the children within a school district and for all decisions related to the operation of the local school district. Boards of education may be either elected or appointed, and their memberships usually vary between five and eleven members.

Bonded Indebtedness is the amount of money owed to pay off bonds (principal and interest).

Caucus refers to the private union team's or management team's single party meetings held during negotiations, when proposals and counterproposals are considered, and strategies and tactics are discussed.

Certification Election is a supervised employee election that results in the formal designation of an organization to act as exclusive representative for all employees in the bargaining unit.

Certified Employees are those employees who hold professional state-level certification; usually teachers and administrators.

Chief Negotiator is the person appointed to do all the communication at the table for one side or the other in the presentation of proposals or counters and to discuss content and intent of the language. She/he is empowered to call caucuses, initial (temporarily approve) all items as agreed upon, set the calendar for at-the-table bargaining, and, in general, be responsible for the conduct of the team at the table.

Class Grievance   is a com.,laint that may be filed when it is felt that the grievance relates to a group of union members rather than to a single individual.

Classified Employees   are those school district employees who are not required to be certified; it refers to such employees as custodians, food service workers, transportation personnel, etc.

Clients   refers, in the context of the book, to the students first, and to the community at large, second. The community constitutes the parents and all other taxpayers who have a stake in the outcome of the bargaining being done.

Closed Hearing   refers to the type of impasse procedural hearing that may occur if either party objects to a public, open hearing. Most experts in the field recommend closed hearings. This also refers to closed negotiating sessions.

Closed Shop   refers to a situation wherein any person wishing to become employed by the school district, must become a member of the union prior to being hired. Closed shops are prohibited in public school settings.

Co-Curricular Activities   are those student activities that are not part of the main course of study, such as athletics.

Collective Bargaining Law   is the statute governing representation of certified employees and governing the employer-employee negotiations.

Collective Bargaining   is the legally required process wherein both the school district's board of education's negotiation team and the exclusive representatives of a union's negotiation team meet, confer, and bargain in good faith for the purpose of executing a written master contractual agreement that incorporates all of the agreements reached during the bargaining process.

Comparable Data   refers to economic and noneconomic statistical information about neighboring or demographically and financially similar school districts; those systems to which the negotiating district will have to be ultimately compared.

Contract Arbitration   refers to the situation when an outside arbitrator comes into the school district as a step in an impasse procedure.

In this case, the union and management cannot reach agreement on one or more proposed master contract articles, and an arbitrator is hired to come in to resolve the outstanding contractual issues in order that a total master contractual agreement can be reached and ratified. Contractual arbitration can be mandated or permissive, depending on the specific state's laws and regulations governing collective bargaining.

Contract Article   refers to individual provisions of a master contract, such as salary or a particular benefit.

Contract Erosion   refers to the result when a member of management is not following both the strict interpretation of the contract and the direction of her/his supervisor in the operation of the contract following ratification by allowing the union members a freedom not allowed in the contract.

Contract   is a written document between an employer (the board of education) and an employee organization, usually for a definite length of time, defining the conditions (salaries, etc.) of employment, the rights of both parties to the contract, and the procedures to be followed in settling disputes or other issues arising during the course of operating the contract.

Contract Language   refers to the specific terminology and written technical structure of the master contract. Some words, such as ''shall'' and ''will,'' are words that mandate compliance, whereas words like ''may'' or ''should'' allow the party flexible decision-making power when it comes to compliance.

Contract Management   is the administrative process that ensures that the employees receive all benefits of the negotiated contract and that the day-to-day operations conform to the contract language.

Contract Ratification   occurs when employees of a particular group vote in an open meeting to accept a contract offer, and when the board of education also votes to accept it.

Contract Violation   is a misinterpretation of the wording of the master contract that results in action, bringing about a charge by the offended party of noncompliance with the contract.

Cost of Living Index   is an economic percentage indicator used in the expression of normal living expenses, including inflation.

Cost/Benefit Analyst   is a member of the negotiation team who carries the basic responsibility of determining the financial cost of every potential proposal being developed by management's negotiation team.

This person also is responsible for determining the financial cost of every at-the-table proposal being made by the union's negotiation team.

Counterproposal   is a proposal made in response to a proposal from the other side in collective negotiations.

Court Recorder   is a person who is sometimes hired when fact-finding procedures are taking place, in order to have a verbatim record of the proceedings. A court recorder is also sometimes hired during arbitration hearings.

Decertification Election   is a formal procedure removing the negotiations representation status of an employee organization.

Demographic Data   are data such as pupil population figures, density across grade levels, age of residents, average family income, etc., which are collected about the school district and its students, in order to inform the fact-finding procedure.

Dental Insurance   is a fringe benefit intended to provide preventive, diagnostic, and basic dental care services for employees.

Dividing and Conquering   is a technique used when the union team's members represent different interests; to create proposals that are divisive in nature and aimed at internally polarizing the individual union's negotiating team members.

Documentation   is the administrative recording of each step in the employee disciplinary process. Documentation must take place at every step of the disciplinary process, and the documentation must be in writing with a copy to be placed in the employee's personnel file and a copy given to the employee.

Due Process   is the act of following legal steps to ensure that employees are treated fairly and according to law.

Economic Contract Proposals   involve fund expenditure, such as salary or fringe benefits proposals.

Employee and Union Rights   are those rights that are specified in the collective bargaining law of the state and those rights written into a ratified master contractual agreement between union and management.

Employee Compensation   means wages and fringe benefits provided to employees as part of contractual obligations.

Employee Evaluation   refers to the performance assessment of individual workers in the school district.

Employee Leaves   are release times, given with or without pay, to employees desiring temporary relief from job assignment for such purposes as sick leave, maternity leave, sabbatical leave, etc.

Employee Termination refers to the discharge of an employee by the school district, within existing and legally appropriate personnel procedures and guidelines.

Employee Transfer refers to the reassignment of employees, usually between buildings or classroom assignments.

Employment Conditions refers to such conditions as contract time, length of work day, length of work year, etc.

Empowerment is the process of allowing employees to make decisions related to assigned work tasks, involving them in the creation of ways to maintain a productive and satisfying work environment, and involving them in day-to-day problem solving and decision making.

Exclusive Representation is the right and obligation of an employee organization that is designated as the sole representative authorized to negotiate for all district employees.

Expedited Bargaining refers to a situation whereby both parties to the negotiations agree to attempt to achieve a TA (tentative agreement) on a total contract over a very short period of time. Often the time period could be one week or less, and it usually occurs with both negotiating teams meeting at some location removed from the school district's environs.

Fact-Finding is a step in the impasse phase of bargaining. This resolution procedure usually follows mediation and precedes arbitration. It is used to allow an outside individual or panel to review all presented documents from each side of the conflict, and to make a determination as to her/his recommended settlement, whether in money, empowerment, or policy.

Fallback/Alternative Proposals are those proposals that are readied in advance to be used in case of abandonment or modification of original at-the-table proposals.

Federal Mediation and Conciliation Service (FMCS) is a federal agency that provides independent mediation to groups involved in negotiations or labor disputes, and it supplies arbitrators and fact finders upon request.

Financial Impact refers to the economic effect of a union negotiations proposal, such as a proposal involving an across-the-board salary increase.

Financial Status   refers to the income and expenditure status of the district budget, its historical allocations, and the amount of money available for all purposes—including negotiations.

Focus Groups   are comprised of employees and management, and are usually assembled to deal with a specific problem that is facing the school district. Focus groups usually meet for very short periods of time; and the task of a focus group is usually one of isolating a problem, analyzing the variables that impact the problem, and brainstorming possible solutions.

Focused/Limited Bargaining   has a purpose similar to that of expedited bargaining—achieving a quick and win/win agreement on a master contract. In many cases, limited bargaining, like expedited bargaining, takes place at a motel or at some other off-school district location. In focused bargaining, both parties agree to carry forth into the successor master contractual agreement most items that are currently contained in that agreement, but each party selects two or three areas where formal bargaining will take place.

Fringe Benefit Costs   are those costs accruing to specific employee benefits, such as health insurance coverages.

Fringe Benefits   are those benefits that the employee receives but that do not become direct salary. Fringe benefits usually consist of paid holidays; health, life, dental, vision, and other insurance; retirement provisions; severance considerations; workman's compensation; unemployment compensation; leaves of absence; etc.

Future Items   are those new desired items introduced into current negotiations, which are not expected to be met, but which do establish a future agenda that can be pushed during subsequent contractual negotiations of replacement master contractual agreements between union and management.

Good-Faith Bargaining   occurs when the board of education's or union's negotiating team agrees to meet regularly, listens intently to the other side's proposals, and offers rational counterproposals.

Grievance Arbitration   is the study of mandated or suggested rulings by an arbitrator when there is disagreement about the specific management actions taken that may or may not violate the actual wording or the intent of the written and ratified master contractual agreement.

Grievance Handling   is a step-by-step process followed by management that assures that employees will be handled with consistency and fairness. A grievance becomes a quasi-legal document once submitted, and must be handled as such.

Grievance is an employee complaint or problem of dissatisfaction with some aspect of employment. It may be solved by means already bargained into the contract, depending on the scope of existing grievance procedure.

Ground Rules are those mutually agreed-upon rules under which the bargaining proceeds. They usually involve such things as place and time of meetings, who attends meetings, etc.

Health Maintenance Organization (HMO) a type of employee health coverage that limits the range of health care providers in order to make the coverage more cost effective.

High Ball Proposal an exaggeratedly overinflated negotiations demand, intended to achieve a greater negotiating range; this usually occurs during adversarial negotiations.

Horizontal Salary Step is a salary placement that reflects an employee's degree level or level of training.

Hot Issues are those issues sometimes headlined and dramatized to provide a biased perception that all negotiations issues are of this nature.

Impasse is a term used to define persistent disagreements between the employee organization and the employer, requiring further steps to be taken by an outside force to bring about settlement through appeal procedures.

Impasse Procedures vary from state to state; some allow either party to declare impasse and request a mediator from the state's PERB (Public Employment Relations Board) or other state agency that has been designated to oversee the collective bargaining of public agencies in the state. Procedures include mediation, fact-finding, and arbitration.

Incompetency is failure to perform to the levels or standards of efficiency accepted by the profession.

Instruction Expert is the one who knows the what and why of the instructional programs being offered in the district. This expert can alert the management's negotiation team to the impact, positive or negative, of any instructionally related proposal that the team is considering bringing to the table.

Insubordination is the failure to follow a legal, ethical, and reasonable request or demand of a person in a supervisory or administrative position which can bring about disciplinary procedures against the employee who is insubordinate.

Interest Arbitration   is aimed at achieving a settlement of the terms and conditions of a new bargaining contract. It is a process conducted by an outside third party, and it may lead to recommended or mandated terms of settlement.

Item-by-Item Arbitration   addresses arbitration of individual contract articles, and the arbitrator may rule in favor of one party on some items, and in favor of the other party on other items in dispute.

Just Cause   is a determination made that the action taken by an employer had reasonable evidence to take discipline against an employee, and that the specific discipline was justified.

Labor Arbitration Reports   is a publication of the Bureau of National Affairs, and lists information about arbitrators. Other sources are the *Martindale-Hubbell Law Directory,* or the *Summary of Labor Arbitration Awards.*

Last Best Offer Arbitration   occurs when the arbitrator must rule in favor of a single party's total last best offer, and the arbitrator cannot rule on an item-by-item basis.

Last Best Offer   is the final contract proposal offered by either side in negotiations.

Lose/Lose   is a term utilized to describe an adversarial relationship between labor and management that deteriorates to the point that an employee strike is called, the end result of which is a long-term loss, in many respects, for both labor and management.

Low Ball Proposal   is an exaggeratedly underinflated management negotiations demand, intended to achieve a greater negotiating range; this usually occurs during adversarial negotiations.

Management   is the collective body of individuals who are employed to oversee and to operate the day-to-day affairs of a school district within the policies and directives of a board of education.

Management Rights   are those statutory (or otherwise established) rights or prerogatives of employers, such as personnel decisions, that are to be made without consultation with or notification to the employee organization(s).

Mandated Subjects   of collective bargaining are those items required to be collectively bargained by a state's law, usually including matters of salary and fringe benefits.

Master Agreement is a formal written agreement detailing all of the specific details reached between the union and management. It is the end result of successfully concluded negotiations.

Master Contract is the document bargained and agreed to by both sides in the negotiations process. This term is sometimes used instead of the term *master agreement.*

Master Contract Violation is a process that usually involves management taking a specific disciplinary action and informing the employee (and sometimes the union) of the specific contract violation and the specific discipline that is to be administered. At this time the employee or the union, in cases of class grievances (those that involve two or more members of the union in the same grievance situation), will file a grievance against management. This begins the grievance procedure that is spelled out in the master contract document.

Maternity Leave is a fringe benefit for pregnant employees that allows time off from the employee's job assignment, usually without pay.

Mediation is an impasse process conducted by a third party to attempt to resolve the differences between the two parties' bargaining proposals, usually through a federal or state mediation agency. Recommendations by mediators are customarily advisory and not binding on either party.

Mediator is an impartial third party who tries to reconcile an impasse between employer and employee organization.

Medical Insurance is a fringe benefit intended to cover regular medical care for employees, including preventive care and outpatient services.

Multi-Contract Bargaining refers to the process in which individual contracts are negotiated separately with each group of unionized employees.

National Education Association (NEA) is a teacher organization that is the nation's largest professional organization.

Need is a requirement. It also can be used to define the difference or discrepancy between the *what is* and *what should be* or *what could be* state of affairs.

Negotiation is the active and formal give-and-take between members of a union's negotiation team and a management's negotiation team, which ultimately ends in a master contract that governs the provisions, activities, and accommodations agreed to by both union and management.

Negotiations Guidelines are those guidelines provided to the negotiating team by its referent group (board of education or union membership), which govern the parameters of negotiations.

Negotiations Status Notebook is a running diary of the status of proposals, intended to serve as a reference to the negotiating team during bargaining.

Noneconomic Contract Proposals do not involve fund expenditure.

Observer is a member of the negotiating team responsible for observing the behavior of the opposite negotiating team's members.

Official Minutes are the official narrative record of negotiations proceedings, usually electronically recorded and transcribed.

Open Hearing refers to the type of impasse procedural hearing that may occur if both parties agree to open the process to the public. The arbitrator, however, may or may not agree to allow the hearing to be open.

Packaging Proposals involves combining those proposal items that have some relationship into one group, and insisting that all interrelated items are bargained as a unit.

Past Practice is a means of grievance handling by considering the manner in which a similar problem was previously handled.

Per Pupil Expenditure is a budgetary and negotiations figure that reflects dollar expenditure on a student unit cost base; all costs, such as salary and operational costs, are included in the calculation.

Permissive Statement is language within the master contract that indicates actions or specifics that may be met; there is an intent of guidance and latitude in the decision-making process.

Permissive Words such as ''could'' or ''should,'' are flexible contractual terminology and indicate a noncompulsory requirement situation.

Permitted Subjects include practically anything that can be agreed to by both parties, and which is not contradictory to any existing law.

Picketing is the constant presence of dissenting, sometimes striking, employees at various key administrative locations (such as the central office), usually carrying signs and intending to attract media attention and to gain support.

Post Hearing Brief is a written document filed by either the union, management, or both, elaborating on the points made at the arbitration hearing, and adding additional information to support their position.

Posturing is an at-the-table technique that implies presenting an artificial position or attitude in negotiations in order to pretend that you feel strongly about or take seriously an item that may not actually be one about which you feel strongly. Posturing is intended to throw the opponent off balance in her/his deliberations.

Potential Strike Items are those items that could trigger a strike if they are entered into the arena of negotiations. They might well deal with such items as the right of administrators to evaluate the degree of employee performance, with the right of management to make employee assignments, or the amount of new dollars that will ultimately be allocated to settle the contract with the employees' union.

Power Impact refers to the noneconomic effect of a union negotiations proposal, especially with reference to any impact on managerial purview.

Precedent is a detail that has been a common practice in the organization. It can be a resultant action or determination made in a prior situation closely related to the one being considered at the time.

Progressive Discipline is a definitive step-by-step process whereby the employee is given more severe discipline for each time the same (or very similar) violation of management's rights takes place. The first step may be a verbal reprimand, the second will constitute both a verbal and written reprimand, the third a deduction in pay, and, lastly, the dismissal of the employee from the organization.

Prohibited Subjects normally include the right to strike. In some cases such items as hiring, supervision, job assignment, recruitment, discharge of employees, and evaluation of employees are prohibited by the state's collective bargaining law.

Proposal Analysis involves analysis of the other party's proposals and counterproposals in order to prepare adequate counters and to anticipate items that may be approved or items that may be areas of disagreement.

Proposal is a suggested negotiations item, such as a specific salary increase, which is part of a negotiations package.

Public Employee Relations Board (PERB) is the state agency appointed to oversee collective bargaining.

Pupil-Teacher Ratio reflects the average number of students assigned to an individual classroom teacher.

Quality Circles generally, are groups of six to eight employees who identify problems within their workplace; develop potential solutions to each problem; present their proposed solution to management; and, if management approves, implement its solution.

Quality of Work Life can be defined as a *philosophy* which states that employees are capable of and desirous of improving their work environment and level of production; as a *goal* which attempts to make the work environment for employees the best possible work environment; and as a *structure and process* which involves employees in continuously improving the quality of their work life.

Quid Pro Quo proposals are those proposals that the negotiating team determines can be obtained at equal or greater value than those they would give as a compromise to the other team.

Rationales logical justifications that accompany negotiations proposals, and they are accompanied by comprehensive and convincing data.

Reopeners usually refer to a timeline, such as three months prior to the expiration of the existing master contractual agreement, when negotiations are initiated on a successor contract. This timeline is agreed upon to allow both parties to the upcoming negotiations sufficient time, hopefully, to negotiate a successor contract prior to the date of expiration of the current master contractual agreement.

Recognition Clause is the initial clause or article in any printed master contractual agreement. It specifies which employees the union represents and which it doesn't represent, and it gives sole representation rights to a specific union in all matters of collective bargaining throughout the length of the ratified master contractual agreement.

Recorder is a member of the negotiation team who has the responsibility for accurately and comprehensively keeping a written record of every significant discussion or agreement point made at the table by the union, management, or by both parties.

Restructuring is the name given to any idea that dramatically changes the structure of school districts or that changes the manner in which they operate.

Retroactive Pay is an amount, accumulated daily, which the arbitrator may ultimately award to an employee after a disciplinary action process, if she/he rules in favor of the union's position.

Sabbatical Leave is a fringe benefit provided for employees who request leave for scholarly purposes, such as pursuit of advanced degrees. Frequently these employees continue on the payroll at a reduced salary rate, as an inducement for such pursuit.

Salary Differential refers to the monetary difference paid to teachers with advanced degrees or years of service.

Salary Schedule is an array of employee salaries coded by years of experience and/or to level of professional preparation.

School-Based Management is a structure and a process that delegates greater decision-making power related to any or all of the areas of instruction, budget, policies, personnel, and all matters related to governance to the local school building level, and it is a process that involves a variety of stakeholders, including employees, in the decisions that relate to the local individual school building's programs and operations.

Sick Leave is a fringe benefit provided for employees for personal illness, or sometimes, for illness of a family member.

Sick Outs are when union members use sick leave or personal leave, in concert, on the same day in hopes that a normal school day will be interrupted. Sometimes there will be a staggered usage of this tactic wherein the employees in one building will all call in sick or take personal leave one day, another building's teacher staff will do this on another day, and so forth. This tactic is usually utilized after a lengthy impasse, to apply pressure on the school board to settle a contract.

Sidebar Agreements refer to actions taken away from the official negotiation's meetings by the chief negotiator for both the union and management.

Single-Contract Bargaining refers to the process in which one contract is negotiated on behalf of all groups of employees, regardless of their individual union affiliation.

Spokesperson is the person selected to be in complete control of communication at the table. This person must possess the ability to think on her/his feet, must be able to manage conflict and disagreement within the team and between the union and management teams, must possess leadership skills that will cause consensus within the team members, and will share responsibility for the training and overall preparation for upcoming negotiations with the various negotiation team members.

Stakeholders   are the local community residents, including parents, students, or other persons who have an interest or stake in what takes place in the school district.

Strategy   is the design to achieve a clearly defined goal. It is the *what* to be achieved, while a tactic is the *how* or maneuvers used to achieve the goal.

Strike   a temporary cessation of work by a group of employees, undertaken in order to communicate a grievance, achieve media and community recognition, or to enforce a threat related to negotiations demands.

Strike Plan   is an emergency backup plan intended for damage containment and for effectively dealing with typical employee tactics during a strike. It usually addresses such critical areas as coverage/supervision of students in each school, and specific counter measures and contingency strategies.

Sunshine Law   is a statute in many states that requires open public sector meetings, such as board of education meetings.

Superintendent of Schools   is the CEO (Chief Executive Officer) of a school district.

Supervision   is one of the three basic operations in management; the function of assisting others in improving upon their abilities.

Tactic   is a maneuver or action designed to achieve a goal or objective.

Target District   is a district that the regional, state, or national union selects to establish some negotiations or contractual precedent.

Taylor Law   is the labor negotiations law in New York that heavily penalizes striking teachers and that defines an impasse when both parties fail to achieve an agreement at least 120 days prior to the end of the fiscal year of the public employer.

Teamsters   are a separate, mostly transportation-related (trucker) union.

Telegraph   means a mannerism displayed by many people in negotiations who demonstrate their feelings by verbal cues or by tone of voice.

Tentative Agreement (TA)   is an agreement between the two bargaining teams that later has to be ratified by the union membership and the board of education in order to become official.

Throwaway Proposals are proposals that are seriously presented, but that are not considered absolutely necessary to secure before reaching a contractual settlement with the other party to the negotiations. These proposals assist in the give-and-take that accompanies every negotiation.

Transcript is a verbatim record of the proceedings of an impasse hearing. In cases where a transcript is allowed, there should be prior agreement as to which parties besides the arbitrator are to receive transcripts, and who will pay the expenses of the court recorder and for the preparation and distribution of the transcripts of the hearing.

Tripartite Arbitration Panel is an arbitration panel consisting of three arbitrators — one selected by the union, one selected by the board of education, and one selected by the two previously named arbitrators.

Tripartite Bargaining is bargaining that refers to the negotiations between the spokesperson and her/his team members; the bargaining between the union team and the management team at the table; and the bargaining between the negotiating team and its referent group (union membership or board of education).

UAW is the United Auto Workers of America.

Unfair Labor Practice is a labor practice that can be charged against a union when: (1) an employee organization or its agents deliberately interfere with, restrain, or coerce employees in the exercise of the rights granted them under the collective bargaining law, or (2) when the employee organization or its agents does not collectively negotiate in good faith with the public employer. The public employer or its agents can be charged with an unfair labor practice when: (1) it conducts itself in the same manner as the union's unfair practices listed above, (2) it attempts to dominate or interfere with the formation or administration of any employee organization, for the purpose of depriving employees of their rights under the collective bargaining law, (3) it attempts to discriminate against any employee for the purpose of encouraging or discouraging membership in, or participation in the activities of any union, and (4) it refuses to continue the terms of an expired agreement until a new agreement is negotiated. Management can also file a charge of unfair labor practice against a union.

Union is the officially recognized bargaining unit that has the authority to collectively bargain a master contractual agreement with the management of a school district, and that has the authority and responsibility to represent all union employees on a day-to-day basis.

Union Rights   refers to those rights, such as representation, that accrue to the union.

Union Shop   refers to a situation wherein employees are required to join the majority union organization that has been recognized by the board and by the National Labor Relations Board or comparable state's governing agency as the exclusive employees' representative. This is generally not permitted in public education situations.

Union Steward   is the individual elected by the members of the union to serve as their representative, usually at the building level.

Union/Management Relations   refers to the interface, both officially and unofficially, between formal representatives of a union and of management. The degree of positive interface, to a large part, determines the working environment within which collective bargaining and the day-to-day operation of a school district takes place.

Union/Management Teams   are various sized groups that are comprised of official representatives of the employee's union and the official administrative representatives of the school district. The union/management teams meet for a variety of time periods depending on the issue upon which the team is focusing.

Uniserve Director   is a full-time, state-level union employee assigned to one or more local school district—affiliated union groups.

Vertical Salary Step   is a salary placement that reflects an employee's years of service in the district.

Vertical Work Team   is a type of team that is vertically representational of top-to-bottom levels of the school district, with single or multiple members drawn from the ranks of central office personnel, supervisors or coordinators, principals, teachers, and classified personnel.

"What If" Game   is the anticipation of the union's or management's proposals and the potential reactions that the other party's negotiating team may have to the proposals.

Win/Lose   is a term utilized to describe an adversarial relationship between labor and management in which as one party wins a point, matter or conditions, the other party loses.

Win/Win   is a term that indicates that a positive and collaborative relationship exists between management and labor which is highly beneficial to both parties.

Wordsmith is a member of the negotiation team who carefully prepares the wording of each proposal offered by the management's negotiation team, and is responsible for the detailed analysis of every word of every proposal brought to the table by the union's negotiation team.

Work-to-Rule actions are those whereby employees are instructed by the union leaders to refuse to perform any duties that are not specifically mandated by the contract. In many cases, this means that teachers will not provide homework, will not meet with students who require help after normal school hours, and will not meet with parents to discuss their child's progress at any time, other than normal school hours.

Worst Case Scenario is the most disastrous thing that could be predicted to happen with regard to the results of negotiations.

Zipper Clause is language within an existing master contractual agreement that allows re-negotiations of a specific article in the contract while all other contractual conditions remain in effect until the end date of the existing contract. Many times a situation will exist wherein a multiple-year ratified master contractual agreement will contain a zipper clause that allows yearly negotiations of the salary provisions in the existing master contract.

Aaron, B., J. M. Najita and J. L. Stern. 1988. *Public Sector Bargaining*. Washington, DC: Industrial Relations Research Associates.

Adams, R. J. 1989. "North American Industrial Relations: Divergent Trends in Canada and the United States," *International Labour Review,* 128(1):44−64.

Ambrosie, F. 1989. "The Case for Collaborative, versus Negotiated, Decision Making," *NASSP Bulletin,* 73(518):56−59.

American Association of School Administrators. 1971. *Critical Incidents in Negotiations*. Washington, DC: American Association of School Administrators.

Anderson, B. 1981. "Teacher Unions Brace for New Battles," *American School Board Journal,* 168(10):24−25, 28−29.

Andree, R. G. 1970. *Collective Negotiation: Guide to School Board−Teacher Relations*. Lexington, MA: D. C. Heath and Company.

Bacharach, S. B. and E. J. Lawler. 1984. *Bargaining−Power, Tactics, and Outcomes*. San Francisco, CA: Jossey-Bass Publishers.

Bacharach, S. B., J. B. Shedd and S. C. Conley. 1989. "School Management and Teacher Unions: The Capacity for Cooperation in an Age of Reform," *Teachers College Record,* 91(1):97−105.

Barrett, J. T. 1985. *Labor-Management Cooperation in the Public Service: An Idea Whose Time Has Come*. Washington, DC: International Personnel Management Association.

Beamer, J. B. 1985. "An Introduction to the Public Employees Relations Act," address by the Chairman of the Public Employment Relations Board of Iowa. *Public Employment Relations Act,* pp. 13−18.

Beer, M. et al. 1985. *Human Resource Management*. New York, NY: Macmillan.

Blum, M. C. 1990. "Managing Perception to Change Reality: A Guide to Bargaining for Professionals," *Education Libraries,* 15(2):20−29.

Bramson, R. M. 1981. *Coping with Difficult People*. Garden City, NY: Anchor Press, Doubleday.

Braun, R. J. 1972. *Teachers and Power−The Story of the American Federation of Teachers*. New York, NY: Simon and Schuster.

Brock, J. 1982. *Bargaining Beyond Impasse−Joint Resolution of Public Sector Labor Disputes*. Boston, MA: Auburn House Publishing Company.

Bucholz, S. and T. Roth. 1987. *Creating the High Performance Team,* New York, NY: John Wiley and Sons, Inc.

Candoli, I. C. et al. 1978. *School Business Administration−A Planning Approach, Second Edition*. Boston, MA: Allyn and Bacon, Inc.

Castetter, W. B. 1986. *The Personnel Function in Education,* New York, NY: Macmillan Publishing Company.

Cloyd, S. 1990. "Involving School Board Members in Negotiations," *School Business Affairs,* 56(12):24−27.

Coleman, C. J. 1990. *Managing Labor Relations in the Public Sector,* San Francisco, CA: Jossey-Bass Publishers.

Colon, R. J. 1990. "Job Security Issues in Grievance Arbitration−What Do They Tell Us?" *Journal of Collective Negotiation,* 19(4):243−251.

Commission on Educational Reconstruction. 1955. *Organizing the Teaching Profession,* Glencoe, IL: The Free Press.

Coulson, R. 1981. *The Termination Handbook.* London: Collier MacMillan Publishers.

Cresswell, A., M. Murphy and C. Kerchner. 1980. *Teachers Unions and Collective Bargaining in Education,* Berkeley, CA: McCutchen Publishing Company, Inc.

Cresswell, A. M. and C. N. Gerdin. 1990. "Risks and Constraints in New York State Teachers' Strikes," paper presented at the *1990 AERA Annual Meeting, April 16−20, Boston, MA.*

Daria, R. 1978. "The Future Impact of Collective Bargaining on School Systems," paper presented at the *1990 AERA Annual Meeting, April 16−20, Boston, MA.*

Davis, W. M. et al. 1990. "Collective Bargaining in 1990: Health Care Cost a Common Issue," *Monthly Labor Review,* 113(1):3−10, 27−29.

DeFigio, N. F., D. J. Miller and J. Werlinich. 1990. "Patterns of Employee Discipline That Emerged from Arbitration of Grievances," paper presented at the *1990 AERA Annual Meeting, April 16−20, Boston, MA.*

Dilts, D. A. and E. C. Leonard, Jr. 1989. "Win/Loss Rates in Public Sector Grievance Arbitration Cases: Implications for the Selection of Arbitrators," *Journal of Collective Negotiations,* 18(4):337−344.

Dilts, D. A., A. Karim and A Rassuli. 1990. "Mediation in the Public Sector: Toward a Paradigm of Negotiations and Dispute Resolution," *Journal of Collective Negotiations,* 19(1):49−60.

Dilts, D. A., L. J. Haber and S. W. Elsea. 1990. "Selection of Fact Finders in Iowa Public Sector Labor Disputes: Characteristics of Acceptable and Unacceptable Neutrals," *Journal of Collective Negotiations,* 19(3):207−216.

Doherty, R. E. and W. E. Oberer. 1967. *Teachers, School Boards, and Collective Bargaining: A Changing of the Guard.* Ithaca, NY: New York State School of Industrial and Labor Relations, Cornell University.

Donley, M. O., Jr. 1976. *Power to the Teacher.* Bloomington, IN: Indiana University Press.

Durity, A. 1991. "The Fine Art of Compromise," *Personnel,* 68(3):1.

Eaton, W. E. 1975. *The American Federation of Teachers, 1916−1961.* Carbondale, IL: Southern Illinois University Press.

Eberts, R. W. and J. A. Stone. 1984. *Unions and Public Schools.* Lexington, MA: D. C. Heath and Company.

Elkouri, F. and E. A. Elkouri. 1973. *How Arbitration Works, Third Edition.* Washington, DC: Bureau of National Affairs, Inc.

Elsea, S. W., D. A. Dilts and L. J. Haber. 1991. "Factfinders and Arbitrators in Iowa: Are They the Same Neutrals?" *Journal of Collective Negotiations,* 19(1):61−67.

Employee Benefit Plan Review. 1990. "Costs Create Tensions at Bargaining Table," *Employee Benefit Plan Review,* 44(11):64−66.

Feiock, R. C. and J. P. West. 1990. ''Public Presence at Collective Bargaining: Effects on Process and Decisions in Florida,'' *Journal of Collective Negotiations,* 19(1):69−82.

Fisher, R. and W. Ury. 1981. *Getting to Yes−Negotiating Agreement without Giving in,* Boston, MA: Houghton Mifflin, Co.

Fox, M. J., Jr. and D. Cooner. 1990. ''Arbitration: Preparing for Success,'' *Journal of Collective Negotiations,* 19(4):253−260.

Freeman, R. B. and C. Ichniowski. 1988. *When Public Sector Workers Unionize.* Chicago, IL: The University of Chicago Press.

Gallagher, D. G. and P. A. Veglahn. 1990. ''Changes in Bargaining Behavior as a Result of Experience under a Statutory Impasse Scheme: Theory and Evidence,'' *Journal of Collective Negotiations,* 19(3):175−188.

Goldschmidt, S. 1990. ''Labor-Management Cooperation in Schools: A Case Study,'' paper presented at the *1990 AERA Annual Meeting, April 16−20, Boston, MA.*

Gorton, R. A., G. T. Schneider and J. C. Fisher. 1988. *Encyclopedia of School Administration and Supervision.* Phoenix, AZ: Onyx Press.

Granof, M. 1973. *How to Cost Your Labor Contract.* Washington, DC: The Bureau of National Affairs, Inc.

Guthrie, J. W. and R. J. Reed. 1986. *Educational Administration and Policy−Effective Leadership for American Education, Second Edition.* Boston, MA: Allyn and Bacon.

Hample, S. R., ed. 1981. *Coping with Faculty Reduction.* San Francisco, CA: Jossey-Bass, Inc.

Heisel, W. D. 1973. *New Questions and Answers on Public Employee Negotiation,* Washington, DC: International Personnel Management Association.

Helsby, R. D., J. Tener and J. Lefkowitz, eds. 1985. *The Evolving Process−Collective Negotiations in Public Employment.* Fort Washington, PA: Labor Relations Press.

Hendrickson, G. 1990. ''Where Do You Go after You Get to Yes?'' *The Executive Educator,* 12(11):16−17.

Herman, J. J. 1982. ''Improving Employee Relations with QWL,'' *Michigan School Board Journal,* 29(7):10−13.

Herman, J. J. 1984. ''The Quality of Work Life: Has It Come of Age?'' *Journal of the New York State School Boards Association* (August): 19−21.

Herman, J. J. 1990. ''School-Based Management,'' *Instructional Leader−*Texas Elementary Principals and Supervisors Association, 3(4):1−5.

Herman, J. J. 1991. ''The Two Faces of Collective Bargaining,'' *School Business Affairs,* 57(2):10−13.

Herman, J. J. and J. L. Herman. 1991. *The Positive Development of Human Resources and School District Organizations.* Lancaster, PA: Technomic Publishing Co., Inc.

Herman, J. J. and J. L. Herman. (In press.) ''What's New in Educational Administration, Part Two−School-Based Management,'' *The Clearing House.*

Hill, R. L., et al. 1990. ''Fact-Finding as a Bargaining Impasse Resolution Procedure: A North Dakota Study and Related Literature Review,'' *Journal of Collective Negotiations,* 19(3):217−242.

Huber, J. and J. Hennies. 1987. ''Fix on These Five Guiding Lights and Emerge from the Bargaining Fog,'' *School Board Journal,* 174(3):31.

Janes, L. 1984. ''Collective Bargaining,'' *NASSP Instructional Leadership Booklet,* pp. 22−23.

Johnson, D. W. and F. P. Johnson. 1982. *Joining Together — Group Therapy and Group Skills, Second Edition.* Englewood Cliffs, NJ: Prentice-Hall, Inc.

Justin, J. J. 1969. *How to Manage with a Union — Book Two — The Rules of Collective Bargaining, Grievance Handling, Corrective Discipline. Book One of How to Manage with a Union.* New York, NY: Industrial Relations Workshop Seminars, Inc.

Kaufman, R. and J. Herman. 1991. *Strategic Planning in Education.* Lancaster, PA: Technomic Publishing Co., Inc.

Kearney, R. C. 1984. *Labor Relations in the Public Sector.* New York, NY: Marcel Dekker, Inc.

Keith, S. and R. H. Girling. 1991. *Education, Management, and Participation — New Directions in Educational Administration.* Boston, MA: Allyn and Bacon.

Kennedy, J. D. 1984. "When Collective Bargaining First Came to Education: A Superintendent's Viewpoint," *Government Union Review,* 5(1):14 − 26.

Kerchner, C. T. 1988. "A New Generation of Teacher Unionism," *Education Digest,* L111(9):52 − 54.

LaNoue, G. R. and L. R. Smith. 1973. *The Politics of School Decentralization.* Lexington, MA: D. C. Heath and Company.

Lavan, H. 1990. "Arbitration in the Public Sector: A Current Perspective," *Journal of Collective Negotiations,* 19(2):153 − 163.

LeRoy, M. H. 1990. "Drug Testing in the Public Sector: Union Member Attitudes," *Journal of Collective Negotiations,* 19(3):165 − 173.

Lewis, A. 1989. *Restructuring America's Schools.* Arlington, VA: American Association of School Administrators.

Lieberman, M. 1981. "The Teacher Union Wants to Endorse Your Re-Election? Step Right into the Den, Daniel," *American School Board Journal,* 168(9):32 − 33.

Maddux, R. B. 1988. *Successful Negotiation — Effective "Win/Win" Strategies and Tactics.* Los Altos, CA: Crisp Publications, Inc.

Maier, M. M. 1987. *City Unions.* New Brunswick, NJ: Rutgers University Press.

Many, T. W. and C. A. Sloan. 1990. "Management and Labor Perceptions of School Collective Bargaining," *Journal of Collective Negotiations,* 19(4):283 − 296.

McGregor, D. M. 1960. *The Human Side of Enterprise.* New York, NY: McGraw-Hill Book Co.

Metz, E. J. 1981. "The Verteam Circle," *Training and Development Journal,* 35(12):79 − 85.

Miller, M. H., K. Noland and J. Schaaf. 1990. *A Guide to the Kentucky Education Reform Act.* Frankfort, KY: Legislative Research Commission.

Moskal, B. S. 1991. "Is Industry Ready for Adult Relationships?" *Industry Week,* 240(2):18 − 24.

Murphy, M. 1990. *Blackboard Unions — The AFT and the NEA 1900 − 1980.* Ithaca, NY: Cornell University Press.

Namit, C. 1986. "The Union Has a Communications Strategy — And Your Board Should, Too," *American School Board Journal,* 173(10): 30 − 31.

Nash, P. G. and J. R. Mook. 1990/1991. "Strike Replacement Legislation: If It Ain't Broke, Don't Fix It," *Employee Relations Law Journal,* 16(3):317 − 332.

National Education Association Research Division. 1990. *Postretirement Health Care Benefits for Public Employees.* Washington, DC: National Education Association.

Neal, R. 1980. *Bargaining Tactics—A Reference Manual for Public Sector Labor Negotiations.* Richard G. Neal Associates.

Neal, R. G. 1988. "At Arbitration Hearings, Justice Favors the Well Prepared," *Executive Educator,* 10(11):17−18.

New York State Public Employment Relations Board. 1983-1984. *The Taylor Law.* Albany, NY: New York Public Employment Relations Board.

Nickoles, K. W. 1990. "Future Shock: What's Coming to the Bargaining Table," *School Business Affairs,* 56(12):36−38.

Nyland, L. 1987. "Win/Win Bargaining Pays Off," *Educations Digest,* L111(1): 28−29.

Pace, R. W., P. C. Smith and G. E. Mills. 1991. *Human Resource Development—The Field.* Englewood Cliffs, NJ: Prentice-Hall, Inc.

Paterson, L. T. and R. T. Murphy. 1983. *The Public Administrator's Grievance Arbitration Handbook.* New York, NY: Longman, Inc.

Peck, L. 1988. "Today's Teacher Union Are Looking Well Beyond Collective Bargaining," *American School Board Journal,* 175(6):32−36.

Rawson, D. V. 1990. "A Comparison of the Statutory Framework and Perceived Role of the Superintendent in Teacher Negotiations in the States of Kansas and Nebraska," *Journal of Collective Negotiations,* 19(4):297−303.

Rebore, R. W. 1991. *Personnel Administration in Education—A Management Approach, Third Edition.* Englewood Cliffs, NJ: Prentice-Hall, Inc.

Richardson, R. C. 1985. *Collective Bargaining by Objectives: A Positive Approach,* Englewood Cliffs, NJ: Prentice-Hall, Inc.

Rock, M. L., ed. 1984. *Handbook of Wage and Salary Administration.* New York, NY: McGraw-Hill Book Company.

Ross, V. J. and R. MacNaughton. 1982. "Memorize These Bargaining Rules Before You Tackle Negotiations," *American School Board Journal,* 169(3):39−41.

Rynecki, S. B. and J. H. Lindquist. 1988. "Teacher Evaluation and Collective Bargaining—A Management Perspective," *Journal of Law and Education,* 17(3): 487−525.

Sandiver, M. and H. Blaine. 1980. *TEACHNEG—Collective Bargaining Simulation in Public Education,* Columbus, OH: Grid.

Schwerdtfeger, R. D. 1986. "Labor Relations Thrive When You Control Collective Bargaining," *American School Board Journal,* 173(10):41−44.

Seifert, R. 1990. "Prognosis for Local Bargaining in Health and Education," *Personnel Management,* 22(June):54−57.

Silberman, A. D. 1989. "Grievance Mediation," *The Arbitration Journal,* 44(4): 41−45.

Smith, S. C., D. Ball and D. Liontos. 1990. *Working Together—The Collaborative Style of Bargaining.* Eugene, OR: ERIC Clearinghouse on Educational Management, University of Oregon.

Splitt, D. A. 1991. "How Much Can Unions Charge Nonmembers?" *Executive Educator,* 13(9):18.

Thompson, B. L. 1991. "Negotiation Training: Win/Win or What?" *Training,* 28(6):31−35.

Tooredman, K. J. 1990. "The Impact of Win/Win Negotiations on School District

Working Relationships,'' paper presented at the *1990 AERA Annual Meeting, April 16–20, Boston, MA.*

Trotta, M. S. 1976. *Handling Grievances—A Guide for Management and Labor.* Washington, DC: The Bureau of National Affairs, Inc.

Venter, B. M. and J. Ramsey. 1990. "Improving Relations: Labor Management Committees in School Districts," *School Business Affairs,* 56(12):20–23.

Walsh, W. J. and F. Witney. 1990. "Indiana Teacher Salaries and the Teacher Collective Bargaining Act," *Journal of Collective Bargaining,* 19(3):197–205.

Walter, R. 1975. *The Teacher and Collective Bargaining,* Lincoln, NE: Professional Educator Publications.

Webb, L. Dean, J. T. Greer, P. A. Montello and M. S. Norton. 1987. *Personnel Administration in Education—New Issues and New Needs in Human Resource Management,* Columbus, OH: Merrill Publishing Company.

Webster, W. G., Sr. 1985. "Effective Collective Bargaining in Public Education," Ames, IA: Iowa State University Press.

White, R. N. 1990. "Positive Negotiations Tactics," *School Business Affairs,* 56(12):28–35.

Wynn, D. R. 1983. *Collective Bargaining: An Alternative to Conventional Bargaining.* Bloomfield, IN: Phi Delta Kappa Educational Foundation.

Zack, A. 1980. *Understanding Fact-Finding and Arbitration in the Public Sector.* Washington, DC: U.S. Department of Labor, Labor Management Services Administration.